CASE STUDIES IN
ECONOMIC SECOND EDITION
DEVELOPMENT

CASE STUDIES IN
ECONOMIC SECOND EDITION
DEVELOPMENT

STEVEN C. SMITH

An imprint of Addison Wesley Longman, Inc.

Reading, Massachusetts • Menlo Park, California • New York • Harlow, England
Don Mills, Ontario • Sydney • Mexico City • Madrid • Amsterdam

Reproduced by Addison-Wesley from camera-ready copy supplied by authors.

ISBN 0-201-42188-7

Copyright © 1997 by Addison-Wesley Publishing Company, Inc.

7 8 9 10-VG-04 03 02 01

An excellent aid to classroom lectures. *Case Studies* links economic development theory to events in economic development. It does not do this in the dry statistical manner found in so many textbooks, but weaves theory and numbers into a colorful fabric. Most importantly, *Case Studies* supplies us with an accessible and up-to-date guide to how the problems development economists deal with are real problems. It provides development students with perspective they cannot get elsewhere.

— IRA GANG, RUTGERS UNIVERSITY

Table of Contents

CASE STUDIES IN

ECONOMIC SECOND EDITION
DEVELOPMENT

Introduction

In fourteen years of teaching development economics I have found that students grasp general principles and models of development much better if they also are presented with case studies that clearly illustrate those principles. At the same time, where there is sharp controversy, students appreciate the debate much better if the contending approaches are presented in a context of case studies.

Economists participating in multidisciplinary courses, or teaching courses largely attended by noneconomics students, often need to be attentive to making connections to approaches of other disciplines but wish to do so in a way that does not compromise the integrity of economics as a discipline.

Moreover, development economics is made much more interesting if current development issues that students may be following in the news are integrated into the course. Students demand a real-world feel from their development courses, and better appreciate core theory material if they can see how it relates to that real world in more than just passing anecdotes.

Use of the right case studies can help accomplish these objectives. Unfortunately, no text has stressed case studies, although Michael P. Todaro's *Economic Development* contains 18 country overviews, as well as four comparative case studies. Nevertheless, no conventional text can hope to stay current on development topics and countries in the news. The case studies in this book have grown out of these goals and concerns. The sequence of the studies is designed in part to follow the chapter order of Michael Todaro's *Economic Development, Sixth Edition,* 1997.

Case Studies in Economic Development strives to represent alternative points of view on development in a balanced way. In doing so, the central role and importance of market based development is stressed without overlooking the role of government policy. The prevalence of market failure in development is examined without overlooking the recurring problems of government failure. Finally, although at its core the text is one of mainstream economics, it is open to contributions of other disciplines and nonmainstream approaches in development economics when they may help guide wise implementation of policy.

I would like to thank Ira Gang, Sanjay Jain, Anindita Mukherjee, and Michael Todaro for their very valuable comments. I would also like to thank Catherine Bealin and Usha Pitts for their truly outstanding research assistance on the first and second editions, respectively.

1. The Meaning of Development: Brazil and Costa Rica

Economic development is the presumed solution to absolute poverty and to many of the world's other most pressing problems. But what is development, and how do we know it when we see it?

The term, *development,* has been used in several ways. Traditionally, it was equated with growth of per capita income. Since the 1970s, other indicators of development have become widely used by development scholars and development agencies such as the World Bank. The meeting of basic needs (or, equivalently, reduction in absolute poverty), the creation of modern employment opportunities, and the achievement of a less unequal distribution of income and farmland have all become important criteria in determining the level of development.

Traditional measures of growth, especially in developing countries, may be misleading in that they fail to account for the environmental destruction that often accompanies spurts in temporary and unsustainable economic growth; and economists are devising measures of the national capital stock that includes environmental wealth. The United Nations has placed both educational attainment and health standards on equal footings with per capita income as development criteria, in the widely followed United Nations Development Program human development index (HDI). Some leading development scholars, such as Denis Goulet, Dudley Seers, and Michael Todaro, have gone farther. They argue that more intangible goals, such as expanded ability to choose (including political as well as market freedoms), enhanced self-esteem, and self-actualization, must be considered development criteria in their own right, if not its only meaningful measures.

Thus, development is not necessarily the same as growth, although in poor countries growth is generally a precondition for meeting important development goals, such as poverty reduction. But if growth is a necessary condition for development in poor countries, it is not a sufficient condition. This case study comparing Brazil and Costa Rica brings out some of these contrasts in national development performance when different aspects of development are stressed.

These two Latin American countries are good cases to examine carefully because while Brazil is often cited as an example of a country experiencing growth without development and Costa Rica is often cited as a case of successful development, a close examination of these two countries reveals the great complexity of these issues.

Costa Rica is of special interest because it has stood virtually alone as an example of democracy and slow but steady economic development in an otherwise violent and stagnant Central America. In fact, the Costa Rican government was very active in efforts to bring peace to the Central American region.

Brazil is of special interest because its growth performance from the 1960s through the 1980s was the best in Latin America, with at least some parallels with East Asian policy and performance (see Cases 3, 4, and 18). At the same time, other indicators of development in Brazil lagged, eventually undermining growth prospects.

Average Income and Human Development Levels. Costa Rica's per capita income in 1989 was $4,413 in purchasing power parity terms. The country is ranked as a "high human development country," number 42 of 160 countries on the 1992 index. In contrast, Brazil's per capita purchasing power parity income in 1989 was some 12% higher than Costa Rica's, at $4,951. But Brazil is ranked as a "medium human development country," number 59 of 160 countries on the 1992 index. Costa Rica is ranked 25 countries higher on the HDI ranking than would be predicted from its income ranking, while Brazil ranks five countries lower than predicted.

These differences are accounted for in health and education. Costa Rica's life expectancy at birth in 1990 was 74.9 years, compared with 75.9 in the United States. But despite Brazil's higher average real incomes, life expectancy at birth in 1990 was just 65.6 years. Similarly, Brazil's under-five mortality rate is 83 per thousand, compared with just 22 in Costa Rica. In the education sphere, Brazil's adult literacy rate is 81.1%, while that of Costa Rica is 92.8%. Helping to explain this difference, Brazil's people have 3.9 years of schooling on average, compared to 5.7 years in Costa Rica. In Costa Rica, six years of school attendance are mandatory and 99% attendance is reported.

Inequality. A comparison of the distribution of income in the two countries can be seen in the following table, derived from the *World Bank World Development Report*.

	Percent share:	
Quintile	Brazil	Costa Rica
Lowest 20%	2.1%	4.0%
Second quintile	4.9%	9.1%
Third quintile	8.9%	14.3%
Fourth quintile	16.8%	21.9%
Highest 20%	67.5%	50.8%
Highest 10%	51.3%	34.1%
Gini coefficient, early 1970s	.56	.45

| Growth, GNP per capita, 1965–90 | 1.4% | 3.3% |
| Growth, GNP per capita, 1980–92 | 0.4% | 0.8% |

Gary Fields concluded that relative inequality substantially increased in Brazil from the early sixties to the early seventies. This trend continued through the 1970s, as the World Bank estimated the Gini coefficient in Brazil to have risen from .565 in 1970 to .590 in 1980. Increases in inequality were largest in the agricultural sector. In 1980 the top 5% of farms comprised 69.3% of the farmland in Brazil. Most observers have concluded that an even steeper increase in income inequality took place in Brazil during the 1980s, as is confirmed by comparing income distribution data in successive World Development Reports. But inequality in Costa Rica is also high and only appears low in comparison to an extremely unequal country like Brazil.

Poverty. Fields concluded that the proportion of Costa Ricans below the absolute poverty line fell from 20% to 10% from the early sixties to the early seventies. In Brazil in this period Fields estimated the decline as from 37% to 35.5%. Today, absolute poverty is even closer to being eradicated in Costa Rica, while it has declined little in Brazil (see *World Development Report, 1990*).

What lies behind these very different outcomes?

Costa Rica's background. Costa Rica's modern development history begins with its 1948 revolution, and the broad-based development policies that emerged in its wake. The country has retained its democratic system since then, a rare exception in a region in which most countries have experienced extended periods of military rule in the postwar period. This democratic system should not be overly glamorized—the president holds substantial personal power; the legislative branch has tended to be inefficient and politically weak; central government power has expanded at the expense of local jurisdictions; and citizen participation is modest at best. The tax system in Costa Rica is quite regressive, like most countries in Latin America. The country experienced a 1980s armed right-wing movement associated with the contras. U.S. military and economic aid has been significant, but two-edged. A 1980s scandal involved allegations that American aid funded a "parallel state"—one that drew part of its budget from high central bank interest payments on undisbursed USAID funds—and whose activities were directed at undermining Costa Rica's government-directed development policies.

But elections are open and fair; the press is free; and there is substantial feedback from the governed to the government. In the 1980s, democracy survived encroachment by contras and their local supporters, and Nicaragua's Sandinistas fighting them. The dominant party since the 1948 revolution has been the National Liberation Party (PLN), traditionally social democratic but market-oriented in economic policy outlook. The stability of its democracy and consensus of its moderate development policies were confirmed when the moderate conservative Rafael Angel Calderon was elected president in 1990. In large measure he continued the policies of the previous PLN president Oscar Arias. In sum, Costa Rica has had among the most democratic histories in the developing world, even if it falls short by Western standards.

In the traditional view of Costa Rica's economic history, its better human development performance in relation to its Latin American neighbors is largely explained by its agrarian system, one that is said to be comprised mostly of humble but secure and solvent yeoman farmers. This differs from Latin America's characteristic Latifundia-Minifundia system, with its highly unequal distribution of land and sharp class distinctions. In this view, the historical differences are due in part to Costa Rica's lack of factors such as natural resources or a large native American population that would otherwise have drawn Spanish elites, who created the Latifundia-Minifundia system elsewhere in Latin America, to Costa Rica in the colonial period.

Historically, Costa Rica has had a larger yeoman farmer sector than most other countries in Latin America. But this difference of degree should not be exaggerated into a difference of kind, as it has often been. Latifundia have always been an important part of the rural economy in the northern Pacific region and elsewhere. An agricultural census found that 36.9% of the landholders hold only 1% of the farmland. The land Gini coefficient, a standard measure of inequality, was a staggering .86, exceeded elsewhere in Latin America but perhaps nowhere else.

Costa Rica's land reform efforts are commendable in the Latin American context, but should also not be overemphasized. The 1961 Law of Lands and Land Settlement, passed despite the strenuous resistance of land owners, provided for possibilities of land redistribution. But in the first decade of its implementation only about 4% of farmland was affected. A spurt of implementation in the mid-1970s came to a halt by the end of the decade. James Rowles concluded that implementation of the law has depended on the balance of political forces, not on the law itself. In sum, although the people of Costa Rica have benefitted from its comparatively better agrarian system, including its better opportunities for rural economic mobility, the agrarian system is an incomplete explanation for the country's human development performance.

Other policies have been important contributors to development in Costa Rica. In the early 1960s, Costa Rica shifted attention from import substitution to export promotion. This was a timely change: countries that made this shift in the early 1960s, notably South Korea and Taiwan, have had striking development success. Costa Rica differs from those economies, however, in that its exports have been more concentrated in agriculture. The largest traditional crop is coffee, which together with bananas, meat, sugar, and cocoa comprised 70% of export earnings in the 1970s. Costa Rica has had some success in nontraditional agriculture, such as decorative yucca, however. Costa Rica also emphasized agricultural infrastructure and extension programs.

Development policy in Costa Rica paralleled that of the successful experiences of Taiwan and South Korea in a number of ways. Several of these policies, including mandatory education, led directly to human development. Until the mid-1980s, Costa Rica continued to have a highly state-directed economy.

Costa Rica experienced an economic crisis from 1980 to 1982, including a rise in oil prices, sharp inflation, a serious debt crisis, recession and high unemployment, and, in response, moved to a more market-directed economy.

Brazil's background. GDP in Brazil in the 1965 to 1980 period grew at an extraordinary 9% rate, and while the growth rate in the 1980s fell to 3.3%, this performance was still significantly better than most other countries of Latin America.

Industrial and export policies played an important role in Brazil's successes prior to 1980 and to its comparative success among Latin American countries since 1980. Its percentage share of manufactured exports in total exports has grown dramatically, owing in part to this extensive industrial policy system. Manufactures now comprise 42% of total exports, tied with Uruguay for the highest share in Latin America. Actually, in 1980, the figure was substantially higher, nearly 57%, up from just 18% in 1965, all using World Bank data. Since 1982, Brazil has been forced by its debt crisis to expand exports in the quickest and easiest ways possible; this has often meant commodity exporting, often at high environmental cost as well as longer-run economic cost as primary prices decline. Costa Rica also has a huge foreign debt and has suffered similarly under its weight.

Brazil has had an export policy stressing incentives for manufacturing exports, with numerous parallels with Taiwan and South Korea (see Cases 3 and 18). Its pattern of combined import substitution and export promotion policies is strongly reminiscent of East Asian policy. For example, the World Bank found a "pro-export bias" in 11 of 21 industrial subsectors. Further, Fabio Erber found that tax incentives have been combined with the requirement that importers of parts and components export certain levels of final goods, in order to encourage exports in the electronics industry. A study by Renalto Bauman and Helson Braga of the role of selective financing in Brazil and concluded that "the subsidies involved in official credit have an important individual role in (explaining) exports, especially as regards industrialized products." Brazilian capital goods exports have grown dramatically since the late 1960s when they were targeted for industrial policy promotion. Morris Teubal concludes on the basis of in-depth case studies that their success is due to first building up reputation and learning by doing in protected domestic markets. It is at this point (and not before), he concludes, that the export subsidy has been effective at encouraging a switch to export activities.

As Werner Baer argues, Brazil has taken major strides toward industrialization since World War II. It has impressive production statistics in the growth of its systems of paved roads, electricity generation, and industrial output, including over one million cars, three million televisions, and two million refrigerators per year. Agricultural output has similarly grown. The average material standards of the country have improved substantially. Progress on social development has also been made; although the child mortality rate is quite poor by the standards of comparable countries today, like most developing countries Brazil has made great progress from 1960 when its rate was 159 per thousand to today's 83 per thousand. But this has been more by default than through any proactive social policy. And such strides do not automatically propel a nation to advanced industrial status, a lesson underscored by the economic history of the former Soviet Union. Brazil's human development statistics compare unfavorably with many other middle-income countries such as Costa Rica, and quite a few low-income countries, let alone with the advanced industrialized countries. A third of all children under the age of five suffer from malnutrition in Brazil, despite the nation's plentiful food supply. The dramatic contrasts of Brazil are often expressed with the saying that it is "a Belgium inside an India," which is an exaggeration but a telling one.

Brazil labors under the developing world's highest debt, at over $110 billion, and has been one of the last debt crisis countries to arrive at a debt reduction agreement. A debt pact for Brazil was finally reached in 1994. From 1982 to 1995, the rate of investment was actually negative (−0.9% annually in the 1980–87 period), absolute poverty has increased significantly, and income distribution, already one of the worst in the world, has worsened further. It is not enough to say that industrialization and social progress have been derailed by a debt crisis, for a debt crisis is in large part endogenous, or the result of previous economic and social policies. A country that finds it easier to take on foreign debt than institute needed reforms will eventually suffer consequences.

Land reform has been repeatedly blocked by the political power of Latifundia owners. In Brazil, unequal land distribution produces political incentives to encourage poor farmers to establish inefficient rain forest settlements. The northwest state of Rondonia has experienced the most devastation, beginning with the 1970s construction of roads to the area and the encouragement of low-income farmers to move there. This policy represented a politically inexpensive—but ecologically disastrous—alternative to land reform. In fact, highly unequal patterns of land ownership soon asserted themselves in Rondonia (see Case 14).

Brazil and Costa Rica: Further Contrasts. Gary Fields, in his classic book *Poverty Inequality and Development,* examined Brazil and Costa Rica among other countries and concluded that "deliberate unevenness is the central feature of Brazilian growth," while Costa Rica's "emphasis on agricultural exports helped spread the benefits of growth throughout the country" and that "the Costa Rican economy grew, creating more modern sector job opportunities and educating the skilled labor force needed."

The size of Brazil in comparison to Costa Rica is not an adequate basis to dismiss the differences. For example, a 1993 World Bank study found that while Brazil's average per capita income grew by 220% from 1960 to 1980 with a 34% decline in the share of the poor in the population, similarly-sized Indonesia grew 108% from 1971 to 1987 with a 42% decline in poverty incidence. Much ground on poverty was subsequently lost in Brazil in the 1980s. Brazil today is one of the slowest growing and highest inflation countries in Latin America. One interpretation is that in the 1990s, Brazil's growth without, at least, much social development has created conditions in which growth itself is no longer possible unless attention is given to broader development goals.

Brazil has been described as a nation of voter apathy and weariness with politicians. Brazilians called on to choose among a king, a prime minister, or a president to run their country voted to retain the presidential system of government in a plebiscite. As president, Fernando Collor de Mello ordered a price freeze and the temporary seizure of 80 percent of private savings—over $110 billion—in an attempt to squeeze out liquidity, which he assumed would cause hyperinflation. The savings seizure destroyed confidence in financial assets and in the government itself, especially because government debt comprised 80 percent of the assets seized, offering the state an expedient means of reducing its expenses. Brazil's chronic inflation resides mainly in expectations and in government credit and credibility. President de Mello was impeached on corruption charges and resigned in 1993. The 1993 resignation of Paulo Haddad, Brazil's second finance minister to resign in a two-month period, sapped an already low level of confidence.

Some hope was returned to Brazil in October 1994 when Fernando Henrique Cardoso was elected president. Cardoso had devised a more effective anti-inflation campaign as finance minister in 1993 to 1994. A former leftist sociology professor turned moderate free-market reformer as leader of the Social Democratic Party, Cardoso is a politician of considerable skill and determination. It was widely perceived that if any leader were capable of bringing both political and economic reform to Brazil, it was Cardoso. By mid-1996, however, it became clear that Brazil's enormous institutional inertia would be very difficult for even a leader of Cardoso's remarkable abilities to overcome.

Costa Rica's foreign policy is "permanent neutrality"; it has no army by constitutional statute, and its police force has no modern military weaponry. In contrast, the military has long been powerful in Brazil, frequently playing a decisive role in politics and acting in its own institutional interests or siding with the landed oligarchy.

Race and racial discrimination is another area in which Brazil and Costa Rica differ markedly. Few discussions about poverty in Brazil pay much attention to race. But about half the population of Brazil is African or Mulatto in origin. This makes Brazil the second largest black nation, after Nigeria. And most of the poor in Brazil are black. While racism is a crime in Brazil, no one has ever been sent to jail for it. Hundreds of children living on the streets of Brazil's large cities are murdered each year; and most of these are black. The average black worker receives only 41% of the salary of the average white worker. Most of the million-plus Brazilians living in the worst *favelas,* or slums, are black.

In Costa Rica, descendants of the Spanish are a majority, while a sizable minority are Indian or Mestizo (compared with just 1% in Brazil). About 5% are black, generally of West Indian descent. Though there is widespread racism and discrimination against blacks, they have achieved a great deal of upward mobility compared with most countries in Latin America. Many have become landowners employing nonblacks as farm workers.

Conclusion. In this case study, a close examination of Brazil and Costa Rica has revealed the great complexity of the "growth without development" issues. Structural features of the two countries differ more by degree than by kind. In the case of Brazil, it might be more accurate to say that there has been considerable economic development without much social development, rather than the more blanket term "growth without development" that applies better to a few Middle Eastern and other energy-exporting countries. And other differences between Brazil and Costa Rica, besides policies that might account for human development performance, are obvious: for example, Brazil is by far the largest and most populous country in Latin America, while Costa Rica in contrast is a small open economy. But although broad generalizations cannot be made, the case study does bring out vividly the important idea that growth and development can be two very different matters, and that inattention to social aspects of development will likely act as an eventual brake on continued economic development.

Sources

Baer, Werner. *The Brazilian Economy,* 3d ed. New York: Praeger, 1989.

Bauman, Renato, and Helson C. Braga. "Export Financing in the LDCs: The Role of Subsidies for Export Performance in Brazil." *World Development 16* (1988): 821–833.

Binswanger, Hans P. "Brazilian Policies that Encourage Deforestation in the Amazon," *World Development 19,* no. 7 (1991): 821–829.

Denislow, David, and William Tyler, "Perspectives on Poverty and Income Inequality in Brazil: An Analysis of Changes During the 1970s." *World Bank Working Paper 601,* 1983.

Dinsmoor, James. *Brazil: Responses to the Debt Crisis.* Washington: Inter-American Development Bank, 1990.

The Economist, Dec. 7, 1991.

Edelman, Marc, and Joanne Kenen, eds. *The Costa Rica Reader.* New York: Grove Weidenfeld, 1989.

Erber, Fabio Stefano. "The Development of the Electronics Complex and Government Policies in Brazil." *World Development 13* (1985): 293–310.

Fields, Gary. *Poverty Inequality and Development.* New York: Cambridge, 1980.

Fishlow, Albert. "Some Reflections on Comparative Latin American Economic Performance and Policy." *World Institute for Development Economics Research Working Paper 22,* August 1987.

Heubel, Edward J. "Costa Rican Interpretations of Costa Rican politics." *Latin American Research Review 25,* no. 2 (1990): 217–225.

Lizano, Eduardo. "Lessons in Economic Policymaking." *Finance and Development,* Dec. 1991.

New York Times, April 26, 1993.

Roett, Riordan. *Brazil: Politics in a Patrimonial Society, 4th ed.* Westport, CT: Praeger, 1992.

Rowles, James. *Law and Agrarian Reform in Costa Rica.* Boulder, CO: Westview, 1985.

Sahota, Gian S., and Carlos A. Rocca. *Income Distribution: Theory, Modeling and Case Study of Brazil.* Ames: Iowa State University Press, 1985.

Sercovich, Francisco Colman. "Brazil," Special Issue: Exports of Technology by Newly Industrializing Economies. *World Development 12,* nos. 5/6 (1984): 575–600.

Teubal, Morris. "The Role of Technological Learning in the Exports of Manufactured Goods: The Case of Selected Capital Goods in Brazil." *World Development 12* (1984): 849–866.

United Nations Development Program. *Human Development Report.* 1992, 1994. New York: Oxford.

Washington Post, April 22 and Aug. 17, 1993, and other issues.

World Bank. *Implementing the World Bank's Strategy to Reduce Poverty.* Washington, DC: 1993.

World Bank. *World Development Report.* 1990, 1992. New York: Oxford.

2. Zaire: Immiseration Amidst Riches, with the Counterpoint of Botswana

How bad can things get in a developing country? Zaire provides one of the best case studies on what a country should avoid in the struggle for economic development.

The state has a vital role in economic development, building education and skills, health, infrastructure, and offering guidance in industrial development. When the state plays a healthy role it can improve economic development outcomes. But when civil servants are corrupt, when policy is made for private gain, when political power of top leaders is abused, the state can also make development prospects much worse than if it played virtually no role at all.

Zaire is one of the world's most tragic stories of economic development in the Third World, where one of the countries best endowed in natural resources has been devastated by government corruption. In the midst of natural resource riches, nearly 40 million Zairians are not only among the poorest people in the world—only Ethiopians are poorer in real terms according to the United Nations Development Program—they are steadily getting poorer.

GNP has been declining since 1990. The World Bank estimated that Zaire's economy shrunk 40% between 1988 and 1995. With rapid inflation and a plummeting currency, a one million zaire note is in circulation. Western aid has been largely suspended, although this made little difference for basic needs, because so little of it was getting through to the people who needed it anyway. But the economy is in a state of total collapse that is almost impossible to convey with such statistics alone.

Zaire is has been estimated to have enough arable land to feed the entire continent of Africa and enough hydro power to provide for all of the electricity in Africa, where food production is declining and industry has ground to a complete halt. The case of Zaire demonstrates that "political development" is a necessary condition for modern economic development (see Case 25). It provides a vivid reminder of just how bad things can get in a developing country even in the late 1990s. In extreme form, Zaire also illustrates the unfortunate legacy of the Cold War for development in Africa (see Case 26).

Copper and cobalt are abundant enough to make Zaire one of the world's major producers of these commodities, but there has been a severe decline in mining and processing these commodities. Mining at the dominant *Gecamines* copper mine in 1993 was at 10% of 1990 production levels. Similar declines can be seen in gold, production of which dropped from 4.6 tons in 1990 to 1.4 tons in 1993. Diamond production was at 22 million carats in 1986, but fell to 15.6 million carats in 1993.

Zaire has farming conditions appropriate for cotton, rubber, coffee, palm oil, and sugar, but none of these potential sources of wealth and income have been well developed. Zaire lacks basic agricultural services, such as access to credit, extension services, and means for transport. Therefore, the country must import staples such as rice, wheat, meat, and fish in order to feed the population. Zaire imports sugar when it could be a world supplier.

Zaire's infrastructure is in a state of collapse, only part of which can be explained by the episodes of rioting by the armed forces that scared off thousands of Westerners who held vital technical and managerial positions in the country. Zaire does not possess skilled personnel to fill those positions. The result is a dramatic fall in production. The deterioration has been heightened by an overall lack of spare parts, skilled labor, and maintenance equipment. Industry has not been able to withstand successive looting, administrative harassment, and severe monetary and institutional instability.

Roads, one of the most basic forms of infrastructure, are steadily disappearing into the undergrowth. Of the 150,000 kilometers of road networks, only a third are maintained by the Highways Authority. With the withdrawal of international aid, highway maintenance has halted altogether. Only armed convoys and a few trucks travel the roads that are still passable. This has left huge regions of the country without access to the government or to foreign food aid. The *New York Times* reported in 1994 that some 85% percent of roads are reverting to bush. Government absenteeism means that there are no buses or other forms of organized transportation. There is no through highway connecting North to South. Even as the highways deteriorate, there are fewer cars to drive on them. Gas stations often go without delivery of fuel for weeks. The country has 5000 kilometers of rail tracks, but they are so badly damaged in some places that usage is only 20 to 30%.

Health conditions are appalling. While much of the world's attention has been focused on Zaire's 1995 outbreak of the deadly Ebola virus, this is really the least of Zaire's problems. Besides the scourge of infectious and parasitic diseases that would be preventable or curable at modest costs with an efficient public health system, Zaire has a very serious AIDS epidemic. Most other African nations have typically adopted an attitude of denial about AIDS and done little to attack the problem. But in Zaire, a progressive environment existed for research, treatment, and education in the late 1980s. But with the collapse of the central state and the withdrawal of economic aid from Western donors after 1990, progress on AIDS was virtually halted. Zaire's infection rates may now exceed those of even the worst situations, such as Uganda (see Case 8). Medical workers lack funds to test blood for HIV infection. A USAID project of the early 1990s, which once employed about 70 Americans and several hundred Zairians, has been dismantled.

In 1990, Zaire abandoned an IMF economic recovery program. In 1994, the World Bank has completely closed down operations in the country because of long-standing arrears in debt payments. This is the strongest action the bank has ever taken against a member country. There have been no major lending commitments on the part of principal institutions or foreign investors. The U.S., France, and Belgium have virtually cut off assistance because of arrears in debt payments, erratic economic policy, and Mobutu's refusal to allow political freedoms.

The historical background of Zaire offers important insights into how such a promising country came to such a state of affairs.

Zaire gained independence from Belgium in 1960. Once called the Belgian Congo, this huge country, almost as large as the United States east of the Mississippi, was long the private personal possession of Belgian King Leopold. For decades the Belgians governed the colony essentially as a private, profit-making business venture, operating mines under virtually slavelike conditions, in which untold numbers perished. Only after World War II did Belgium begin to make significant efforts on behalf of the development of its colony.

This colonial experience fostered an understandably antagonistic attitude toward government that carried over from colonial times to the cynical, rapacious attitudes toward government and public service that have prevailed in the post-independence period. This kind of carryover from conflict with harsh colonial administrations to perceptions of the state as a means of self-aggrandizement is seen in many African countries and is one of the most bitter fruits of the colonial legacy. But perhaps nowhere is this legacy more bitter than in Zaire.

Zaire has been ruled for three decades by the dictator President Mobutu Sese Seko Kuku Mgbendu Wa za Banga. Born Mobutu Joseph Desire, his current official name is translated as "the all-powerful warrior who because of his endurance and inflexible will to win will go from conquest to conquest leaving fire in his wake." In his pictures he is always seen in a trademark leopardskin cap.

Five years of wars and rebellions followed Zaire's independence in 1960. Within months of independence, at least four rival administrations had claimed to be the legitimate government. There was concern in the West that support for Communist factions would grow, or at least that they would be able to take advantage of the chaos. Mobutu's rise to power in 1965, despite his support from the CIA, was viewed by many as an improvement over the conditions of chaos that ruled at the time.

Mobutu changed the country's name, from Congo to Zaire in 1971, in a symbolic show of cutting ties with the colonial past. But Mobutu, who was an accounting clerk in the colonial army, has himself run the country in a way reminiscent of King Leopold. Under Mobutu, Zaire has often been described as a "kleptocracy," an economy based on theft; a government of, by, and for thieves. Mobutu himself is believed to have stolen several billion dollars and squandered public funds on personal projects. Mobutu has been said to operate less like a president than as a "franchise system," who will, for example, provide an entrepreneur with the exclusive right to "import chickens from Europe or to sell fish to the army or to operate cellular telephones."

As Lucy Komisar notes, in Zaire bribes are considered part of the normal pay of anyone with any authority. Police arrest passersby at random, extorting money. Schoolteachers sometimes demand bribes before they release grades. Hospital guards demand bribes before admitting sick patients. Men and women in uniform shamelessly compete for payoffs at the ferry dock. The security forces, deprived of regular wages, resort to the populace for income. For example, security forces may station themselves on the roads to collect fines for imaginary traffic violations or rent themselves out as security for hotels and businesses. State employees may go months without pay, so they resort to bribery and stealing government property.

In some ways Mobutu represents more a difference of degree than of kind from the rule of a "big man" as seen in many other African states. The African nationalists who took power from colonialists enjoyed different forms of highly personalized one-man rule, but all represented something of a glorified African chieftain. Similar situations arose under Jomo Kenyatta in Kenya, Julius Nyerere in Tanzania, Kwame Nkrumah in Ghana, Dawda K. Jawara in Gambia. Along with the sadistic Idi Amin of Uganda, and Ahmed Sekou Toure of Guinea, Jean-Bedel Bokassa of the Central African Republic, who changed the country's name to the Central African Empire and spent a quarter of the country's GNP on his coronation, Mobutu represents only the extreme of a continuum of destructive dictators plaguing the region.

Despite the base corruption, political repression, and human rights violations of Mobutu's regime, he generally received continued support from Western Europe and the United States as a Cold War buffer. The United States alone provided Zaire with over $1 billion in aid in the 1970s and 1980s. Mobutu was helpful to the United States in providing a base and supply route for rebels attempting to overthrow the Marxist government of Angola. Western assistance helped put down rebellions in the region of Shaba that began in 1977. When the Cold War ended, this disagreeable marriage of convenience resulted in an abrupt separation, if not quite divorce.

Mobutu attempted to get away with a partial and insincere democratization, having his representatives meet with opposition leaders in a "national political conference in 1992." Things did not go the way Mobutu had expected, and his long-time rival Etienne Tshisekedi was selected as transitional prime minister by a coalition of generally pro-democratic, but often ethnically based, partisan forces. There are now some 200 ethnic groups in Zaire, a bewildering situation that may itself become a further barrier to effective democracy. In partially free 1995 elections, Leon Kengo wa Dondo became prime minister. Despite some U.S. moves to support him, his grip on power has been tenuous, and Mobutu remains entrenched.

Mobutu is now based securely in his marble jungle palace at Gbadolite, deep in the "interior" of the country. Gbadolite is one of eleven palaces he has built for himself with public money. He enforces his will in the capital through his personal army, the Special Presidential Guard, drawn from his Ngbandi ethnic group. The Guard often operates incognito, without the slightest regard for human rights. Dissenters are murdered, or their children are. Prisoners are starving in the jails, where there is no food to feed them.

Mobutu continues to control the country's treasury, which, it is said, he treats as his private purse. He also controls the television and radio system, surrounded by loyal Special Presidential Guards, from which he broadcasts fictitious images of an active presidency from his Gbadolite palace. While these broadcasts are ignored in Kinshasa, they look real in the vast country's villages, and help him maintain power.

Mobutu tried to dismiss Interim Prime Minister Tshisekedi in December 1992, but the result has been a standoff. Lacking real power, Tshisekedi's government has been regarded as virtually as fictitious as Mobutu's. Nor are Tshisekedi and his circle viewed as entirely without taint of corruption and ethnic favoritism by international observers.

In early 1993, Tshisekedi declared illegitimate Mobutu's new 5-million-zaire note, worth about $1.75 at that time. The army, having just been paid in these notes, staged riots for the third time in as many years, and hundreds of Zairians were killed. The French ambassador was shot and killed during these riots while observing them from his window. France, the United States, and Belgium formally demanded that Mobutu relinquish authority to Tshisekedi's interim government.

Ethnic conflicts are often complex and fueled by passionate historic hatreds, as we have seen vividly in recent years in the former Yugoslavia. Opportunistic behaviors can be reinforced by ethnic hatreds. Dictators often manipulate ethnic conflict for their own advantage. Tension between two ethnic groups, the Kasai and the Katangans, has been stewing since colonial times. The Belgian colonial administration forcefully brought the Kasai to the region to work in the diamond mines. But resentment has been growing for a long time. The Katangans, native to Shaba province, where much of the mineral wealth is located, have long felt exploited by the rest of the country. But in August 1991 after Tshisekedi was elected prime minister, members of the Kasai, an ethnic group based in the center of Zaire, were driven from their homes in Shaba province, in the southwest. In Shaba, Tshisekedi was perceived less as a reformer than as a member of the hated Kasai ethnic group (Mobutu is Katangan). Rather than celebrate discreetly, as might have been more prudent, resident Kasai conducted boisterous street celebrations. Shaba's governor, Kyunguwa Kumwanza, had publicly denounced the Kasai "insects," further fanning the flames of ethnic hostility. Mobs made up of the Katangan ethnic group staged bloody ethnic attacks that local police did nothing to stop, and Mobutu implicitly encouraged. Many Kasai were killed with machetes, knives, and immolation, in a manner later repeated in ethnic massacres in Rwanda. About 400,000 Kasai fled the area, with hundreds of refugees dying of starvation. Some 60,000 live in a tent city where they would starve if not for the efforts of relief agencies.

In the wake of the fighting, many Western businesses also left the country, taking with them capital and expertise. The signs of economic decay are now visible everywhere. Import substitution factories, intended to manufacture locally what had been imported, and viewed as embodying Zaire's future when mineral resources are no longer able to fuel development, have been pillaged and plundered, and finally abandoned, since an earlier outburst of looting and arson that began when soldiers mutinied over lack of pay in September 1991. Even the walls and roofs of factories were stolen. Years of painstaking growth of the modern sector were destroyed overnight, costing close to 100,000 jobs in the Kinshasa area alone. For example, the General Motors assembly plant in Kinshasa suffered so many waves of looters that all that remains is a structural skeleton bearing the GM logo. Once vibrant copper and cobalt mines in Shaba province and elsewhere are now flooded with water. One historical irony is that Congo, a smaller country north of Zaire, and long shunned by the U.S. as a Marxist regime, is now a growing destination of investment. It is actually considered a more stable and well-governed regime.

In the meantime, there are signs that Zaire is splintering. Kivu, a prime agricultural area, cannot move its goods westward, so it trades almost exclusively with Tanzania and Kenya. Kasai still uses the old currency, in a striking example of disintermediation. Shaba has declared its independence amidst an environment of ethnic cleansing. Equateur, the home region of Mobutu's palace, displays conditions reminiscent of the Nineteenth century. (For a look at another African country where central authority has collapsed, see Case 7 on Somalia.)

What can the outside world do in a case like this? Sanctions may be of no avail when a ruler is indifferent to the suffering of the country's people, as the world discovered in the case of Sadam Hussein of Iraq. Diamonds, a principal export, are a very compact and lightweight commodity, and are easy to smuggle. This makes them the perfect sanctions-breaker.

The entire diamond industry in Zaire is corrupt. Diamond export values are in reality up to twice the officially recorded $185 million for 1992. False transfer pricing in the form of underinvoicing of revenues received from exports is used to avoid taxes and to facilitate capital flight. Senior military officers run protection rackets, skimming a percentage of the diamond exporters' sales.

Mobutu, it has been said, proves that diamonds are a dictator's best friend, so eventually they became a developing nation's burden rather than its boon.

But nearby Botswana shows that mineral wealth can be a benefit in a country with the political development in place. The country offers an instructive counterpoint to Zaire. Botswana has had by far the highest rate of growth in sub-Saharan Africa, 8.4% per year over the whole 1965 to 1990 period. In this time Botswana went from being among the very poorest countries in the world to a country that surpassed the per capita income of such countries as Turkey and Chile.

The economy of Zaire, in contrast, shrunk at a –2.2% rate throughout this quarter-century period. This is an appropriate period for comparison because Botswana became independent in 1966, and Mobutu came to power in Zaire in 1965. Botswana's astonishing rate of growth places it higher than any country with a population of more than one million as reported by the World Bank over this period, including South Korea at 7.1%, Singapore at 6.4% and Hong Kong at 6.1%. A chart comparing selected indicators for Botswana and Zaire is found at the end of this case study.

Perhaps even more impressive, unlike its high-growth peers Botswana has been a multiparty democracy, albeit one dominated by a single political party, the Botswana Democratic Party. Elections have been held every five years since 1965. Amnesty International has consistently given Botswana the highest human rights rating in Africa, one higher than the United Kingdom, its former colonial master. There is a free press and no political prisoners. Botswana accomplished these impressive economic and political results while surrounded by white minority regimes (South Africa, Rhodesia, and Namibia) for the first half of its history, nearby civil wars have often spilled over into its territory, and a steady stream of refugees has threatened to upset the social order.

There is no doubt that Botswana's diamond wealth has been central to its towering success. Botswana's 16 million metric carat annual diamond production is almost identical with Zaire's 15 million. But Botswana's population is just 1.2 million; Zaire's is much larger at 34.5 million. And a growth slowdown in Botswana in the mid-1990s was associated with price declines and instability in the diamond market. As we have seen, Zaire has several other important sources of mineral wealth, and although there is no doubt that Botswana's per capita mineral wealth is greater, African countries with strong mineral wealth have typically done worse than those without. Scholars of contemporary national development, such as Michael Porter, have argued that absence of natural resources can be a net competitive advantage. A Harvard Institute of International Development study confirmed this paradoxical disadvantage, which tends to divert resources away from sustainable industrial development, and lets a country avoid hard policy choices for a time. Botswana's landlocked geography is another disadvantage; other things equal, landlocked developing countries have tended to grow more slowly than those with direct access to the sea.

Thus, Botswana's success cannot be attributed only to diamonds. The absence of a dictator like Mobutu has helped, but even this explanation is not enough. What keeps a country like Botswana from falling prey to a Mobutu? It certainly helps to have a democratic tradition, in which there are pressures to allocate resources to genuine development. In this way, Botswana has been an outlier in Africa. What a country spends its wealth on matters, whether that wealth is large or small. Botswana has achieved essentially universal primary education, a rare achievement in the developing world, and a respectable one-third of children enroll in secondary education, compared with the sub-Saharan Africa average of under 20%.

Botswana suffered a brutal drought from 1982 to 1987, and poor rural peoples were severely affected. In many countries their plight might have been unattended to until significant starvation began and caught the attention of the world. Botswana built on its social security system and provided relief to the rural poor through a three-pronged system of maintaining food availability, as detailed by Jean Dreze and Amartya Sen: (1) guaranteeing public employment for cash wages that could be spent on available food, (2) direct food distribution to selected groups and (3) programs to increase agricultural productivity and restore food availability. Botswana's free press and democratic system seem to be a major factor in this response, as contrasted with the harsh indifference to severe poverty in Zaire.

On other human development indicators, such as infant mortality and health professionals per capita, Botswana also scores well. However, the United Nations Development Program (UNDP) 1995 Human Development Index ranks the country 74th out of 174 countries ranked, which is 7 points lower than its GDP rank; in other words, human development is slightly lower than predicted by the level of real per capita income. But if to some degree nonincome measures of development have not quite kept pace with Botswana's astronomical growth rate, its human development performance for Africa is extraordinary. In sub-Saharan Africa only the island of Mauritius rates higher in the UNDP Index.

Finally, it should be noted that not all of Botswana's luck has been good. The five-year drought of the mid-1980s was very harsh by any standards, and other serious droughts, such as that of 1979 to 1980, plague the country with some regularity.

A single ethnic group, the Batswana, dominates Botswana; it is widely considered a development advantage to have a homogeneous population, ranging from political decision-making advantages for selection of public good levels of a population holding similar preferences, to the common historical animosities of neighboring peoples. Minorities often fare poorly in developing—and often in developed—countries. In Botswana one of the few blemishes on the development record is that the minority aboriginal bushmen fare much less well than the majority Batswana, though this problem is a very difficult one to remedy. Botswana will continue to bear watching to see if its human development performance can fully catch up with its income growth, but it already demonstrates the good use a country can make of its natural resources when it has an advanced political development to facilitate economic development.

Taken together, the case of immiseration amidst riches in Zaire with the counterpoint of development success in Botswana shows clearly the vital role of political development, and the importance of the role of the state, whether to do good or ill, in economic development.

BOTSWANA AND ZAIRE:
A Comparison of Selected Indicators

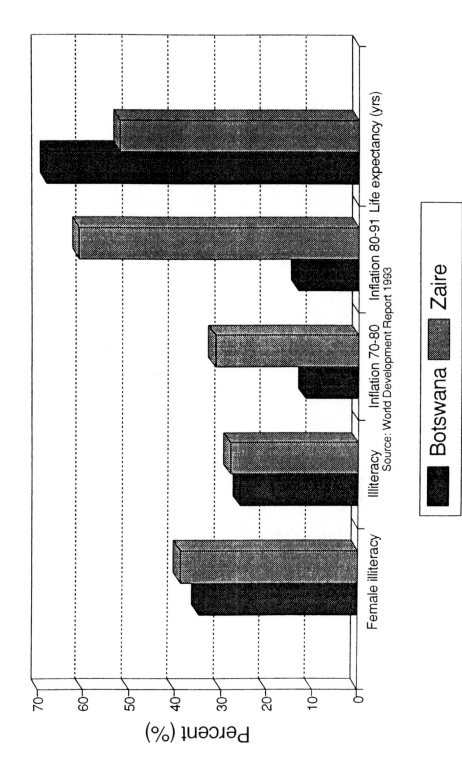

Sources

Africa Research Bulletin, Dec. 1993, July 1995.

Askin, Steve. "Zaire's Tyrant Hangs On," *Christian Science Monitor,* March 9, 1993.

Christian Science Monitor, Feb. 5, 1993.

Dreze, Jean, and Amartya Sen. *Hunger and Public Action.* Oxford: Clarendon.

The Economist, Jan. 23, 1993.

Harvey, Charles, and Stephen R. Lewis Jr. *Policy Choice and Development Performance in Botswana.* New York: St. Martins, 1990.

Komisar, Lucy. "The Claws of the Dictatorship in Zaire: 'The Leopard' Still Rules." *Dissent,* Summer 1992.

New York Times, April 30, 1992; March 21, 1993; July 22, 1993, March 2, 1994; April 3, 1994; May 24, 1994; Oct. 25, 1994.

Picard, Louis A. *The Politics of Development in Botswana: A Model for Success?* Boulder: Rienner, 1987.

Porter, Michael. *Competitive Advantage of Nations.* New York: Free Press, 1990.

Stedman, Stephen J., ed. *Botswana: The Political Economy of Democratic Development* (especially the chapter by Stephen R. Lewis). Boulder: Rienner, 1993.

United Nations Development Program. *Human Development Report,* 1992, 1995.

U.S. Congress, *The Situation in Zaire, Hearing before the Subcommittee on African Affairs.* Washington, DC: Government Printing Office. Nov. 6, 1991.

Wall Street Journal, Dec. 17, 1991.

Washington Post, Oct. 10, Oct. 13, 1991; March 31, 1992; Feb. 23, April 13, 1993.

World Bank. *World Development Report,* 1986, 1991, 1992.

3. Taiwan—Inside the Miracle: A Development Success Story

Taiwan is one of the four East Asian "tigers," or "mini-dragons," whose dramatic economic successes of recent decades, along with South Korea, Singapore, and Hong Kong, have influenced the way economists think about development. With a population of about 21 million, Taiwan is a mountainous, 14,000-square-mile island off the coast of China, about the combined size of Massachusetts, Connecticut, and Rhode Island.

Taiwan's claim to its status as a "development miracle" is as strong as that of any other economy in the world. The island has racked up a measured annual economic growth rate averaging close to 8% over more than four decades. Taiwan grew nearly 10% annually in the widely used benchmark 1965-80 period, higher than any other reported figure. Though growth in various countries has occasionally reached rates as high as 14%, and in some regions as high as 25% or more, Taiwan's average growth performance is the highest ever recorded over such a long stretch of time. In the postwar period, Taiwan has grown from an impoverished annual per capita income of just $100, to a relatively prosperous society with per capita income measured at about $12,000 U.S. dollars in 1995, 18th highest in the world. At least as important, Taiwan has achieved universal elementary and middle-school education (nine years are mandatory), a healthy population with a life expectancy of 71.9 years for men and 77.2 for women, and an infant mortality rate of only five per thousand. Absolute poverty l.as been essentially eliminated, there is very little unemployment, and relative inequality is modest even by developed country standards.

Taiwan thus seems to have achieved almost everything we look for in development. This achievement is in dramatic contrast to many other economies that started in a similar—or even much better—set of circumstances in the postwar world. The question begs itself: how did they do it?

Explanations for Success. Paradoxically, but as is often the case in development studies, the problem is not that we have too few explanations for success or failure, but too many. Taiwan's success in particular has been ascribed to many factors. Here are 14 of the major ones: 1) emphasis on education; 2) extensive infrastructure development; 3) early and thorough land reform; 4) very high rates of savings and investment; 5) a mixture of constructive foreign influences and diffusion of commercial ideas from Japan and the United States; 6) effective government industrial planning; 7) the free market's release of human energies and creativity; 8) the 1960s Vietnam War boom; 9) direct American aid—and Taiwan's use of that aid for investment rather than consumption; 10) the work ethic and productive attitudes of the labor force; 11) a long history as an entrepreneurial culture; 12) the initiation of an export-led growth strategy in the midst of the rapidly expanding world economy of the early 1960s; 13) the movement into entrepreneurship of capable local islanders seeking opportunities for advancement, as they were blocked from the political arena; and 14) the survival instinct: the necessity of economic development as a defense against attack from the mainland (the Peoples' Republic of China).

We will be able to dismiss perhaps four of these explanations as major factors, but any of just a few of the remaining factors might offer sufficient explanation for Taiwan's success. The case of Taiwan's development may thus be "overdetermined." Despite advances in such techniques as cross-national econometrics, we still lack adequate ways of measuring factors of development across countries. Uncovering the key factors in any one "development miracle" thus remains almost as much art as science.

Emphasis on education. Consistent with the historical Chinese cultural veneration for education, six years of education became compulsory on Taiwan in 1950. This was remarkable enough, but more remarkable still in the troubled history of developing economies was that this edict was actually carried out within just a few years. Especially impressive were enrollment rates for girls, which surpassed 90% for those aged 6 to 11 by 1956. (The comparable figure for boys in that year was over 96%.) Emphasis on girls' education is one of the most important factors in successful development, if not the single most vital factor, as the case of girls' education in Pakistan demonstrates (see Case 16).

When compulsory education was expanded to a full nine years in 1968, there were doubts that the economy could afford it. Today, while nine years remains a remarkable minimum educational standard for any developing economy, plans are being considered to expand compulsory schooling to twelve years.

Some other features are: Students go to school seven hours per day, for five and one-half days per week. In 1992-93, the student-teacher ratio was just 26 for elementary school, 21 for junior high, and 22 each for academic and vocational high schools. Teacher salaries are relatively high, comparable to lower-middle management in Taiwan. The U.S. was Taiwan's model for general education and Japan for vocational education. Greater emphasis is placed on general rather than job-specific skills. But incentives for close relationships between education and business are also stressed. In one innovative program, vocational high school teachers are paid to work in industry during the summer months to stimulate the development of curriculum relevant to industry's current needs. Tax breaks are given for company donations of personnel and equipment to schools.

Extensive infrastructure development. Development of infrastructure has been widely cited as a crucial factor in successful development by economists such as Paul Rosenstein-Rodan and Albert Hirschman. A major highway, for example, is argued to represent a "growth pole" around which industrial and commercial development can consolidate and grow. From the period of Japanese colonial rule (1905-1945), Taiwan inherited an infrastructure system that was far superior to that of most poor countries. The Japanese built roads, ports, and railroads to facilitate their own acquisition of rice and other farm products from the island. But this same infrastructure became a vehicle for national industrial growth from the 1950s. This endowment was supplemented by the government's own extensive program in the 1950s and 1960s. Taiwan's army was too large for the island, a legacy of the pre-1949 control of the mainland by the governing Kuomintang, or Chinese Nationalists. Thousands of soldiers participated in a voluntary program to retire from active military service to build infrastructure, including the technically challenging east-west highway projects, a program reckoned in Taiwan to be a major factor in its subsequent success.

Early and thorough land reform. Not burdened by close political ties to landlords, the Taiwan government was politically able to implement a thoroughgoing land-to-the-tiller reform program in the 1950s. Landowners received stock in state-owned enterprises in return for transferring land to peasants. This was a major factor in the extremely rapid growth of agricultural productivity in this period—a crucial foundation for later industrialization. Other countries with similar land reform efforts, such as South Korea and Japan, have seen impressive results. The U.S. analogously benefitted from 19th-century programs such as the Homestead Act. Development in Latin American countries has been severely hampered by the lack of land reform.

Very high rates of savings and investment. Capital formation has long been deemed crucial to successful development. Developed countries have much higher levels of capital per head than less developed countries, one of the factors enabling developed countries to enjoy higher productivity and incomes. Taiwan's savings rates were among the highest ever recorded, reaching 30 to 40% in the 1950s and 60s.

The savings ethic is deeply rooted in Taiwanese culture. Parents teach children the overriding need to save for a rainy day. This cultural pattern is supplemented by public policies that keep real interest rates for savers relatively high and tax free. Interestingly, like fellow tiger South Korea but unlike Singapore, Taiwan has a relatively low foreign capital share in total investment, about 10%. High savings and investment is an important factor in development, but not a sufficient one. India has substantially increased its rates of investment since independence, but not its growth rate, in part because capital equipment is more expensive there, in part because investments have not been made in the most productive sectors at any point in time.

Diffusion of commercial ideas. High saving alone will not create a development miracle without productive ideas among entrepreneurs about what use to make of it. Though hard to document precisely, Taiwan has had considerable success at absorbing commercial ideas from Japan and the United States. Much of this was due to the diligence of thousands of individual small companies. But government also played a role, through agencies like the China External Trade Development Council (CETDC) that combed the world, especially the United States, for ideas on how Taiwan firms could upgrade their technology and adapt to enter industrial markets. The World Bank's Donald Keesing has offered some fascinating insights into its operation:

"Market research in CETDC's New York office as of 1980 was based on an active search for items that could be sold in the United States. The search began with an analysis of the size and origin of U.S. imports, followed by a preliminary study of the price and quality of the more competitive imported and U.S. products. From this the officers in New York reached an estimate of the likelihood of Taiwan, China firms competing successfully against offerings already on the market. (They claimed to understand the manufacturing capabilities of Taiwan, China firms well enough to do this.) Once a likely product was identified, the office asked firms in Taiwan, China to send it samples of the product and price lists. Representatives of the office would then visit importers, wholesalers, and other traders with samples and price lists, prospecting for sales. They would try to get reactions to the product. If the buyers were interested they would telex the manufacturers. If not, they would find out why and then suggest appropriate steps to the manufacturer."

This leads us to perhaps the most complex set of development issues—the roles of state and market in successful development.

Effective government industrial planning. A traditional explanation for Taiwan's success is the operation of the free market. In recent years, Robert Wade and others have effectively championed the idea that Taiwan's success is due in large measure to effective government industrial planning. These policies are in large measure analogous to those of South Korea, though the industrial base of Taiwan is in small firms and that of Korea in large firms. (See Case 18 on South Korea.)

Taiwan has had active industrial policy systems in place to license exports, control direct foreign investment both to and from Taiwan, establish export cartels, and to provide fiscal incentives for investment in priority sectors and concessional credit for favored industries.

Taiwan's economic history began with a very highly dirigiste, or state-directed, import substitution-oriented industrialization, in the 1949-1950 period. The 1958 reforms switched intervention to export promotion and introduced market forces. But what emerged was far from a free market—only a less thoroughly planned economy. Into the 1980s, all imports and exports in Taiwan have had to be covered by a license. Imports are classified into "prohibited," "controlled," and "permissible." Controlled goods include luxuries and some goods produced locally with reasonable quality, in sufficient quantities, and whose prices are not more than a narrow margin (about 5%) above comparable import prices. Even the "permissible" items were subject to strong controls, such as with garments, which until 1980 could only be imported from Europe and America—the least competitive sources. Other goods subject to "competitive origin restrictions" have included yarns, artificial fibers, fabrics, some processed foodstuffs, chemicals, machinery, and electrical apparatus. Because the controlled list is larger than the published one, not all "permissibles" are automatically approved. As Wade shows, a potential importer of an item on the hidden list has been asked to provide evidence that domestic suppliers cannot meet foreign price, quality, and timing-of-delivery terms. Wade presents evidence that their function is to jump-start growth industries by providing domestic demand for products targeted by government. Then aggressive incentives are provided to induce companies to begin to export these products.

Wade's interpretation of the relative success of this import substitution program, however, is consistent with an emphasis on market incentives. He argues that because it controls quantities of foreign goods entering the local economy, the government can use international prices to discipline the price-setting behavior of protected domestic producers. The government demands to know good reasons why domestic prices of protected items are significantly higher than international prices, especially in the case of inputs to be used for export production. In this way, domestic prices for controlled goods can be kept near world price levels through the threat of permitting imports, even without free trade of goods across national borders. Wade concludes that an effective government threat of allowing in more goods can itself be sufficient to hold prices down, despite the current trade protection. Wade's argument can be interpreted as analogous to the theory that monopolists will keep prices low to the extent that they fear the entry of a rival firm seeking to take advantage of a prevailing high price in an industry. Thus the argument is that government is able to play an active role in industrial planning without compromising the vitality of market incentives.

But some observers feel that Taiwan's government has been quite happy to promote the developmental state explanation, perhaps finding greater domestic political benefits in the implication that it has been more competent in formulating economic policy than diplomatic costs, in that it will be viewed as interventionist and anti-free market. Clearly, Taiwan's economy has been very far from a free market, but explanations for Taiwan's success other than its actively interventionist policies can be given. In particular, general policies such as support of basic education and encouragement of high savings cannot be said to have been ruled out as more important factors in Taiwan's success. Many small entrepreneurs in Taiwan seem to feel that government has done more to harass them than help them. And the stable, consistent macroeconomic policies in Taiwan and elsewhere in East Asia also stand in dramatic contrast to much of the rest of the developing world, especially the poorest-performing regions.

Free market incentives. Claims that an economy's success is due to government industrial policies, rather than the action of the free market, are impossible to fully prove. There is always the danger of corruption and inefficiency when government is excessively involved in the economy. Some anti-interventionist economists have gone so far as to argue that Taiwan would have done even better without its industrial policies; part of their contention is that "government failure" is almost always worse than market failure in developing countries.

At the same time, while entrepreneurial dynamism is hard to measure precisely, it is plain for all to see throughout the island. Taiwan is a case in which incentives to produce wealth rather than merely to seek a share of existing wealth ("rent-seeking behavior") are established with solid property rights and not significantly undermined by other policies.

Certainly, the government of Taiwan has not always been a highly efficient engine of progress. There would seem to be plenty of room for inefficiency merely because the Republic of China is in the unique situation of administering both a central and a provincial government covering exactly the same territory. This is a legacy of the Chinese civil war, which Taiwan's governing Kuomintang lost. Moreover, until 1991, the government ruled Taiwan under martial law. This would seem to have offered ample opportunities for corruption. Indeed, since 1993, new corruption scandals seem to be reported almost daily in Taiwan's many independent newspapers. The free election of Lee Teng-hui as President in 1996 was the culmination of a smooth five-year transition to democratic governance.

Listening to Taiwan's government and opposition leaders, one might conclude that there are not only two Chinas, but two Taiwans. One is clean, efficient, has a free press, and is democratic. The other is corrupt, inefficient, features government control of television, and has democratic institutions that are little more than a figleaf over Kuomintang dictatorship. The truth about the government role lies somewhere in between. Taiwan is best understood as a case in which the dynamism of the marketplace is sustained and harnessed with a generally, though not universally, effective role of government in correcting market failure and promoting sustainable development. Taiwan might indeed have done better if government activities had been scaled back in some fields—but on net there is little doubt that its industrial policies have helped more than hurt. The reverse is true of many other developing countries, and it is difficult to draw general conclusions. Of course, now that Taiwan is approaching developed country status, earlier government economic policies may no longer be applicable. The emergence of an effective opposition in the independence-minded Democratic Progressive Party is a factor keeping government failure in check.

Other factors. The other explanations listed earlier were also somewhat important, but are unlikely to have been critical given the decisive role of the seven factors just discussed. They are also special features that other economies cannot easily encourage through policy measures. The 1960s Vietnam War boom affected countries such as the Philippines as much if not more, but without lasting effect; this suggests that other conditions were more important in Taiwan's success. American aid to Egypt has been far larger, and substantially used for investment purposes, but with less impressive results. Undoubtedly the work ethic and attitudes of the labor force were important. At the same time, they could not be called into play without the right incentives being in place, and without the availability of economically productive ideas. And a work ethic can be stimulated by the right incentives. A long history as an entrepreneurial culture may also be important, but in the long term these will similarly be influenced by incentives for entrepreneurship.

The fact that Taiwan benefitted from beginning export-led growth in the early 1960s, a time of unequaled world growth and a wide-open American market, was an undoubted advantage. On the other hand, other countries, such as Thailand, have successfully grown through manufactures exports in the 1980s, despite far slower U.S. and world income and trade growth rates. Export-oriented Guangdong province of China is growing far faster in the 1990s than Taiwan ever did, despite continued sluggish world trade growth (see Case 4). The idea that local islanders had little opportunities outside of entrepreneurship has not been proven; in any case, Taiwan seems hardly to differ in this regard from the situation under many other authoritarian regimes around the developing world that have suffered negative per capita income growth.

As to the necessity of economic development as a defense strategy, one can hardly single out Taiwan. The United States guaranteed Taiwan's defense after President Truman sealed off the island in 1950, in response to the Korean crisis. Other developing countries lacking the natural defenses of an island and are gravely threatened by hostile neighbors have made little development progress in the same period. Military necessity more often represents a diversion of resources needed for development than a productive stimulus.

Conclusion. It seems that Taiwan's success is best explained by a combination of emphasis on education, absorption of productive ideas from abroad, extensive infrastructure development, thoroughgoing land reform, very high rates of savings and investment, effective industrial policy, and last but not least, ensuring that incentives of the marketplace to produce wealth rather than seek a share of existing wealth are established with solid property rights and not undermined by other policies.

Today, Taiwan seems well-characterized by Walt Rostow's notion of an economy in a "drive to maturity," in which the range of the world's most advanced technology and skills are mastered. Government is focusing on collaborating with the private sector on more advanced research and development (R&D), as Taiwan moves into high technology fields. In 1991, a huge $300-billion-plus infrastructure development project was announced as part of the ambitious 1991–1996 Development Plan, designed to propel Taiwan into the ranks of the developed economies. Unfortunately, the program had to be scaled back considerably for budgetary reasons, and corruption has hampered the program's effectiveness, as organized crime moved into the construction sector. The private sector is being encouraged through incentives and exhortation to take up the slack, but it is unlikely that it can fully do so. Only time will tell how soon Taiwan can reach the status of a fully developed economy.

Are there any drawbacks to Taiwan's growth? Certainly environmental considerations have taken a backseat to economic growth until very recently. Taipei suffers from exceedingly noxious air pollution, for example. Despite a nominal beginning at land use planning, a driver down the island's West coast will find a dizzying jumble of various agricultural, industrial, commercial, and residential uses, defying any economic rationale, let alone land use aesthetics. She will find industrial sites perched on landfill over rice paddies and prawn pools, into which some waste products inevitably seep. Attention is given to matters such as endangered species only after much Western pressure has been applied. Even then, as one Taiwan official put it, "the private sector is flexible and vibrant in Taiwan—where there is profit, there is activity."

Moreover, GNP per capita, measured in U.S. dollars, often understates a country's real living levels, because equivalent personal services, from haircuts to advanced training courses, cost so much less. To compensate, adjustments are made to what is termed *purchasing power parity*. A few countries, such as Japan, have their living standards overstated when incomes are expressed in dollars. Taiwan is also almost certainly such a case; for example, its distribution system is biased against consumers in a way very similar to that of Japan. But because the economy does not appear in United Nations and World Bank reports, agencies in which only the Peoples' Republic of China is represented, purchasing power parity estimates comparable to other countries are not readily available. But Taiwan's purchasing power parity income level is more likely under $10,000 rather than significantly over that figure.

Housing remains small and basic in Taiwan; and motorbikes outnumber cars, a large fraction of which are taxis. (Some of this may be due to incentives of the tax code). Left behind by the miracle, homeless derelicts can be seen sleeping on the streets of Taipei and Kaohsiung—though these cities differ little in this regard from New York and Washington, DC. With the opening of China, many Taiwan companies are moving lock, stock, and barrel to the mainland; fears of the hollowing out of the economy, such as has been seen in the U.S. and U.K., are being voiced. But this is likely to bring as much opportunity as problems. And even with such caveats, Taiwan has come exceptionally far; the caveats only qualify Taiwan's success, and point to some necessary future directions; they do not in any way negate its impressive accomplishments.

In sum, Taiwan illustrates well the complex mix of factors behind the kind of rapid economic and social progress often termed a development miracle. The factors that stood out were education, infrastructure, land reform, high savings and investment, absorption of commercial ideas, effective industrial policy, and market incentives.

Sources

Due to Taiwan's peculiar status as a non-member of the United Nations and the World Bank, little authoritative scholarly work is available. This study is based largely on government documents, interviews of the author with government and opposition leaders, and other firsthand observations. Additional sources:

Amsden, Alice. "Taiwan's Economic History: A Case of Etatisme and a Challenge to Dependency Theory." *Modern China 5* (1979): 341–80.

Amsden, Alice. "Taiwan," Special Issue: Exports of Technology by Newly Industrializing Economies. *World Development 12,* nos. 5/6 (1984): 627–633.

Balassa, Bela. "The Lessons of East Asian Development: An Overview." *Economic Development and Cultural Change 36,* Supplement, S273–290, 1988.

Borus, Michael, and Denis Fred Simon. "High Technology in the Pacific Basin: Analysis and Policy Implications." Paper presented at the State Department-NAS Conference on Foreign Competition in Science and Technology, National Academy of Science, May 11, 1989.

Bradford, C.I. "Trade and Structural Change, NICs and Next-Tier NICs as Transitional Economies." *World Development 15* (1987): 299–316.

Hollis, Chenery, Sherman Robinson, and Moses Syrquin. *Industrialization and Growth: A Comparative Study.* New York: Oxford, 1986.

Chu, Wan-Wen. "Export Led Growth and Import Dependence, the Case of Taiwan 1969–1981." *Journal of Development Economics 28* (1988): 265–276.

Cline, William. "Can the East Asian Model of Development Be Generalized?" *World Development 10* (1982): 81–90.

Dahlman, Carl J., Bruce Ross-Larson, and Larry E. Westphal. "Managing Technical Development: Lessons from the Newly Industrializing Countries." *World Development 15,* (1987): 759–75.

Jacobsson, Steffan. "Technical Change and Industrial Policy: The Case of Computer

Numerically Controlled Lathes in Argentina, Korea and Taiwan." *World Development 10* (1982): 991–1014.

Keesing, Donald B. "The Four Successful Exceptions. Official Export Promotion and Support for Export Marketing in Korea, Hong Kong, Singapore and Taiwan, China." *United Nations Development Program–World Bank Trade Expansion Program Occasional Paper 2,* 1988.

Lal, Deepak. *The Poverty of Development Economics.* London: Hobart, 1984.

Pack, Howard, and Larry Westphal. "Industrial Strategy and Technological Change: Theory versus Reality." *Journal of Development Economics 22* (1986): 87–128.

Rostow, Walt W. *The Stages of Economic Growth: A Non-Communist Manifesto.* London: Cambridge University Press, 1960.

Smith, Stephen C. *Industrial Policy in Developing Countries: Reconsidering the Real Sources of Export-Led Growth.* Washington, DC: Economic Policy Institute, 1991.

Wade, Robert. *Governing the Market.* Princeton University Press: 1991.

Wade, Robert. "The Role of Government in Overcoming Market Failure: Taiwan, Republic of Korea and Japan." In Helen Hughes, ed., *Achieving Industrialization in East Asia.* New York: Cambridge University Press, 1988.

Wade, Robert. "State Intervention in Outward-looking Development: Neoclassical Theory and Taiwanese Practice." in Gordon White, ed. *Developmental States in East Asia.* New York: St. Martins, 1988.

4. Guangdong, China: Fastest Growth in Economic History

The larger the productivity gap between countries, the quicker income can grow once modern economic growth has begun. It seems the gap between traditional and advanced technology can be crossed about as quickly today as a century ago, although the gap between the most advanced and the most backward regions in the world is larger than ever. While Britain doubled its output per person in the first 60 years of its industrial revolution, and America did so in 45 years, Korea accomplished this in the ten years from 1966 to 1977. Incredibly, Guangdong province in China (adjacent to Hong Kong) recently performed this feat in less than five years in the second half of the 1980s, and probably accomplished this again in the first half of the 1990s. In 1991, Guangdong grew at an annual rate of 27% and in 1992 at 23%. Changan County China, in Guangdong Province, a current destination of much foreign investment, had a 30% increase in foreign-investment projects in 1995. Foreign companies signed investment agreements there worth $257.3 million in 1995. For example, Guangdong province exported some $2.12 billion worth of toys in 1995, up from $1.94 billion in 1994. Guangdong exports about 95% of its toy output. Some of the data showing Guangdong's remarkable economic progress are summarized in three charts at the end of this case study.

Guangdong is the province of China adjacent to the British colony of Hong Kong and the Portuguese colony of Macao. Between those cities and up the Pearl River lies its capital, Guangzhou, once known in the West as Canton. This Pearl River Delta region is one of the main engines of the recent rapid growth of China, and the driving locomotive for Guangdong, today the wealthiest Chinese province, with a population of about 65 million.

A tour of Guangdong vividly brings out the almost inherent unevenness of rapid growth. Large parts of the province give the impression of a vast forest of construction cranes. This itself is unremarkable—the cities, at least, of many developing countries have a similar appearance. The remarkable difference is that the cranes are almost always moving. Though Shenzhen does have some signs of underdevelopment in the form of beggars, bicycle rickshaws, and the like, for the most part it is now a modern extension of Hong Kong. Factories in Shenzhen and other Guangdong export zones could perhaps be best described as high-tech sweatshops. Internal Chinese passports are still required to move to these areas, although some Chinese are apparently living illegally in the zones, or just outside them. The province is very mixed, but on net the impression matches the statistics that suggest that Guangdong has now joined the ranks of the lower middle-income countries. The dynamism of the market is very visible in cities such as Guangzhou. Amidst a construction boom, the streets are filled with energetic entrepreneurs engaged in every conceivable market activity. The contrast with the more languid pace of the streets in sub-Saharan Africa or the Indian subcontinent is striking to an observer.

The larger state-owned enterprises (SOEs), often operated as joint ventures with foreign partners, appear surprisingly efficient, with relatively modern capital equipment from sources such as Japan and Italy. Typically, about half of Guangdong's SOE workers will be on a five-year contract, automatically renewed in most cases. Permanent workers, who may have 12 years of schooling and three months of intensive on-the-job training, typically earn about $100 per month. Much emphasis is given to product quality, although quality circles and other forms of employee participation are rare.

Guangdong benefits from a history of an entrepreneurial culture and exposure to Western business practices dating to the early 19th century. The market savvy of the province was never fully extinguished in the command economy period of the mid-1950s to mid-1970s.

Modern Guangdong economic history of rapid development begins in Hong Kong, the British enclave city-state surrounded by Guangdong. Hong Kong will revert to Chinese sovereignty in 1997, and has had a long and complex relationship to Guangdong.

Given its proximity to Hong Kong, Guangdong became the local symbol of hated capitalism in the Maoist 1950s, 60s, and early 70s. It was relentlessly portrayed in the Chinese media as a center of exploitation and immiserating poverty.

Hong Kong became an industrial center when many industrialists who had previously concentrated in Shanghai moved their factories to Hong Kong after the Communist takeover in 1949. These industrialists benefitted from a continuous flow of migrants leaving the mainland who were willing to work hard for low pay. Hong Kong's niche as a manufacturing center was a departure from its previous function. Before 1949, Hong Kong had specialized as an "entrepot" (trading and transshipment) center rather than a manufacturing center, for trade between the interior of China and the rest of the world. This role was greatly diminished at the time of the Communist takeover, but the Communists tacitly worked to guarantee Hong Kong's continued viability because of its continued value as a connection—if a covert one—to the outside world.

In a dramatic turnabout, once-despised Hong Kong instead became a symbol of modernity when China reopened to the outside world in the late 1970s. By this time, Hong Kong had become one of Asia's principal centers of industrial know-how and investment capital and one of the famous newly industrialized "four tigers." Hong Kong had benefitted in international commerce from its widespread use of the international language, English. It also gained from the presence of top-quality British civil servants transferred there from all over the once sprawling British Empire, who brought good governance. Much more than any other newly industrialized country (NIC), however, Hong Kong relied on the free market, rather than industrial and trade policies, for its great success.

Technology transfer and direct foreign investment, primarily from Hong Kong or through Hong Kong intermediaries, has unquestionably been the engine of growth for Guangdong. The "demonstration effect," in which the population perceives firsthand relatively high levels of wealth in Hong Kong, at just the time when commitment to Communist values of sacrifice and egalitarianism were waning, should also not be underestimated as a force for entrepreneurial drive, an elusive human factor in development that David McClelland has called the "need for achievement."

For well over 150 years there has been a migrant flow from Guangdong to Hong Kong, and there have always been many family and personal connections between these territories. This has provided a valuable base on which to build industrial development. Business connections between Guangdong and Hong Kong anticipate the return of Hong Kong to Chinese sovereignty in 1997. This return carries some risks for Guangdong development if Hong Kong declines as a result; but it offers mostly prospective benefits, provided Beijing carries out the reintegration without jeopardizing the continuation of Hong Kong's special commercial advantages.

Guangdong leaders were more oriented toward market reform and ensuring development progress over ideological objectives than leaders of a majority of the other provinces. From the beginnings of the opening in the 1970s, these leaders became adept at determining what would be permitted by the Communist rulers in Beijing, and in leveraging these specific areas of greater economic freedom to the province's maximum advantage. The most popular local saying revived the ancient Chinese adage that "the mountains are tall and the emperor is far away."

Agricultural reforms stressing more incentives for individual farmers and agricultural markets in place of state distribution were pursued first, and farm output rose dramatically, doubling in the late seventies and early eighties. It does have to be acknowledged that Guangdong benefits from rich delta soil, and its success may not be easily duplicated. Moreover, the growth rate in agriculture probably cannot be sustained. Much of this increase in agricultural output probably represents what economists call a "once-for-all shift," as existing resources are used more efficiently, rather than a large permanent increase in the *rate* of growth. But the gains have been remarkable despite the caveats.

At the same time, village-owned and collective enterprises were encouraged and grew very rapidly, providing productive employment for farmers no longer needed on the land. Guangdong's leaders then took advantage of special autonomies granted the province in economic matters and of the special economic zone status in three parts of the province, including the dynamic Shenzhen, across the border from Hong Kong's New Territories.

But the leaders also took all other opportunities for pursuing reform that presented themselves. No doubt part of their stance was influenced by their own proximity to Hong Kong as well as the attitudes of their local citizens who could see Hong Kong television. But their attitudes and the favorable climate they created for the private sector has been a factor in Guangdong's success in its own right.

The dynamism and success of the township and collective enterprises represent a unique aspect of the emerging Chinese economy. Whether standing alone or as joint venture partners with foreign firms, these companies have led the growth and export success of the province. Some are really little more than private firms that are employee- or municipality-owned only on paper. But a majority seem to represent a distinctly Chinese form of quasi-public enterprise that spread the benefits of export success widely to all the employees or town residents while maintaining incentives for hard work. Information on these township and collective enterprises are hard to come by, but from preliminary indications they will bear close watching in the coming years as a possible model (see Case 24).

One should not underestimate the development damage inflicted by the Cultural Revolution turmoil of 1966–76. On the surface this conflict was ideological in nature, but it reflected in large measure a power struggle over who would succeed Mao Tse-tung after his death. Riots and factional fighting brought with them some damage to industrial machinery and buildings, but the most significant losses of the period were of human capital. Schools failed to function normally for almost a decade. Scholarship of all kinds became politically suspect and discouraged. Work habits flagged and institutions of incentives were sabotaged. If any real ideology prevailed in this period it could be called "anti-incentivism."

Much of the potential accumulation of skills and knowledge lost in the Cultural Revolution period can never be fully recovered, but some progress has been made in training those affected, improving work habits, and restoring and upgrading the quality of schools and universities. Unquestionably, part of China's very rapid growth of the past dozen years represents catch-up to lost potential output.

Then the question becomes whether the phenomenal growth of Guangdong, and indeed the impressive growth of China as a whole, represents a once-for-all shift as existing resources are used more efficiently, or represents sustainable growth. In much of China it seems to have been the former, especially in the agricultural sector. But in Guangdong, a permanent higher growth path seems to have been reached in the industrial and service sectors.

Many development scholars have argued that colonies and some other very dependent regions may find their development progress retarded by their dependent status. Modern economic growth, they argue, may be difficult to initiate under these circumstances. Economic history suggests that there are some important insights to be gained from this view. But certainly, the case of Guangdong shows that if the right conditions are met, trade can be a true engine of modern economic growth. Note that China and Guangdong have strong government with significant bargaining power.

Are the phenomenal economic statistics for real? There is a widely held view among foreign businesses involved in Guangdong that, if anything, the growth numbers are systematically understated. There is concern about igniting jealousies elsewhere in China and ideological reactions in the Communist Party if Beijing were to realize the amount of profits being made in joint ventures.

But the foreign investment numbers—over $15 billion were said to have been invested through 1992 with about the same level in new commitments—are somewhat exaggerated. Because foreign investment gets special treatment, Guangdong capital is increasingly "laundered" in Hong Kong, after which it reenters Guangdong as "clean" foreign capital. Front companies are known as "false foreign devils." But, if anything, there is little reason to believe that the total private investment figures are understated.

On July 1, 1997, Hong Kong officially becomes part of China. Guangdong in the end may become part of a "double-headed tiger" with Hong Kong, rather than a fifth East Asian tiger in its own right. In this scenario Hong Kong would be the regional center for top management and advanced services. But Guangdong also brings much bargaining power to the relationship. The economic consequences for China and the region as a whole bear close watching.

Industrial Output in Guangdong
1985-1992

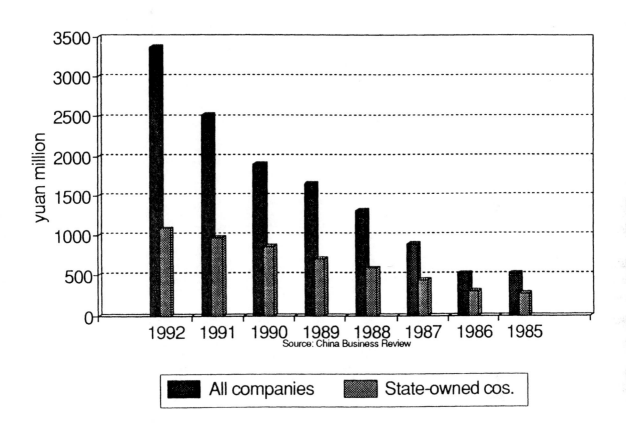

Source: China Business Review

All companies   State-owned cos.

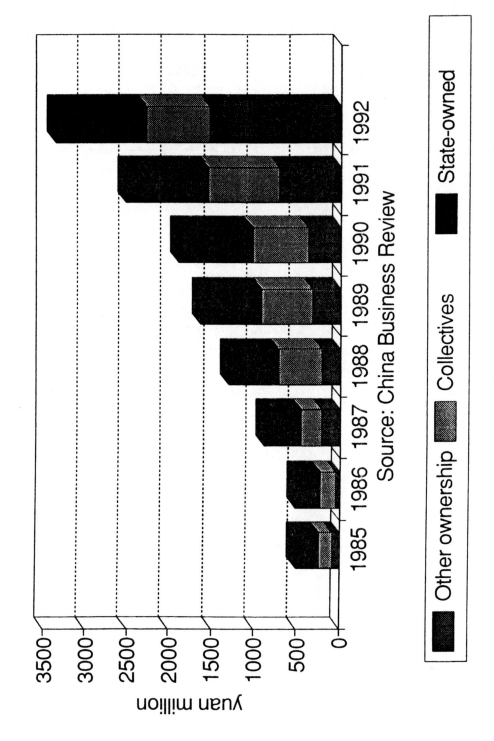

GUANGDONG
Industrial output by ownership

Source: China Business Review

Other ownership   Collectives   State-owned

yuan million

3500 3000 2500 2000 1500 1000 500 0

1985 1986 1987 1988 1989 1990 1991 1992

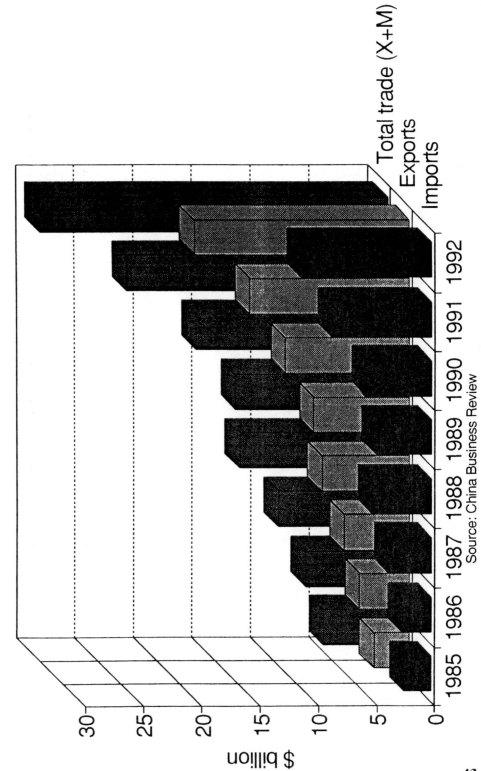

GUANGDONG
Foreign Trade

Total trade (X+M)
Exports
Imports

1985 1986 1987 1988 1989 1990 1991 1992

$ billion

30
25
20
15
10
5
0

Source: China Business Review

43

Sources

Balassa, Bela. "The Lessons of East Asian Development: An Overview." *Economic Development and Cultural Change,* 36, Supplement, S273–290, 1988.

Borus, Michael, and Denis Fred Simon. "High Technology in the Pacific Basin: Analysis and Policy Implications." National Academy of Science, 1989.

Byrd, William, and Lin Qingsong, eds. *China's Rural Industry: Structure, Development and Reform.* New York: Oxford, 1990.

Financial Times, Feb. 22, 1993.

Keesing, Donald B. "The Four Successful Exceptions. Official Export Promotion and Support for Export Marketing in Korea, Hong Kong, Singapore and Taiwan, China." *United Nations Development Program–World Bank Trade Expansion Program Occasional Paper 2,* 1988.

Smith, Stephen C. *Industrial Policy in Developing Countries: Reconsidering the Real Sources of Export Led Growth.* Washington, DC: Economic Policy Institute, 1991.

Vogel, Ezra. *One Step Ahead in China.* Cambridge, MA: Harvard University Press, 1989.

Wall Street Journal, Jan. 10, 1992; April 8, 1996; Aug. 28, 1995.

Washington Post, May 28, 1992.

White, Gordon, ed. *Developmental States in East Asia.* New York: St. Martins, 1988.

5. Hope for the Rural Poor: The Grameen Bank of Bangladesh

One of the biggest problems facing the poor is access to credit. For the poor urban peddler, access to credit can mean a chance to build a bigger inventory, so she has items on hand when customers request them, and can eventually move from the insecurity of being a petty street hawker to the stability of being a established vendor. For the poor rural peasant, access to credit can mean a chance to purchase tools, a draft animal, and small capital goods that can enable him to greatly improve his productivity, diversify crops and move toward commercial farming by producing some cash crops for the market, and eventually move from marginal peasant or landless agricultural laborer to established commercial farmer. For the poor rural landless laborer, access to credit can mean a chance to learn skills, purchase raw materials (such as cloth) and tools (such as a sewing machine), and eventually move from the edge of survival to established business person. The Grameen Bank of Bangladesh is an excellent illustration of how this credit can be provided to those who need it, while minimizing the risk that resources will be wasted.

The Grameen Bank was conceived by Muhammad Yunus, a former Chittagong University economics professor, as a private nonprofit development "action and research project." Professor Yunus had become convinced from his research that the lack of access to credit on the part of the poor was a binding constraint on their economic progress, a conclusion that has been confirmed by later studies from around the developing world. Yunus wanted to demonstrate that it was possible to lend to the poor without collateral, and to determine the best system for doing so.

Yunus said in an interview that "all human beings are born entrepreneurs. Some get the opportunity to find this out, but some never get this opportunity. A $5 loan can be a ticket to exploration of personal ability. All human beings have a skill—the survival skill. The fact that they are alive proves this. Just support this skill and see how they will choose to use it."

Yunus began the operation in 1976 with—at least as legend has it—a capitalization of just $30. He was able to convince the Bangladesh agricultural development bank (BKB) to provide some initial loan money. The first loans through BKB were guaranteed personally by Yunus. A series of expansions convinced the government of Grameen's value, and the Grameen Bank was formally incorporated under government charter in 1983. The Bank continued to grow very rapidly and now has well over 1000 branch offices throughout the country and about two million members. The branch office, covering 15 to 20 villages, is the basic organizational unit, and is responsible for its profits and losses.

Since its founding, the public-cooperative Grameen Bank has enabled nearly two million poor Bangladeshis to start or upgrade their own small businesses. Most of these borrowers are virtually landless, and more than three-quarters of the borrowers have been women. Borrowers are generally limited to those who own less than one half acre. Representatives of Grameen branches often go door to door in the villages they cover to inform people, who are generally illiterate and very reticent about dealing with banks, about Grameen's services.

Before opening a new branch, the new branch manager is assigned to prepare a socioeconomic report covering the economy, geography, demography, transportation and communication infrastructure, and politics of the area. Among other things, this ensures that a branch manager becomes familiar with the region and its potential borrowers before the branch begins operations.

Grameen, which alternatively means "rural" or "village" in the Bengali language, is incorporated as a publicly supported credit union, with borrowers owning 75% of the bank's stock and the government owning the remainder. The bank sets its own policy with strong borrower input, independent of government control. Grameen's annualized interest rate on loans is 16%. This excludes, however, a 25% surcharge on loan interest amounts that borrowers pay into an insurance Emergency Fund; it has been little used. The average annual inflation rate in Bangladesh has been about 9.1% over the 1980–1993 period, making the real interest rate about 7%.

Grameen's 16% loans can be compared with traditional moneylenders' loansharking rates of 120 to 200%. These moneylenders generally have a great deal of monopolistic power. Sometimes, though by no means always, they use extraeconomic coercion to get peasants to borrow from them at these high rates of interest and to ensure repayment; built into these moneylenders' rates are such costs as wages for maintaining thugs who enforce the moneylenders' dictates. These rural moneylenders' interest rates are not the result of competitive market forces. True, the traditional system may not be as inefficient as some writers have claimed. Because they are locally based, even though they do not move in the same social circles as low-income borrowers, these lenders have access to information about the credit-worthiness of borrowers that would be very hard for traditional banks to obtain. But one of the beauties of the Grameen Bank is that it trumps these moneylenders' informational advantages by using information held by the close peers of the borrowers.

Moreover, Grameen does not just substitute for existing moneylenders. Not only do few Grameen borrowers ever receive loans from formal borrowers, but it has been estimated by Grameen that only about one-fifth are served by the informal lenders. Another two-thirds can sometimes get small interest-free loans from relatives or friends. The remainder have no access to any form of credit.

To qualify for uncollateralized loans, potential borrowers form five-member groups. Each member must undergo a two-week training session before any member can secure a loan, and the training sessions are followed up with weekly group meetings with a bank officer. Grameen relies on what could be called the "collateral of peer pressure." Once a member of the group receives a loan, no other member may borrow until a regular repayment record has been established; and no repeat loans are approved until all members' accounts are settled. Members know the characters of group members, and only join groups with members they believe likely to repay their loans. Dr. Yunus recently said that the credit-worthiness of the poor is now established beyond doubt, and the real "question is whether banks and credit institutions are people-worthy."

A significant proportion of new borrowers pay installments in advance, presumably to qualify quickly for a larger loan. The five-person group size was not decided arbitrarily, nor on prior insight, but on the basis of experimentation. Initially, loans were awarded directly to individuals, but this required too much staff time to control the use and repayment of the loan. After the idea of mutual responsibility was developed, large groups of ten or more were tried at first, but this proved too large for intimate and informal peer to peer monitoring to be effective. Groups of five proved in practice to work best.

Peer oversight has contributed to Grameen's astonishing 98% ultimate repayment rate. By contrast, the country as a whole has a repayment rate of 30 to 40%, and the Industrial Bank of Bangladesh has been infamous for having almost all of its loans to the relatively wealthy in default. The list of defaulters is said to read like a "Who's Who in Bangladesh."

Group members are trained in such practical matters as bank procedures, the group savings program, the role of the center chief and the chairperson of the 5-member group, and even how to write their signatures. In addition, training has a moral component, stressing the Bank's 16 principles, or "Decisions," to be adhered to by each member. These Decisions were formulated in a national conference of 100 female center chiefs in 1984. They emphasize modern values, including self-discipline and hard work, hygiene, refusal to participate in backward practices like demanding bridal dowries, and mutual assistance. Adherence to these principles and attendance at rallies featuring the chanting of the Decisions are not formal requirements for receiving loans, but they are said to have become effective, implicit requirements.

Here is a sample from the 16 Decisions: #3- We shall not live in dilapidated houses. We shall repair our houses and work toward constructing new houses as soon as possible. #4- We shall grow vegetables all the year round. We shall eat plenty of them and sell the surplus. #6- We shall plan to keep our families small. #8- We shall always keep our children and the environment clean. #11- We shall not take any dowry in our sons' weddings, neither shall we give any dowry in our daughters' weddings. We shall not practice child marriage. #13- For higher income we shall collectively undertake higher investments.

Much has been written anecdotally about the structure of the Grameen Bank and the beneficial impact it has had on the lives of its members. But most of the solid quantitative information we have of the effects of the Grameen Bank comes from surveys conducted by Mahabub Hossain for the International Food Policy Research Institute.

The group structure facilitates the formation of cooperatives or joint ventures among the participants, encouraging ventures too large or too risky for poor individuals to undertake alone. Grameen also works to facilitate the accumulation of savings among its members through savings requirements or incentives for its borrowers to save. Hossain found that the working capital of borrowers tripled on average within 27 months.

Loans are only made for income-generating activities and have financed a wide range of activities, most of them not based on crop production. Activities financed have included dress (sari) weaving, shoe repair, livestock and poultry raising, small-scale food processing, paddy and rice trading, and grocery shopkeeping. Mahabub Hossain found that 46% of loans went to livestock and poultry raising, 25% for processing and light manufacturing, and 23% for trading and shopkeeping, thus almost no loans went to finance farm crop activities.

Opportunities for expansion of agricultural activities are limited in Bangladesh. About two-thirds of its 56,000 square miles is under cultivation, and the cost of expanding into the remaining uncultivated area is excessively high. Nearly three-quarters of the labor force is already working in agriculture, and opportunities for women are especially limited. Small scale "microentrepreneurship" offers the best opportunity for most of the functionally landless rural poor to improve their economic circumstances. In addition, it is difficult to operate the weekly or biweekly loan repayment system with loans for agriculture, which normally yield a return only at the end of a crop cycle. The Grameen Bank's focus on rural women microenterprise borrowers is probably optimal, providing the highest marginal social benefits under the conditions found in rural Bangladesh.

The average loan size in 1994 was $140, over half the annual income of many borrowers. In 1995, loans over $100 were common, but generally did not exceed $300. Loans have generally reached the absolutely poor. Hossain found that only 4.2% of borrowers own as much as a half acre of cultivatable land. The average income of borrowers has been found to be about half the national average. Though incomes of most borrowers remain below the poverty line, they get much closer to the line. In other words, Grameen has only slightly reduced poverty by the headcount measure, but has significantly reduced it by the income shortfall measure.

Grameen borrowers have had notable success in capital accumulation. Cattle raising is a major activity of borrowers. Hossain found that the number of cattle owned increased by 26% per year. Though the numbers involved are small—going from 61 per 100 borrowers before becoming a Grameen member to 102 per 100 borrowers at the time of the survey—these are impressive improvements for Bangladesh's absolutely poor.

But completely landless agricultural laborers appear to remain significantly underrepresented in the pool of borrowers: Hossain found that they represent 60% of Grameen's target group but only 20% of its actual borrowers—and this includes those who reported hired agricultural labor as a secondary economic activity as well as those who reported it a primary economic activity. There is certainly a stigma attached to being from an agricultural-labor household, and its incidence among borrowers could perhaps be understated—though likely not by much given Grameen's good information about its borrowers. In any case, to be both landless and an agricultural laborer by occupation is to be among the very most downtrodden groups in any developing country. Note that in Bangladesh, most laborers own a small plot of land for their house, but too little to form the basis for a viable farm. Some 60% of Bangladeshis are "functionally landless" in this sense.

But underreaching the hired agricultural laborers is probably not the fault of the Grameen Bank. Landless farm laborers are extremely hard to reach for any development program in any country. They also tend to be the least educated and are probably the least well prepared to move into viable entrepreneurial activities. The fact that the Bank has reached as many landless farm laborers as it has is itself very impressive. These laborers also benefit indirectly from the general development that Grameen affords, as it raises demand for labor and reduces the supply of agricultural labor. They will need other services besides those the Grameen can provide. But they must be the target of renewed, concerted aid efforts.

Grameen makes some loans to finance cooperative enterprises as well as to individuals. The goal is to take advantage of economies of scale and make the use of more modern techniques financially feasible. Though the share of such loans has been well under 10%, it has financed some of the most impressive undertakings, including the purchase and use of power looms, rice hullers, oil mills, and irrigation machines. But both the Bank and its borrowers have lacked the technical expertise to make these activities viable, and this is an area of needed improvement.

Grameen's emphasis on serving poor women is especially impressive. According to Hossain's survey, half the women borrowers said they were unemployed at the time they became Grameen members (compared with less than 7% of the men). The share of women among borrowers has climbed steadily over the years and reached 94% by the end of 1995.

Is Grameen subsidized, and how much subsidy makes sense? Costs at the bank are quite high by commercial bank standards. They have been estimated at 26.5% of the value of loans and advances. This is some 10% higher than the nominal interest rate charged, or 39% of the costs of lending are subsidized from all sources. Adding in estimated opportunity costs, Hossain has calculated an effective subsidy of 51%. But also note that about half of the excess of costs over interest receipts are attributable to the expense of opening new branches, which should be treated as a capital cost.

These high cost numbers indicate at first glance that there is room for greater economy measures. But it may also indicate that interest rates charged borrowers are at least 10 percentage points too low. We have seen that these rates are only about a tenth that charged by traditional moneylenders and that repayment rates are over 97%. Most borrowers would already be better off paying an interest rate of, say 27%, because they are either paying far more already; or, they may have to rely on loans from family members that have a high opportunity cost even if no interest is paid, and that may not always be available; or the poor simply have no source of borrowing at all. Only comparatively few current borrowers may be expected to find their investments no longer profitable at a modestly higher interest rate.

However, there is no doubt that a public subsidy of Grameen loans is justifiable on the basis of the loans' effect on absolute poverty alleviation and other positive externalities. Ideally, these benefits should be quantified to get a better handle on the level of subsidy that can be supported on efficient grounds. Because funds for subsidies are limited, the more the subsidy per loan, the less subsidized loans can be made. There may be some combination of reduced operating costs, modest increases in interest rates, and continued subsidy that is optimal for creating the most welfare gains with the available resources.

A small loans development bank like Grameen may be a vital—if not necessary—condition for improving the well-being of the poor. But it is not a sufficient condition. Bangladesh suffers many tornados and excessive floods. For example, in 1992 up to 200,000 people died in flooding following a major cyclone. For the survivors, these recurrent disasters can also wipe out years of economic progress nurtured by Grameen. This shows that small-scale projects like Grameen are not enough and must be undertaken in conjunction with large-scale projects like Bangladesh's flood control project. The point is not that large-scale projects should be abandoned in favor of smallscale ones, but that the two must be made to work together. Neither offers a sufficient development strategy by itself.

Only about 9% of the labor force in Bangladesh are women, a figure that has risen little over the past decades. The Grameen Bank has proven itself one of the few effective attempts to involve poor women in economic activities. Women borrowers have higher repayment rates than men, and are more likely to spend their increased income on their children's welfare. Rising women's incomes, self-esteem, and business clout has begun to cause some backlash in the conservative Islamic culture of rural Bangladesh, in which under the Purdah system women are expected to be secluded from social activities. Grameen and other programs, such as the nontraditional schools run by the Bangladesh Rural Advancement Committee, are seen as a challenge to this traditional status quo, over which men have traditionally presided. Schools have been burned, and women have been driven out of their villages and worse for challenging traditional cultural norms, including participating in market activities. Yunus has stated that some husbands have viewed Grameen as a threat to their authority. In some cases "the husband thought we had insulted him and were destroying his family. We had cases of divorce just because the woman took loans." A leading fundamentalist cleric in Dhaka was quoted in the *Washington Post* as saying, "We have no objection to improving the lot of women, but the motives of the Grameen Bank and other organizations are completely different. They want to eradicate Islam, and they want to do this through women and children." The future of the Grameen Bank will depend on a creative response to this difficult environment of economic and cultural change.

Despite challenges, today the Grameen Bank continues to break new ground in development projects. In a strikingly original scheme, a Grameen Telecom subsidiary has recently been established, with the participation of Norwegian and Japanese telecommu-.

nications companies. The business plan is simple: to provide the poorest woman in each village with a cellular phone. Most of these villages are still without a phone system. "Now you may wonder," says Dr. Yunus, "what would the poorest woman in such a Bangladesh village want with a cellular phone? Well, everyone in the village who wants to make a call will have to come to her." The Grameen Bank is also pioneering a low-cost cooperative health insurance scheme, in which an annual fee of $1.25 provides half of the health costs for an entire family for a variety of services.

The general value of the Grameen experience depends on whether it can be replicated and sustained. Its replicability has already been demonstrated in good measure both in Bangladesh ai d outside it. It has spread to villages in several regions of the country. Even so, it has still only covered less than 5% of its target group in Bangladesh. Only time will tell whether Grameen can continue to expand at its previous impressive rates. Of course, while the goal of a village banking system like Grameen must be to work itself out of a job, realistically millions of Bangladeshis will remain poor for several decades to come under the very best assumptions.

Though on a smaller scale, other developing countries have benefitted from imitating the Grameen Bank, including Malaysia, Sri Lanka, and Malawi. It has even been borrowed with some success as a model by some of America's inner cities, as Lewis Solomon has chronicled. Of course, it would be unrealistic to expect Grameen to be replicable everywhere. For example, training and oversight activities are very labor-intensive, and would be hard to operate efficiently with a highly dispersed population without viable roads, let alone communications. Corruption might engulf similar activities elsewhere. But although none of the existing replications have yet demonstrated that they can approach Grameen's scale and durability, their benefits to date are substantial. Grameen's own sustainability seems clear with a solid track record of over two decades.

No discussion of replicability and sustainability would be complete without noting that Grameen has greatly benefitted from the dedication of the motivated and idealistic bank staff. The Grameen Bank "organizational culture" emphasizing service to the genuinely poor has helped maintain honorable attitudes. Importantly, staff incentives are also maintained: quick promotions have been regularly awarded to those whose performance in the field has been exemplary.

A major key to Grameen's sustainability will be to keep high motivation, anti-poverty orientation, and rewards for good work intact, and to guard against the lethargy, arrogance, and corruption that mar so many other developing country bureaucracies and quasi-public financial institutions. A system of cooperatives begun among rickshaw pullers in the 1960s and once considered a model for the country lost its vitality after it was taken over by the government in the 1970s. Grameen's continued independence may be essential to its future success.

Finally, the role of a dedicated founder like Muhammad Yunus cannot be underestimated. If development aid agencies only knew better how to identify, encourage, and support individuals who are motivated, technically competent, skilled at organization, charismatic, and genuinely altruistic, a major step toward development progress would be made. By all accounts this is the character and achievement of Dr. Yunus, a man of great ability who could clearly have made much more money in other endeavors. Such leaders can never be fully paid for the value their good works add to society, but for some potential leaders of this caliber, the prestige and renown they gain from their works might be an added incentive to pursue an altruistic career combining compassion and competence. In this case, ordinary development scholars can perhaps do no better service than to publicize their achievements.

Sources

Anderson, Dawn, Kimberly Hoffstrom, Karin Schelzig, and Yutaka Odagiri. "The Grameen Bank: Women Challenging Tradition." Processed, George Washington University, 1994.

Christian Science Monitor, July 8, 1992; March 5, 1991; March 15, 1989.

The Economist, Oct. 18, 1986.

Hossain, Mahmoub. "Credit for Alleviation of Rural Poverty: The Grameen Bank in Bangladesh." *International Food Policy Research Institute Research Report No. 65,* 1988.

Osmani, S.R. "Limits to the Alleviation of Poverty through Non-Farm Credit." *The Bangladesh Development Studies 17* (1989): 1–17.

Singh, Inderjit. *The Great Ascent: The Rural Poor in South Asia.* Baltimore: Johns Hopkins University Press, for the World Bank, 1990.

Solomon, Lewis D. "Microenterprise: Human Reconstruction in America's Inner Cities." *Harvard Journal of Law and Public Policy,* winter 1992.

Wahid, A. *The Grameen Bank: Poverty Alleviation in Bangladesh.* Boulder, CO: Westview, 1993.

Wahid, A. "The Grameen Bank and Poverty Alleviation in Bangladesh: Theory, Evidence and Limitations." *American Journal of Economics and Sociology. 53,* no. 1 (1994): 1–15.

Washington Post, August 4, 1994; Feb. 14, 1993; August 16, 1992.

Weaver, M. "Letter from Bangladesh: A Fugitive from Injustice." *The New Yorker,* Sept. 12, 1994, 48–60.

Yunus, Muhammad. Speech and interview with World Bank, Oct. 4, 1995.

6. Agricultural Extension for Women: The Case of Kenya

Absolute poverty is disproportionally concentrated among women, in rural areas, and in the agricultural sector. Thus, a key part of a strategy for poverty reduction must be to improve the productivity and incomes of women farmers.

The crucial importance of a solid agricultural extension program for successful rural development has been appreciated by development specialists for decades. Support for agricultural extension has played a central role in the activities of most multilateral and bilateral development agencies. Historically, agricultural extension programs played a vital development role in the United States, one of the world's great agricultural productivity success stories.

That is the good news. The bad news is that extension in developing countries has been aimed almost exclusively at training men, but women do most of the agricultural work. In sub-Saharan Africa, women generate some 70% of staple foods production. They are also active in growing and marketing cash crops, in food processing, and animal husbandry.

In part, the prominent role of women in agriculture reflects long tradition, but women's roles have expanded in recent years as men have increasingly migrated to urban areas and taken on other nonagricultural tasks. Where men and women both do agricultural work, there still tends to be a gender-based division of labor. As a result, techniques relevant to the work of men are often not relevant to the work of women. Where they are relevant, for various reasons men tend not to pass on what they have learned to their wives (what has been called "trickle across").

The role of women in agriculture has been widely publicized in development circles in recent years. The first breakthrough was Ester Bosrup's 1970 book, *Women's Role in Economic Development.* Her work began a trend of important research in this area and a slowly dawning realization on the part of the profession that the issue of women in agriculture was at the very core of prospects for genuine development—and not a narrow concern of a faction of feminists, as some perceived it at first.

Moreover, the focus on training men has generally been more by default than by deliberate design. For example, training is copied from developed countries like the United States, where men do the majority of agricultural work; and in LDCs male extension agents may simply be more comfortable talking to men. But the agricultural extension program response to the problem has been all too slow. And in some countries, program design reflects explicit bias against providing women with too much independence.

A major problem is the segregation and exclusion of women in large parts of Africa and Asia. Gender relations in rural areas are characterized by extreme inequality. In many cases this is a symptom of backwardness and an unacceptable violation of human rights. But one does not have to be an ardent cultural relativist to recognize that the development specialist usually can have little impact on culture.

In the present period, before progress on women's rights can be made, development specialists will have to learn to work around such practices. One emerging strategy is to make use of radio and television, audiotapes and, increasingly, even videotapes. Women may listen to or watch the materials in groups, in houses, or at village centers. Katrin Saito reports that female farmers question extension agents in Ghana about subjects they have heard discussed on the radio.

A recent World Bank study showed that most male African extension agents perceived women as "wives of farmers," rather than as farmers in their own right. And almost all extension agents are themselves male. Female agents must be trained. This is only one reason why education of rural girls is a key in development (see Case 16).

Agricultural extension for women is interconnected with a number of other important rural development and women in development issues. Five key issues are:

1. *Human capital.* Women have far less education than men on average in most rural developing areas. The bias in agricultural extension may in some part be a bias to train the more educated spouse, but the practice has also exacerbated this relative deficiency.

2. *Appropriate technology.* Because women tend to be involved in different farm activities than men, they will often have different technology requirements. Most technology development has been focused on activities of men.

3. *Land reform and agrarian design.* On average, women farm on much smaller, more fragmented plots than men; are less likely to have secure ownership; and often cultivate less fertile soil. This distribution is likely to be inefficient as well as distributionally inequitable.

4. *Credit.* Women have little access, if any, to financial credit, a key input in efficient agriculture.

5. *Work requirements.* Many women who work as many hours per day as men in agricultural pursuits also have to perform several hours of domestic work that does not apply to men. Working days for poor women farmers in Africa have been estimated at 16 to 19 hours. The attention mothers can give to children will be limited by long agricultural hours. The implication may be that women should receive an even higher priority for technical education and technology development and access. Duncan Thomas reports evidence that fathers allocate resources disproportionately toward sons and mothers toward daughters in countries as disparate as the United States, Brazil, and Ghana. The priority of womens' agricultural productivity goes hand in hand with the priority of educating girls.

The latter point has particular relevance to the design of structural adjustment programs. As Rekha Mehra has noted, one intent of structural adjustment programs in many African countries is to encourage the shift to exportable cash crops. But these are the crops over which men tend to have control. A woman's profit share after working with these crops may be as little as one part in twenty. But she is still responsible for growing consumption crops and feeding her children. Mehra concludes that structural adjustment programs tend to place even more time requirements on women already burdened with 16 hour days and longer.

Many development specialists have called for the removal of agricultural price controls to allow the prices farmers receive to move toward world market levels. This would give more accurate price signals to farmers, and encourage a switch to more economically productive crops. But an International Food Policy Research Institute (IFPRI) study showed that after diversification to commercial crops, Kenyan women still try to grow the same amount of consumption crops. Thus, more is needed than price adjustments; reform must address structural problems faced by women that will prevent them from responding to price signals efficiently. A good example is the larger profit share taken by the husband and often not shared with his wife or wives. But as David Sahn and Lawrence Haddad have stressed, blame cannot be placed primarily on structural adjustment programs for the predicament of women farmers in Africa today; conditions for women were abysmal prior to reform.

None of these problems are limited to Africa. For example, Carmen Deere, in a review of 13 Latin American agrarian reform experiences, found that most have directly benefitted only men. This was mostly because farmers were thought of as men and the reforms were designed to target only men as beneficiaries. Her review found that women only benefit in the rare instances when their well-being is a specific objective of the reform and rural women are made an explicit part of the design of programs from the outset.

In sum, taken as a whole these points show why women farmers need the help of extension programs. It is also efficient to do this because of an application of the law of diminishing returns to training for men. The evidence suggests that the theory of "trickle across"—that trained husbands will in turn train their wives—rarely occurs in practice, at least in Africa.

At last, progress is being made, and Kenya is a good example both of successful improvements made and of the work that remains to be accomplished. The Ministry of Agriculture operates a National Extension System (NES) in concert with its agricultural research efforts.

Before 1983, the NES worked almost exclusively with male farmers, while a separate "home economics branch" advised women on household and cottage industry management, and domestic hygiene, but only peripherally on farming matters. Research by the Institute of Development Studies in Nairobi, and other agencies, confirmed that extension was much more likely to have reached men than women farmers. In 1983, Kenya's present training and visit (T&V) system was established with the express purpose of training women as well as men in efficient agricultural practices.

The design of the T&V system is very creative. It is based upon providing "technical messages" to selected "contact farmers," who are regularly visited on their farmsteads. Unfortunately, resources are insufficient to reach all farmers; and if the T&V system did try to reach all farmers, the quality of training would be poor. As a result, only 10% of all farmers are chosen as "contact farmers." These selected participants are expected not only to adopt advice brought to them in these "messages," but to help spread this new technical knowledge by persuading other farmers in the villages to adopt them as well. A number of "follower farmers" are expected to attend meetings with T&V officials on the contact farmer's farmstead. In this way, it is hoped that technical "diffusion" is maximized in a cost-effective manner.

Obviously, the selection process is vital. Farmers must be selected who are capable, likely to diligently follow through on new information, and to be locally respected so as to encourage emulation. In choosing contact farmers, T&V officials meet with farmers and generally consult with local communities and their leaders.

At first, messages focus on procedures that offer the prospect of significant productivity gains, but do not require any cash expenditure, such as spacing and pruning. The messages being diffused in any one month are linked to farm activities underway in the annual crop cycle, such as planting or harvesting whichever crops are cultivated at a given point in the course of the year. Only as farmers see results from this initial advice, and so come to trust the T&V messages, are measures requiring modest cash outlays introduced, such as fertilizer use and crop spraying. In a later stage, measures requiring purchase of capital goods may be introduced.

Recent Kenyan and World Bank studies confirm that while not all women are yet being reached by extension services, significant progress has been made. Increasing numbers of women function officially as contact farmers. Even more serve unofficially in this role, as their husbands farm only part-time or not at all.

The messages of the T&V program, at least ideally, are supposed to be transmitted in both directions. T&V agents are supposed to gather information about how well previous advice has worked in practice, and about continued problems, in order to guide research efforts. This is in the spirit of the often-touted but seldom-fulfilled "participation in development" ideal.

Economic advancement of women farmers is also important for promoting environmentally sustainable development. In addition to their responsibility for agriculture, especially on more marginal and often ecologically fragile lands, women have a customary role in traditional societies as the "guardians of natural resources," such as the water supply. This is also an important domain for agricultural extension work with women. In Kenya the T&V system is not yet strongly involved in environmental problems.

But thousands of women are taking part in the Green Belt Movement (GBM), established in 1977 by the National Council of Women. Its main objective, as reported by Wangari Maathai, is to "halt desertification by encouraging tree planting and soil and water conservation in rural communities." It also works to promote sustainable development and poverty alleviation in parallel projects. While initiated and run privately, seedlings are provided by the government at low prices, and GBM volunteers receive advice and support from government forestry officials, a type of extension service.

The GBM emphasizes grass-roots participation and self-help, and strives to educate people on the link between deforestation, erosion, poor soil quality, and subsequent low crop yields. With the help of outside funding, women are paid to work at about 1,000 nurseries. Seedlings grown at these nurseries are given to small farmers, schools, and churches, which have planted an estimated 10 million surviving trees. The estimated survival rate is 70 to 80%. The GBM is now striving to disseminate its model throughout Africa.

Another shortcoming of the T&V system is that it has made too little progress in the field of women's credit, and private voluntary organizations have not been able to take up the slack. A study by Kathleen Staudt found that of eighty-four female farm managers interviewed in the Kakamega District in Western Province, only one knew about the credit program, and no female manager had received any credit. Informal indications are that this is the area that has improved least over the subsequent years.

As Christina Gladwin and Della McMillan have argued, much more must be done; for example, women should be consulted at the design stage of technology development, extension specialists should receive training on how to approach a male farmer about training his wife or wives, and governments should target funds to women's organizations and clubs.

Training and provision of credit and other inputs for women farmers is one of the critical areas where development professionals can have the biggest impact in fostering genuine development, while reducing poverty and relative inequality.

Sources

Bosrup, Ester. *Women's Role in Economic Development.* New York: St. Martin's Press, 1970.

Davison, Jean, ed. *Agriculture, Women and Land: The African Experience.* London: Westview Press, 1989.

Deere, Carmen Diana. "Rural Women and State Policy: The Latin American Agrarian Reform Experience." *World Development 13* (1985): 1037–1053.

Deere, Carmen Diana. "The Division of Labor by Sex in Agriculture: A Peruvian Case Study." *Economic Development and Cultural Change 30* (1982): 795–81.

Gladwin, Christina H., and Della McMillan. "Is a Turnaround in Africa Possible without Helping African Women to Farm?" *Economic Development and Cultural Change 37* (1989): 345–369.

Due, Jean M., and Christina H. Gladwin. "Impacts of Structural Adjustment Programs on African Women Farmers and Female Headed Households." *Amer. J. Agr. Econ.* Dec. 1991, 1431–1439.

Maathai, Wangari. "Kenya's Green Belt Movement, Ecological Movement Headed by Women," *UNESCO Courier,* March 1992.

Mehra, Rekha. "Can Structural Adjustment Work for Women Farmers," *Amer. J. Agr. Econ.* Dec. 1991, 1440–1447.

Sahn, David E., and Lawrence Haddad. "The Gendered Impacts of Structural Adjustment Programs in Africa: Discussion." *Amer. J. Agr. Econ.* Dec. 1991, 1448–1451.

Saito, Katrin, and C. Jean Weidemann. "Agricultural Extension for Women Farmers in Sub-Saharan Africa." *World Bank Discussion Paper No. 103,* 1990.

Saito, Katrin. "Extending Help to Women Farmers in LDCs," *Finance and Development,* Sept. 1991.

Staudt, Kathleen K. "The Effects of Government Agricultural Policy on Women Farmers: Preliminary Findings from Idakho Location in Kakamega District." Institute of

Development Studies, Nairobi, 1975.

Staudt, Kathleen K. "Women Farmers and Inequities in Agricultural Services." In Edna Bay, ed., *Women and Work in Africa.* Boulder, CO: Westview, 1982.

Thomas, Duncan, "Gender Differences in Household Resource Allocations." *World Bank Living Standards Measurement Study Paper 79,* 1991.

von Braun, Joachim. *Commercialization of Smallholder Agriculture: Policy Requirements for Capturing Gains for the Malnourished Poor.* Washington, DC: International Food Policy Research Institute, 1989.

7. Population, Famines, and Entitlement Theory: Application to the Case of Somalia

The images of famine appear and disappear from the television screens and the public awareness, just as do images of unemployment lines following the irregular fluctuations of the business cycle. We have the searing images of fly-covered children with protruding bones, bloated bellies, and sunken eyes in Biafra, Bangladesh, Ethiopia, Sudan, and recently in Somalia. Horrified by these pictures, the world springs into action and sends food. For this is how we usually think of famine: the absence of food.

The media and the public would find support for their use of the word "famine" in Webster's dictionary: "an extreme scarcity of food; a great shortage." But in Somalia, the world learned that simply sending food might do nothing to solve the problem. So troops were sent along with the food, which ensured that food reached most people for a time. But this approach did not prevent people from starving there again once the troops left, nor did it prevent similar disasters from cropping up elsewhere.

In many cases, such as the terrible Bangladesh famine of 1974, famines coexist with bumper crops of food. Famines, as one might expect, may coexist with national economic declines, as with the recent Ethiopia and Somalia famines. Or, they may coexist with national economic booms, in which the incomes and purchasing power of some groups, usually nonfarmers, increase rapidly, leading them to demand more food and force up its price. This means other groups, often rural laborers whose wages do not keep pace with increases in the price of food, are left with too little income to buy the amount of food they and their children need to survive. A likely example of this was the Bengal famine of 1943. In other cases, the national scarcity of food is an effect of something else, not the prime cause of the suffering. Can development economics provide any insights to this complex problem?

This is the puzzle tackled by Amartya Sen in his celebrated theory of famines. In Sen's terminology, the "acquirement problem" is one of "establishing command over commodities." Sen's approach to the analysis of famines disputes the focus on food availability in favor of examining changes in "endowments and exchange entitlements." Food entitlements depend on what can be grown oneself, what can be purchased with wage or other income or through the sale of assets, or, finally, donations from private charity or public welfare.

A peasant who grows her own food may have to sell some—or even most—of that food to meet debt or other obligations. She may suffer a food deficit if impacted by a drought or other weather shock. A laborer may lose his entitlement to food if he loses his job. Or even if he does not lose his job, a laborer may find that he has a decreased "command over" food commodities if food represents a very large share of his expenditure budget and the relative price of food rises significantly. Finally, a poor self-employed artisan, repairer, or other petty service provider who offers a product or service for sale may suffer hunger if the price of the service falls sharply relative to that of food.

In few societies is food divided equally or by need. And few developing countries have an effective "safety net" public assistance system. Thus, those who fail to "establish command over food" may well go hungry and even starve to death. This is obvious enough, but before Sen's work all the discussion in the literature about famines and widespread starvation in developing countries focused mainly on aggregate food availability.

Sen showed that, historically, famines are more closely associated with collapses of "exchange entitlements" of specific impoverished groups of the local population than they are with declines in aggregate per capita food availability. While historians have made some of these observations in the past, Sen's was the first analytically careful and empirically systematic work.

According to Sen's evidence, those affected by famines work in particular occupations, such as farm laborer; occupations affected differ from famine to famine and from country to country. This evidence underlines that the problem is not so much a lack of food in general, but a failure of some subgroups to exert "command" over food.

When a famine is looming it is common to find families hoarding food. Many will stock up on far more food than they really need, for many months in advance. In this way, the fear of famine can become a self-fulfilling prophesy, as hoarding finally creates a real shortage of food for those without it. These surges in demand for food, driven by fear, can dramatically increase its price in the short run. As a result, there can even be "bubbles" in the price of food, just as there have been in tulips, South Sea Islands shares, or Japanese stocks.

None of this means that aggregate food availability is unrelated to famines. Even with a good system of entitlements, distribution, and incentives for production, an exogenous shock, such as a devastating drought or flood, can be a proximate cause of famine. Entitlements will depend on the price of food, as we have seen, and, of course, a major determinant of the price of food is its aggregate availability.

The entitlements approach certainly does not mean that everyone in the developing world should be simply entitled to food without expecting anything in return. Here, as in designing any development program, incentives need to be kept in mind. An excellent strategy is an approach like the Food for Work Program of Bangladesh, Maharashtra State in India, and elsewhere, that guarantees on a daily basis a food allotment to anyone willing to work for it in rural infrastructure projects (the Bangladesh Food for Work Program is the subject of Case 9).

Sen does not focus on expectations of future price changes and the self-fulfilling prophesy of panics over food availability and price. This is important as a dynamic that needs to be prevented, but does not affect the entitlement approach per se.

Since the early 1980s, Sen's analysis has been applied with success to a number of historical cases, as the recent volume *Famines,* edited by G. A. Harrison, attests. But how well does it stand up to a current case, Somalia, perceived by many to be different from other recent famines? How are the recent African famines, and the events in Somalia in particular, understood in the context of Sen's theory of famines?

This is a region with the highest rates of population growth in the world. In Somalia, population growth has been 3.2% over the last 30 years, increasing the population from 2.9 to 7.5 million, according to UN statistics. All of this sounds on the surface very much like a case of a food availability shock.

In the period leading up to the Somalia famine, aggregate food production did decline, some 21% from the mid-seventies to the mid-eighties according to calculations by Dreze and Sen using Food and Agriculture Organization (FAO) data.

But aggregate availability and the ability to gain access to food are two distinct concepts, and the former does not assure the latter. In the case of Somalia, the world addressed the former, rushing food into the country, but proved unable to fully assure the latter, a much harder task.

Somalia's economy was fragile and inefficient for many years. The corrupt regime of longtime dictator Mohammed Siad Barre was a severe restraint on development in the country. But the proximate cause of the civic and economic collapse of Somalia was Barre's ouster in early 1991. In the capital area, rival local and migrant clans and organized crime bands struggled for political control and embezzled wealth with increasing violence.

The country went from inefficient and corrupt government to essentially no government (with the exception of private violence for private gain), so that not even the rudiments of the right to personal safety or basic property rights were available. Under such circumstances there is little incentive to produce anything. Certainly there was a dramatic decrease in the availability of Somalia-produced food—but this was the proximate cause, not the root cause of the famine.

At the height of the famine in late 1992, thousands of people were dying daily and millions were at risk of imminent starvation. Under weakened conditions of undernutrition, people, especially small children, became much more susceptible to disease. The immediate cause of death for many was dehydration caused by diarrhea, and bacterial infections, especially pneumonia.

We still have no reliable estimates of the number of deaths that occurred during the Somalia famine; one effect of the evaporation of central government was the cessation of any collection of health statistics beginning in early 1991. But preliminary indications are that Somalia will represent one of the deadliest famines in recorded history. Upwards of 300,000 Somalis are estimated to have starved to death or died of complications of starvation in 1992. About 30,000 died in the accompanying violence.

A report by the Atlanta-based Center for Disease Control on two Somali towns it surveyed in late 1992 concluded that mortality rates were among "the highest ever documented in a population survey among famine-infected civilians." More than half of the population of 30,000 in the town of Baidoa, one of the warlord strongholds, is estimated to have died, including 70% of children under age five, between April and November 1992. The report concluded that conditions were substantially worse than during the peak mortality periods of the Ethiopian famine of 1984–85.

Somalia showed that Sen's term, "command over commodities," is applicable to many circumstances. When the economy is collapsing and people have no entitlements, control of food means power over hungry people, plain and simple. What went on in Somalia under the invading warlords does not remotely represent the "magic of the marketplace," nor did the exchange that went on between warlords and terrified people resemble anything like a free market exchange.

In some ways the case of Somalia is as direct an example of Sen's theory as could be found in recent history. A member of a warlord's gang or favored circle has command over food, and others do not.

In the case of Somalia, the government had in 1987 formulated a basic minimum needs program based on community participation and integrated rural development modeled on the program in Thailand, one of the first of its kind. By 1991 it had been implemented in 36 villages with a total of about 20,000 people. International organizations such as the World Health Organization were deeply involved. Significant progress in areas such as immunizations, safe drinking water, reduction of malnutrition, and primary school attendance was recorded within a year of the program's operation.

The program was small in relation to Somalia's population of 7.5 million people. Government was corrupt in the large even if small parts of it were honest and dedicated. It is very unclear that the program could have been successfully expanded even without the collapse of its government.

Although the program was interrupted by the collapse of central governmental authority in Somalia, the small program did show that an entitlements approach to famine prevention and development is possible in Somalia. The causes of its problems are internal, socioeconomic ones, not the caprices of rainfall and climate. While drought afflicts Somalia as it does many other countries in the region, the permanent solution to its problems is not food aid or necessarily even increased food production, but to establish sustainable "command over commodities" for the poorest of the poor. The influx of food into Somalia caused the market price of food to drop significantly. Price elasticities have not been estimated, but it is feared that local production will be substantially affected.

More important is what goes on at the local level. The image of ruthless anarchy occurring throughout the country is something of an exaggeration of the reality. This characterized the southwest region near the capital, and the region around two other cities. But in other parts of the country, traditional governance of elders reasserted itself and provided for a relatively peaceful society, one producing at least the minimum basic needs for most of the people.

Sen's "exchange entitlement" approach can be applied to the problem of effective famine anticipation and action. Shifts in food entitlement are the best early warning system that famine may soon emerge. Policies that address entitlement needs rather than just aggregate food supply are likely to represent the most effective anti-famine strategies.

The contrast between Somalia and some other African countries, such as Zimbabwe, as well as some other developing countries such as India and Botswana, is striking. A long period of racial conflict came to an end in Zimbabwe when democracy was established there in 1980. Robert Mugabe's Zimbabwe African National Union made social services, especially in health, nutrition, and education, its top priority; and it began to make immediate progress.

But the government was quickly tested by a severe three-year drought lasting from 1982 to 1984. The drought caused a collapse in the production of corn, Zimbabwe's staple crop. Coupled with the still highly dualistic distribution of farmland, starvation was a very real possibility for many Zimbabweans. But the government acted quickly, initiating substantial food distribution measures for the adult population and targeted supplementary feeding programs for children under five years of age. Studies vary in their estimates of how many people benefitted, but are unanimous in their conclusion that food got to the many who needed it in sufficient quantities to prevent starvation and even to improve the health status of the poor in this period.

Jean Dreze and Sen conclude, along with many other foreign academic and journalist observers, that an important factor in Zimbabwe's success was its free society, notably its no-holds-barred press, grassroots political participation, and active political debate.

Dreze and Sen note that other countries that have earned high marks for avoiding threatened famines, such as Botswana and India, are relatively stable democracies.

This finding that democracy matters for the alleviation of poverty is the basic needs justification for making progress toward democracy a precondition for all but emergency aid, a trend in most aid agencies. The principle of noninterference in internal affairs in the face of undemocratic and corrupt regimes is an idea whose time has passed when it comes to the provision of foreign aid. From a development perspective, democracy is often as significant in improving efficiency as it is in fostering human rights.

Sen's theory of famines is better at explaining the terrible recent events of Somalia than are traditional ideas based on the availability of food. War and civic collapse are one more way that peoples' entitlements to food may be taken away. As Sen has noted, the frequent association of famine with war is not just the result of the destruction of productive capacity that war brings, or the diversion of resources to military uses, or even the disruption of social services and relief operations. Conditions such as we have seen in Somalia also greatly reduce the incentive to produce food, and local aggregate food availability may fall. But the democracy link is also strong. War provides the excuse and the method for suppressing freedom of the press and other democratic institutions. This in turn blocks the channel for popular outcry that could rally public resources for food entitlements.

68

As relief grain piled up on Somali docks while thousands died daily, it became clear that famines are not caused by the unavailability of food, but by lack of entitlements to it by the afflicted segments of society.

When the UN finally pulled out of Somalia in March 1995, it terminated the jobs of nearly 15,000 Somalis, employed as police agents, guards, mechanics, construction workers, and office workers. Many of these employees provided for up to ten family members. Thus, in a final irony of the Somalia operation, the UN lowered the command over food for its own employees. Famines are a matter of entitlements, and food availability may be of little consequence.

Sources

Barzgar, M. A., and I. A. Kore. "A Solid Base for Health." *World Health Forum 12* (1991): 156–169.

Dreze, Jean, and Amartya Kumar Sen. *Hunger and Public Action.* New York: Oxford University Press, 1989.

Harrison, G. A., ed. *Famines.* New York: Oxford University Press, 1988.

New York Times, Jan. 19, 1993; Dec. 17, 1994.

Ravallion, Martin. *Markets and Famines.* Oxford: Clarendon, 1987.

Sen, Amartya Kumar. "Peacekeeping and Starvation: On the Somalian and Other Crises in Sub-Saharan Africa." Paper presented at the AEA Annual Meetings, Anaheim, Jan. 1993.

Sen, Amartya Kumar. *Poverty and Famines: An Essay on Entitlement and Deprivation.* New York: Oxford University Press, 1981.

United Nations Development Program. *Human Development Report,* 1992.

Washington Post, Nov. 25, Dec. 1, and Dec. 27, 1992; Jan. 9, Jan. 16, Jan. 30, and Feb. 6, 1993.

8. AIDS: Economic Development Impact and the Case of Uganda

The AIDS epidemic is spreading fast in the developing world, threatening to halt or even reverse years of hard-won human and economic development progress in numerous countries. Though usually thought of as an issue of health care systems and delivery, AIDS is equally an issue of economic development. Uganda has been one of the developing countries hit hardest by AIDS. Yet the case of Uganda shows that even a massive AIDS epidemic need not cause an African economy to deteriorate economically to the extent of a country such as Zaire. Implementing the right policies can help restore growth and development. But a policy of AIDS prevention is the best strategy for successful economic development.

AIDS, the final and fatal stage of infection with HIV, the human immunodeficiency virus, is still widely perceived in the Third World as a disease of developed countries and one primarily afflicting homosexuals. In fact, these perceptions are far from reality. The World Health Organization (WHO) estimates that by 1992, over 10 million people worldwide were infected with HIV, with well over 8 million of these, including over 1 million children, in LDCs. So far, the center of the epidemic has been in tropical Africa, where cases of HIV infection are estimated to have tripled from 2 million to 6 million cases from 1988 to 1992, and passed 10 million by the end of 1994. But it is believed that AIDS has reached a peak rate of new infections of just under 1 million per year between 1992 and 1994.

The emerging epicenter of the disease is in Asia, where the WHO estimates that new infections now total over 1 million per year, and will not peak and level off until 2010. The WHO's estimates that 30 to 40 million people will be infected worldwide in 2000 are considered conservative by some researchers, and alternative estimates have gone as high as 120 million. More conservative computer models project up to seventy million infections by 2015.

Haiti, the Dominican Republic, Brazil, and Mexico are also seriously affected, and homosexual and bisexual men are still the highest risk group in Latin America. But in the developing countries as a whole AIDS is primarily transmitted by heterosexual intercourse; infected blood and drug needles, both by drug abusers and in hospitals, and perinatal transmission (from mother to fetus) also play significant roles. There can be a very long incubation period but average survival once AIDS symptoms set in is under one year in LDCs. Death from AIDS comes much more quickly in Third World than in developed countries. AZT and other expensive treatments are not available to over 99% of the infected. Treatments are generally limited to aspirin, antibiotics for infections, and cortisone for skin rashes.

The problem of AIDS for development is an inherently multidisciplinary problem, involving not just medicine and medical research, but economics and most of the social and behavioral sciences. Sociologists or anthropologists must determine who the prime infection-spreading groups are in various regions, what is most risky about their behavior, and how to effectively change that behavior. Simulation models may also be useful in designing strategy. These models suggest that more significant reductions in the spread of HIV can be realized through changes in sexual behavior than through needle sterilization efforts.

In most cases, in order to halt the spread of HIV, sexual behavior must change. Unfortunately, sexual behavior is far harder to change than medical procedures. For example, a spokesperson for an advertising agency volunteering services for an AIDS awareness campaign in Thailand called attention to the resources that go into persuading people to change simple behaviors like favored brands of soap, a smaller problem than changing sexual behavior that is more basic and ingrained. Persuasion among less-educated people who may be prone to superstitious beliefs is all the more difficult.

Here is a look at six of the most important development issues raised by AIDS.

1. *Population growth.* AIDS could noticeably reduce the rate of population growth in the most affected countries, up to one percentage point per year by some estimates. But even under the worst credible scenarios, nowhere is population expected to decline outright. The occasionally expressed idea that AIDS will reduce the importance of family planning as a top development priority is muddled and irresponsible. The population pyramid is unlikely to change noticeably, because children increasingly are as affected as adults. We can only speculate at this time what the effect of AIDS might be on family fertility choice. On the one hand, women who discover they are infected may stop bearing children. Relatives caring for orphaned children may reduce their own fertility rates. On the other hand, there is evidence that some infected women might decide to have more children while they remain alive, despite the 30% or higher chance the baby would be born infected. Sexual behavior change and a wish to ensure that one does not marry an infected partner might lead to a lowered age of marriage, which could increase total fertility. In the hard-hit case of Uganda, the projections for population growth are for a reduction of growth of up to half a percent per year, which would still leave population growth at an extremely high level of 2.6%. As Mead Over has noted, if the only economic effect of AIDS was to reduce population growth, in any plausible economic model, growth rates of income per capita would increase, because high population growth reduces per capita income growth.

2. *Basic needs.* The grim fact is that AIDS is creating a virtual generation of orphans in some African countries such as Uganda. When economically active adults die of AIDS they leave behind dependents, including children and seniors, who become more vulnerable to absolute poverty. Over one million AIDS orphans have been projected for Uganda and at least ten million Africa-wide by 2000. The World Bank has estimated that in East Africa, each woman dying of AIDS leaves three children orphaned. Providing basic needs for these orphans, ensuring that they are not discriminated against out of irrational fears, and seeing that they are able to obtain the few years of schooling that will help rescue them from absolute poverty will be a major development challenge. It is not a challenge that Africa, with all its problems, is accustomed to. Extended family networks have provided privately for children who have lost their parents. In some parts of East Africa this traditional family adaptation to death appears on the verge of collapse because of the scope of the AIDS crisis. In Uganda, the response to the orphan problem is to try to keep rural children on their farms so they can later support themselves, and otherwise to place children with relatives even if they are not immediate family. The policy to keep orphans living on their farmland is productive in some ways, but serious problems remain. These children are often in need of counseling, and social workers carry staggering caseloads. Orphaned teenage girls living alone on their farmland are sometimes preyed upon by thieves—and rapists who may carry HIV.

3. *Savings and urban modern sector investment.* Modern sector enlargement is dependent on savings. AIDS is likely to lead to national dissavings as earnings fall and the sick have to be cared for. This may be balanced in part by foreign savings. Aid may increase; on the other hand, direct foreign investment may very well decrease. Uganda has received considerable new support, in part because of its very severe AIDS epidemic. Many other countries will soon have an AIDS epidemic of the magnitude of Uganda's, and resources will be diverted to those regions. Companies attracted to cheap and plentiful labor may reconsider their choice of a host country so long as they anticipate lowered supply and higher cost of labor as a result of the AIDS epidemic. Mead Over has shown that an AIDS epidemic can reduce the growth rate of per capita income in the average country in Africa even when it is evenly distributed across high and low productivity workers, provided that at least about 50% of treatment costs are extracted from savings. Either a higher share of treatment costs coming from savings or a greater impact of AIDS on high skill workers increases the negative effect of AIDS, and the interaction of these two effects worsens matters. Over found that under the plausible assumptions that half of costs are financed from savings and the incidence of AIDS increases proportionally with education, growth might be reduced by about one-third of a percentage point per year. Given the severe problems of the sub-Saharan Africa (SSA) region (see Case 26), this is a significant loss.

4. *Migration and the urban informal sector.* There is growing evidence that the spread of HIV is strongly facilitated by active movements of migrant labor. Migrants, especially young males, are more likely to adopt high-risk behaviors, including frequent visits to prostitutes and intravenous drug use. They may bring HIV infection with them when they visit their home village.

5. *Rural/agricultural sector development.* Uganda has one of the world's highest percentages of the labor force engaged in farmwork, some 86%. A decrease in labor supply may mean a threat to "food security," or it may lead to a switch in crop composition away from labor-intensive agriculture. This may mean a switch away from cash crops and thus reduce foreign exchange earnings.

6. *Education and human capital.* AIDS predominantly strikes young adults in their most productive years. Although infectious childhood diseases still kill far more people in developing countries, AIDS strikes those who have successfully run this gauntlet of child killers. Throughout sub-Saharan Africa, AIDS is well on its way to becoming the leading cause of death of adult males in economically active years (ages 15 to 49). Urban areas have been hit first, but the virus is rapidly spreading into rural areas. Their societies are counting on the energies and skills of precisely the part of the population most afflicted. Labor shortages in specific skill categories are already emerging in Africa and will get worse.

Estimates of the net impact of AIDS on GNP would be highly speculative. A computer simulation model of Cameroon, designed to mirror the way its market economy works (a computable general equilibrium model), has confirmed the projection that the economic impact of AIDS is vastly magnified if the highly skilled are most affected. A macro model for Thailand indicated that the economic losses due to AIDS deaths is far greater than that due to increased medical care costs. But extensive reliance on standard multisector macroeconomic models for dependable numbers is very hazardous for the case of AIDS impact. This is because such models assume that the structure of the economy remains the same after a shock, whereas a brutal AIDS epidemic may lead to a collapse of the socioeconomic system as it had existed. Beyond this, GNP counts market activity, whereas the impact of uncounted economic activity of women on the farm and in the household may be large and spill over into the market sectors.

Because AIDS raises not just health issues, but development issues as well, an effective AIDS response must involve all the major development agencies and national ministries. WHO has taken the lead with its Global Program on AIDS. Most development agencies are coordinating AIDS efforts with WHO.

The case of Uganda has received considerable attention. Other African countries almost certainly have a higher rate of infection than Uganda, already a numbingly high 10% of the entire Ugandan population according to the WHO. Infection is unevenly distributed demographically and geographically; in Rakai District, for example, over 40% of men and women between 20 and 30 years of age are HIV positive. Some 20% are infected in the capital, Kampala.

A UNICEF study found that by 1989 there were already 600,000 orphans in Uganda, at least double the number of orphans there would be without AIDS, even given the effects of civil war and other widespread diseases. In hard-hit Rakai district, more than one in eight children are orphans, two-thirds of these because of AIDS.

Uganda illustrates that the course of the disease cannot be separated from the socioeconomic context in which it propagates. Uganda has a history of disastrous development decisions, and reversing some of these would mitigate the development impact of the AIDS crisis. In 1972, the unbalanced dictator Idi Amin expelled a majority of South Asian entrepreneurs from the country and confiscated their property. Asians then formed the nucleus of commercial agriculture and commerce in Uganda, but the moves drove about 70,000 of them into exile. The economy suffered severe hardships following these expulsions and other perverse economic policy decisions, some of which led indirectly to the AIDS epidemic.

Commercial controls led to an extremely active smuggling industry. Illegal, highly paid truck smugglers, often stranded for days in towns along smuggling routes, made frequent visits to prostitutes, encouraging the rapid spread of the disease. At the same time, the harshly dependent status of women, widespread polygyny, and generally weak foundations of marriage as an institution led to high rates of divorce, prostitution, and other types of rapid sexual partner changes.

Women's de facto inability to own land despite the fact that they do most of the farmwork creates incentives for both sexes that anthropologists claim leads to this pattern of rapid sexual partner changes. This behavior is conducive to the spread of HIV, while reinforcing low and declining agricultural productivity. There is little doubt that the horrendous conditions of rural women in Uganda, and Africa in general, is a crucial root cause of the rapid spread of HIV there.

The government of Uganda, a largely Catholic country, long resisted the promotion of condom use and was slow even to acknowledge the widespread presence of the disease. But after this slow start, the Ugandan government now has one of the most active and comprehensive AIDS prevention programs in Africa. Programs are coordinated by the Ugandan AIDS Commission Secretariat. The Commission is charged with "policy formulation and setting of priorities as well as overseeing, coordinating and facilitating all AIDS prevention, control and management activities throughout the country." Funding has been provided by UNICEF, WHO, USAID, the World Bank and the UNDP. Donor countries including the United States are probably more active on AIDS in Uganda than other countries as a result of the extensive attention to the problem there.

In the 1990s, the Ugandan government has been making it easier for Ugandan Asians to reclaim their property, despite resistance from Ugandans who have profited from it. Some have returned only to sell their property. But about 7000 exiles have become permanently resettled in Uganda, and these tend to be the largest business owners. They are making a positive difference, reinvesting in their now-dilapidated factories, training workers, and helping Uganda to return to strong growth. Unhelpful regulation, often established to facilitate corruption, is being dismantled, with exchange controls lifted, state-run marketing boards dismantled, inefficient SOEs slated for privatization, investment tax incentives established, and an ongoing dialogue between private and public sectors. The government has succeeded in implementing a sound macroeconomic policy. Annual inflation has been cut from almost 250% in 1984/85 to about 5% in 1994/95. And annual GDP growth reached nearly 10% in 1994/95 and is now projected to be in the 8% range in the next few years. Thus, in the midst of tragedy, Uganda shows that the positive effects of saner economic policies help compensate for at least the economic losses due to AIDS.

As is so often the case in development, private voluntary organizations (PVOs) are playing the leading role in developing creative, effective responses at the grassroots level. The Ugandan PVO, The AIDS Support Organization (TASO) has played a crucial role in treatment, family assistance, and counseling. Mass media was used, sometimes to good effect, but unpretested commercials have sometimes been misinterpreted or have even backfired. A famous example was the slogan "zero grazing," a locally sophisticated way of saying "stay with one partner," but which many ordinary people did not understand.

Condom use has increased in Uganda and some other African countries, but is still very limited. In particular, there is extremely little acceptance of condom use among married or regular partners, regardless of the amount of extramarital sexual activity. But the AIDS film, "It's Not Easy," was a great success that was viewed by some 90% of Uganda's formal sector workforce. Together, these public and private efforts do have a real effect. T-shirts are seen everywhere, with mottos like "Love Carefully." In Uganda the prostitution industry in towns known to be highly infected has dropped dramatically. These campaigns have paid off. Several recent studies have shown that the rate of AIDS infection among teenagers in Uganda has dropped steeply from 1990 to 1995, most likely due to the adoption of safer sex practices. Other statistics show that the proportion of pregnant women testing positive for HIV in prenatal clinics has also dropped significantly.

But Tony Barnett and Piers Blaikie's report on studies of AIDS in Uganda shows that steep challenges remain. It is widely believed among Ugandans that people who discover they have AIDS deliberately infect others sexually. There is at least some evidence that this actually happens, as men with the disease have admitted trying to infect women, including through rape. This is reportedly motivated by anger at having to "die alone." Women infected with HIV are reported to take a gamble at bearing children so they do not "feel cheated by death." If ghastly attitudes like these are indeed commonplace, it will be a formidable task to get the epidemic under control, whatever economic incentives and social programs are put in place.

The spread of HIV has been demonstrated to be significantly promoted by the presence of other sexually transmitted diseases (STDs). In both Asia and Africa, transmission of HIV is abetted by widespread prostitution, especially in conjunction with other STDs whose sores promote viral invasion, and by poor hospital hygiene due in part to resource shortages. Other core transmitters of the virus have included truck drivers and military personnel. The cost effectiveness of AIDS education campaigns can be highest when aimed at high-risk groups who start with a low rate of HIV infection. A useful rule of thumb for targeting regions and subpopulations is to find groups who combine low HIV infection rates with high incidence of other STDs.

Although the AIDS epidemic has spread most quickly in Africa, Asia has now surpassed it in numbers of new cases, and is projected to soon surpass it in total cases. Much of the attention in Asia has centered on Thailand, where some newly affluent modern sector workers are said to commonly visit prostitutes almost daily, and prostitution is packaged as "sex tours" for foreign businessmen. Some 700,000 people, well over one percent of the Thai population, are already estimated to be infected, and at the current rate of dissemination the figure will reach 10% within ten years. Slowing an effective response is the fact that AIDS has been widely viewed by Asians as a "foreigner's disease."

Thailand may have the highest infection rate today in Asia, but other Asian countries are not far behind. In India, over 1 million people are already estimated to be HIV positive, but over 95% of the blood supply there is not being tested for the virus. Indonesia has not been seriously affected yet, but is estimated to have close to 1 million prostitutes. Malaysia has about 1 million intravenous drug users.

In sum, as the case of Uganda reveals, each sector of the developing economy, and indeed every aspect of human development will be severely, if sometimes indirectly, affected by an AIDS epidemic. AIDS is much more than a health issue, and all agencies concerned with development must work with health officials to halt its spread. The later the development of an effective AIDS policy, the greater the ultimate costs, such as medical care, undereducation of orphans, and output loss. These costs cannot be estimated accurately but the magnitudes are so large that even a high discount rate does not alter the conclusion that early intervention is urgent.

An effective response to the problems of AIDS and development will require a careful balancing act of policymaking. Despite the human tragedy and development catastrophe of the AIDS epidemic, it is important not to let resources for HIV programs overshadow other worthwhile development projects. At the same time, the potential problem is severe enough that development project planners need to keep the problem at the forefront of attention. Each new health, population, and basic needs project is now required by several development agencies to either contain an HIV component or to justify why this is not relevant or cost-effective for the project. This requirement is likely to be adopted by virtually all development agencies in the near future.

Sources

Ainsworth, Martha, and Mead Over. "AIDS and African Development." *World Bank Research Observer 9,* no. 2 (1994): 203–40.

Armstrong, Jill. "Socioeconomic Implications of AIDS in Developing Countries." *Finance and Development,* Dec. 1991.

Barnett, Tony, and Piers Blaikie. *AIDS in Africa: Its Present and Future Impact.* New York: Guilford, 1992.

Business Week, "The Unfolding AIDS Disaster in Asia," Feb. 22, 1993.

Financial Times, April 7, 1993; Feb. 5, 1996.

Kambou, Gerard, Shanta Devarajan, and Mead Over. "The Economic Impact of AIDS in an African Country: Simulations with a CGE Model of Cameroon." *Journal of African Economies,* 1, no. 1 (1993): 109–130.

Lamboray, Jean-Louis, and A. Edward Elmendorf. "Combatting AIDS and other Sexually Transmitted Diseases in Africa." *World Bank Africa Technical Department Paper 181,* 1994.

Lewis, Maureen A. et al. *AIDS in Developing Countries: Cost Issues and Policy Tradeoffs,* Washington, DC: Urban Institute, 1989.

Mann, Jonathan M. et al. eds. *AIDS in the World.* Cambridge, MA: Harvard University Press, 1992.

New York Times, March 22 and March 23, 1993; April 7, 1996.

Over, Mead, "The Macroeconomic Impact of AIDS in Sub-Saharan Africa". World Bank Africa Technical Division, July 1993.

Population and Development. Special Issue on "A Cultural Perspective on HIV Transmission," Jan. 1993.

United Nations Development Program. *HIV and Development,* 1993.

World Bank. *Report on a Workshop on The Economic Impact of Fatal Adult Illness in Sub-Saharan Africa,* July 1993.

9. The Bangladesh Food for Work Program (FFWP)

Success in the struggle against poverty and underemployment must begin in the countryside. However important the role of industrialization for growth, rural development remains a vital condition for development success. Agriculture remains important for the foods, raw materials, and export earnings it provides. Moreover, about three-quarters of the world's absolutely poor are found in rural areas, where they are often chronically underemployed. Rural poverty leads to rapid population growth and excess migration to the cities. It puts great stress on the environment, as those faced with starvation will get what income they can from their land without regard for the effect of their practices on the land. A "vicious cycle" often results, in which the poor are effectively forced to take actions that keep them poor in future periods.

Infrastructure development plays a vital role in achieving rural progress. Many rural areas in poor countries are still without road links to the outside world or lack access to nearby market towns. Communication links may be few, and irrigation nil. But with low levels of nutrition, productivity of laborers is also low. Infrastructure thus conditions rural development through its impact on the various rural markets, and on the health and education of the rural poor.

Bangladesh, like many developing countries, has been seeking strategies for tackling this cluster of rural development problems. With a GNP per capita of just $220 in 1992, Bangladesh is the 10th poorest country in the world among those with at least 1 million citizens. Like many poor countries, it seeks both growth and poverty alleviation. But poverty is so severe—85% are absolutely poor according to UN statistics—that the country cannot afford to wait for the benefits of modern sector growth to eventually trickle down to the poor. At the same time, the country does not wish to sacrifice future growth by its care for the poor today.

Most strategies for responding to these problems introduce new problems of their own. Entitlement transfer programs can stifle incentives for work and divert public funds away from needed infrastructure investments. They can also be very wasteful because much of the benefits go to the nonpoor and many of the poor get no benefits. General food and other subsidies end up benefitting many nonpoor people, who also receive cheaper food and other goods, while missing many of the poor who grow and forage what they can. Successful "means-testing" of poverty programs, or screening program beneficiaries to make sure they are really poor, is very costly—if not impossible to achieve. This not only wastes money on administration, but errors will inevitably be made, and corruption by public officials all too commonly destroys the program.

Bangladesh thinks it has found a solution that will help it respond at once to several of these problems—infrastructure needs, poverty, and the counterproductive incentives and secondary effects created by many poverty programs.

The Food for Work Program (FFWP) was begun in 1974. The FFWP organizes construction and maintenance of agriculture-supporting infrastructure—mainly irrigation, drainage and embankment works, and roads—during the slack agricultural season of December through April. It pays the laborers on an in-kind basis with food. The allocation of food to the program has increased steadily over the years and in the 1990s the program has generated about 100 million days of employment each year. The World Bank estimates that at least 17 extra days of employment are generated for each landless laborer in Bangladesh in construction alone.

The requirement that the poor work in exchange for welfare is not new; it goes back at least as far as the English poorhouses of the 19th Century. Some of the traditional basis for these programs have been moral—the belief that the poor benefit morally by engaging in hard work. The focus of this case study, however, is on the positive rather than the normative aspects of such programs. That is, the focus is on the economic incentives, program efficiency, and creation of political support for the program, rather than on its moral effects. The question is, can work requirements provide an efficient method of poverty relief?

Unlike poverty programs in most developing countries, the FFWP generally reaches the poor rather than subsidizing everyone or even disproportionately favoring the more affluent. The most important reason is that an incentive for self-selection is built into the program. Few non-poor persons can be expected to choose to work in labor-intensive construction all day for pay in basic foodstuffs, a conjecture strongly supported by the available evidence. Thus, such programs play an important screening role. Fewer public resources are used unnecessarily, and more funds are directed to the intended recipients. Such programs always have opportunity costs to the poor, and most participants must give up some farm or nonfarm self-employment work time to participate. But the evidence is that net gains to the poor remain substantial.

There is some attention, although probably not enough, to making the program fit an appropriate seasonal pattern; that is, to have work available through the program when demand for agricultural labor is at its lowest levels in the crop cycles. The need for the program is smaller when agricultural labor demand is higher. Because government-financed labor-intensive construction is probably not a permanent solution to poverty, it is very important to avoid making the program work-replacing rather than work-creating.

The program also benefits rural development, including poor farmers, by producing valuable infrastructure. Moreover, it avoids the reductions in the incentive to work, or moral hazard, caused by some welfare programs. With distribution to the poor concentrated in one place, it is easier to monitor for corruption. Private voluntary organizations such as CARE play an important monitoring role, making sure projects meet development goals as well as sound engineering standards, and observing pay rates actually paid to laborers. Environmental sustainability is an important new project criteria, and the program has begun to incorporate afforestation schemes. The Food for Work Program compares favorably with an irrigation project financed by the World Bank in the 1970s that mostly benefitted well-off farmers.

The distribution of land is highly unequal in Bangladesh, yet it is still better than in many other developing countries. The benefits of the infrastructure created are thus more widely disbursed, though still biased in favor of the larger farmers.

Better land distribution is needed in Bangladesh. Small farmers frequently lose their land to constantly shifting river patterns. As new lands are opened up by these changes, these are supposed to be distributed to those who have lost land. But often local powerful landlords, who control local political machines (and enforce their will with armed paid thugs), take this land for themselves, hiring the poor as sharecroppers. Clamping down on such activities would help ensure that the benefits of the program are better distributed.

This is not a program that works only in one country. For example, Maharashtra state in India has long operated a similar program that has received high marks in independent evaluations. That program has been expanded and is working well in several parts of India.

Development economists cannot design poverty policy based purely on economic theory and divorced from the politics of support for taxation and expenditure for various alternative programs. An added dimension of FFWPs is that it seems easier to ensure political support for this program than for other poverty programs. Because it is available to anyone who requests it, nonpoor people who fear that they may become poor in the future will be more likely to support it as a type of unemployment insurance, or insurance against crop failure. This in turn may encourage poor farmers to take reasonable risks that substantially increase expected farm output but that would otherwise be perceived as too dangerous because of their small savings. More affluent people tend to be more generous with income maintenance policies if they know the poor will have to work to receive benefits. They are more likely to support it if they think they will also receive economic benefits themselves, and infrastructure fits this bill well. Finally, when potential beneficiaries of a welfare program know that they will have to work hard to receive its benefits, they likely to make special efforts, for example saving and making human capital and other investments, to avoid having to rely on the program and engage in this type of work. Work requirements thus reverse the moral hazard problems caused by many welfare programs.

Some of the best evidence of the effectiveness of the Food for Work Program in targeting the poorest of the poor comes from household surveys conducted by the International Food Policy Research Institute (IFPRI) in Washington in conjunction with the Bangladesh Institute of Development Studies (BIDS) in Dhaka. Samples were taken in over 30 locations within walking distance of FFWP construction sites throughout the country. Sites were divided by a number of criteria among "more developed" and "less developed" villages.

One finding is that the infrastructure the projects have created has led to significant gains in output and to the incomes of the poor. Infrastructure endowment is associated with 24% increases in agricultural income, 78% increases in livestock, and fisheries income, and a doubling of wages, while business and industry income increases a much more modest 17%. Moreover, the landless and functionally landless farmers get a larger share of these increases in wages, and in agricultural, livestock, and fisheries income, while the more modest business and industry income gains accrue to large landowners. Thus, overall, the distributional impact of rural infrastructure is very favorable.

Another important finding is that in villages endowed with infrastructure, participation in the labor force increases. A large part of this represents increased labor supply by women, who have traditionally had a very low rate of labor force participation in Bangladesh. In developing countries, such changes generally raise womens' effective income and status, while lowering birth rates, and lead to better nutrition for children.

The IFPRI-BIDS survey showed that infrastructure has important effects on the composition of employment. Development of infrastructure creates opportunities for nonfarm employment, where productivity and incomes are higher while the work is less arduous. Those in villages with developed infrastructure sell more of their output and buy more of the food and other products they need, so that villagers can benefit from a more efficient division of labor. Infrastructure also leads to a shift to voluntary wage employment, from low-productivity self-employment in informal sector activities. This shift increases average annual incomes. Unquestionably, these changes mean that traditional lifestyles are altered, and this may have some drawbacks. But the net result is that infrastructure helps reduce poverty, and villagers jump at the opportunities that it provides them.

Further analysis of these data done for the World Bank by Martin Ravallion confirms the overwhelming concentration of participants in the program among the poorest of Bangladeshis; almost all participants would be considered poor even by local standards. Using the village data survey and other data Ravallion estimated that 60% of the participants in the FFWP came from the poorest quartile of rural households.

The existence of the FFWP probably put upward pressure on wages or otherwise increased the credibility of sharecroppers in their bargaining with landlords. This is important for improving the well-being of poor tenant sharecroppers because under the system of sharecropping under assumptions reasonable for South Asia the landlord can often force tenants to their low income "reservation utility levels" despite the presence of regulations intended to help sharecroppers. Not all the income received from the program represents net gains for participants. The poor must give up informal sector work and work time on their own farm plots to participate. The evidence as a whole suggests that these opportunity costs of participation represent about half of the value of food received from working in the program.

A Food for Work Program is not sufficient for alleviation of poverty. Needed infrastructure work may not be in the vicinity of the poor, and make-work is costly. Some of the poorest of the poor may be too weak to come to work. There is no guarantee that the men who work on these projects will give an adequate share of the food to their wives and children; and orphans and others may simply have no family member who can or will participate. Corruption, such as skimming, overstating work done, and underpayment of participants, has not been (and probably cannot be) entirely prevented. Some roads have washed away, a result that could perhaps have been avoided with better engineering practices. The FFWP has also been criticized for lack of integration with other important local rural development schemes, though this is thought to be improving. Thus Food for Work Programs have some limitations and must be complemented with other poverty programs.

But in a world of uncertainty about who the poor are, moral hazard over incentives to work, and the politics of program support, a program like the FFWP is one of the best places for a low-income country to start.

Sources

Ahmed, Raisuddin, and Mahabub Hossain. *Developmental Impact of Rural Infrastructure in Bangladesh.* Washington, DC: International Food Policy Research Institute with Bangladesh Institute of Development Studies, 1990.

Bangladesh Development Studies, Special Issue, Food for Work Program 11 (1983): 1-235.

Ravallion, Martin. "Reaching the Poor through Rural Public Employment." *World Bank Discussion Paper 94,* 1990.

Singh, Inderjit. *The Great Ascent: The Rural Poor in South Asia.* Baltimore: Johns Hopkins (for the World Bank), 1990.

Stewart, Frances. *Basic Needs in Developing Countries.* Baltimore: Johns Hopkins University Press, 1985.

10. The Choice of Appropriate Technology: Textiles in Kenya and the Philippines

There has been a large debate over the choice of an "appropriate technology" for developing countries. But the debate has been very abstract, and it often seems to professionals concerned with development that little useful progress has been made in the real world. But a World Bank study conducted by Professor Howard Pack of the University of Pennsylvania has pointed the way to making real progress on this problem.

The basic dilemma facing developing countries is that while they generally have abundant labor and scarce capital, innovations are usually made in advanced countries that generally have abundant capital and scarce labor. If a developing country wants to use a more labor-intensive technique, this generally means using an older technique, so it is generally a less productive one. Technological progress is made in the use of capital as well as labor, though labor-saving techniques are often much more visible. (With the drastic price decreases of computers even as their power rapidly expands, consider how much less capital it takes to perform a given computer calculation today as compared with just ten years ago).

In the extreme, some writers have said that there could be a conflict between output and employment. Using a labor-intensive technique might involve a technology so backward that the limited capital involved is utilized so inefficiently that an increase in the number of workers might entail a decrease in the level of output.

That the output-employment tradeoff is possible can be seen from this example. Suppose traditional looms cost 1000 rupees each, with 100 laborers employed at one loom per worker. The modern technique saves not only labor but capital: the same output is now produced by 25 workers in a shop with 50,000 rather than 100,000 rupees of capital equipment. Of course, one can always use modern equipment and pay surplus workers to do nothing—though this is hardly a recipe for international competitiveness. But these arguments generally come from rather casual observation of particular examples. What has been lacking is a systematic and careful study.

This technological progress dilemma makes it seem that developing countries have limited range to take advantage of their abundant labor in international trade. The United Nations and other development agencies have increasingly attempted in recent years to innovate technology for developing countries that is at once labor-intensive and scientifically and technologically modern. Some progress has been made in areas such as small scale pumping and irrigation technology. But the private sector, where resources for applied technical innovation are concentrated, has been little involved and the rate of progress has been rather disappointing.

If innovating technology for developing countries that is labor-intensive and technologically modern would lead to significant gains in efficiency, why has the private sector been so little involved? And does this mean that appropriate technology is less valuable than development economists have maintained? The problem seems to be not so much that appropriate technology is unprofitable, but that the profits cannot easily be appropriated by the innovator. Developing countries where appropriate technology might be used tend to lack intellectual property rights that would provide the innovator a return on investment in creating the technology. The problem of information and opportunism is equally important, and this is especially true for more basic types of technology. By the time the inventor explains enough about the invention to the potential licensee to convince her of the value of the technique, he may already have had to tell her enough about how it works for her to be able to carry on independently. Each of these factors obviously decreases the incentive for private firms to engage in this type of innovation.

At the same time, the use of higher technology production equipment in developing countries, has been, for the most part, disappointing. While there are exceptions, such as South Korean conglomerates and some "Maquiladora" factories operated by U.S. multinational corporations just below the border in Mexico, for the most part the use of advanced technology in developing countries has not resulted in the productivity payoffs claimed by its producers or users in developed countries.

But numerous studies have shown that in many sectors, there is more room for substitution of labor for capital than meets the eye. Simple strategies—such as having extra shifts so that machines are never shut down or specialized personnel to maintain equipment at peak performance at all times, and other straightforward methods—can increase output while decreasing the effective capital-labor ratio. Moreover, older—but not antiquated—technologies do sometimes dominate the most advanced ones at developing country factor prices, such as wages of unskilled workers.

The distinguishing characteristic of industry in the developing world is its low productivity. There are market failures in the transfer of technology from developed to developing countries. That such market failures are endemic to original technological progress is one of the best known propositions in economics. But there are also market failures in the transfer of product, process, and organizational innovations to developing countries. Many developing countries have conducted an active "infant" industrial strategy, designed to protect local industries long enough for them to reach efficient production levels. But the validity of these policies depends in part on the ability of infants to really increase their productivity over time. While a few countries, such as South Korea, appear to have had success with infant industry protection strategies, most attempts, notably in Latin America, have met with failure.

As Pack notes, higher-tech equipment that is projected to be more efficient (in unit production costs) when evaluated using a developing country's lower wages but developed countries' productivity specifications, may prove less efficient than more conventional equipment when evaluated at developing countries' lower productivity norms—norms that tend to hold even after the infant has grown up.

In other words, we must consider realistic production requirements (input coefficients) for a specific country rather than general manufacturers' specifications. With cheaper labor, developing countries do not have to reach the same productivity standards as developed countries, but they cannot compete with low productivity standards that are proportionally even lower than their wages. Thus issues of productivity and the choice of an appropriate technology are closely interconnected.

To address these fundamental issues directly, Pack's study compared companies using identical equipment in Kenya and the Philippines with those in developed countries, primarily in the United Kingdom. The study required Pack, an economist, to venture well beyond the usual range for economic analysis. Rather than take technical specifications as a given provided by engineers, he had to study them directly. In doing so, he had to learn technical details of spinning and weaving technology. But crossing disciplinary boundaries in this way is often the source of real intellectual progress.

Pack analyzed production data from a large number of individual plants in Kenya and the Philippines, and compared their productivity with "best-practice plants" in England. Best practice rather than engineering coefficients is relevant because human factors are crucial in the actual efficiency of a manufacturing plant in a way that engineering specifications simply cannot capture. Total factor productivity (TFP) comparisons were made, which measures difference in output performance once standard inputs like capital and labor have been accounted for. These analyses confirmed that total factor productivity tended to fall well short of best practice norms in both Kenya and the Philippines.

In spinning, plants in both countries achieved about 70% of the total factor productivity as found in plants using the same equipment the United Kingdom. In weaving, only about 55% of total factor productivity was found in the Philippines, and 68% in

Kenya, relative to the United Kingdom. Sources of these differences include inefficiencies in the national economy, in the organization of the plant and other management responsibilities, and in the performance of individual workers. But an important problem was the failure to achieve economies of product specialization, such as can found in Italy. As Pack demonstrates, the international evidence suggests that a liberal trade regime is a necessary but not a sufficient condition to ensure that product specialization economies are realized. Increasing competitive pressure on firms must be only one component of industrial upgrading policy.

Pack's conclusions are both very concrete and specific for the textile industry, and offer general principles for evaluations of other industries. Neither the most modern nor the most traditional technology provided the best practice in the Philippines or Kenya. Most cost-efficient technologies in these countries tended to be intermediate in sophistication. Employing used intermediate-vintage equipment rather than new equipment of intermediate sophistication was also shown to be cost-saving in many cases; there is a tendency for used equipment to be utilized more effectively relative to its best-use potential, and it can often be bought on the international market at favorable prices. As the case of Philippine weaving showed, astute management decisions regarding the amount of labor to use with such equipment can result in large cost savings.

A wide range of evidence from engineering data to interviews led to the conclusion that the mastery of a new technology is not simply the result of the proverbial "learning by doing." Mastery takes more than experience, but requires targeted expenditures and considered management.

The use of inappropriate technology is caused by factors in addition to underpriced capital and overpriced urban modern sector labor. The available information is often poor; managers may think their selection of high technology will sound better on the golf course; and technology is probably not always as flexible as Pack found it to be in the textile industry. But factor pricing policy— removing subsidies for capital use and eliminating large artificial wage premiums for work in the modern sector—has an important role to play.

Appropriate technology availability problems are real. But Pack's important study has demonstrated that there is room for developing countries to maneuver, and shows a strategy for evaluating the best available options.

Sources

Chenery, Hollis, Sherwin Robinson, and Moses Syrquin. *Industrialization and Growth: A Comparative Study.* New York: Oxford, 1986,

Dahlman, Carl J., Bruce Ross-Larson, and Larry E. Westphal. "Managing Technical Development: Lessons from the Newly Industrializing Countries." *World Development 15* (1987): 759–75.

Pack, Howard. *Productivity, Technology and Industrial Development.* New York: Oxford University Press for the World Bank, 1987.

Todaro, Michael. *Economic Development.* 6th Ed., ch. 8. Reading, MA: Addison-Wesley, 1997.

11. Rural Migration and Urbanization in Developing Countries: The Cases of India and Botswana

Nearly half of the world's population lives in cities. But by 2025, nearly two-thirds will live in urban areas. All of the fastest-growing cities are found in the developing world. By 2015, seven cities will have grown to more than 20 million inhabitants. All but one of these will be found in the developing world. These are some of the findings of the UN, presented to the Habitat II conference in Istanbul in 1996.

Urban population growth in the developing world is far more rapid than population growth generally; about half the urban growth is accounted for by migrants from the rural areas. Cities in the developing world are growing far more rapidly than those in developed countries. What drives migration? What effects does this have? The cases of India and Botswana are instructive in showing the value of the development theory of migration, as well as some areas where it needs to be extended.

Relative rates of urbanization are not higher in developing countries today than they were in the period of rapid urbanization of today's developed countries. But in today's developing countries this migration is different for at least two important reasons. First, it is much higher in terms of absolute numbers of migrants, and second, in recent years it has been taking place, in many cases, against a background of stagnant living standards rather than one of growth. Problems caused by urbanization like stress on infrastructure and other urban services are likely greater.

Shantytowns and similar makeshift settlements represent over one-third of Third World urban residences. Unchecked urbanization of the developing world is placing a strain on infrastructure and public health and threatens social stability.

About half of the urban labor force works in the informal sector of low-skilled, low-productivity, often self-employed jobs in petty sales and services. Still, this sector may generate up to a third of urban income, and features a low capital-intensity, low-cost training, waste recycling, and creation of surplus as well as employment creation.

Any economic or social policy that affects rural and urban incomes will influence migration; this in turn will affect sectoral and geographic economic activity, income distribution, and even population growth. Before the Todaro migration models were introduced, migration was widely viewed as irrational or driven by noneconomic motivations, sometimes termed the "bright city lights." Noneconomic factors influence migration decisions, but economic factors are now understood to be primary.

In the economic version of the bright city lights theory, people rationally migrated on the basis of costs and benefits. In this approach, it was assumed that if migrants appeared to be worse off, this was because other benefits were being overlooked, with the effect of making the migrants feel better off (or raising their overall utility).

The Todaro migration models postulate that observed migration is individually rational and that migrants respond to urban-rural differences in expected rather than actual earnings. Urban modern sector earnings are much higher than rural earnings, which may in turn be even higher than urban traditional sector earnings. Migration occurs until average, or expected rather than actual incomes, are equal across regions, generating equilibrium unemployment or underemployment in the urban traditional sector.

The extension of the model to consider equilibrium and effects of actions like increases in wages and probability of employment in the urban areas, undertaken by Harris and Todaro, shows that under some conditions, notably elastic supply of labor, creation of employment opportunities in cities can actually lead to an increase in unemployment by attracting more migrants than there are new jobs.

Despite being individually rational, extensive rural-urban migration produces social costs including lowered output and strains on limited infrastructure. In addition to its costs to crowded cities, excessive migration also imposes external costs on the rural areas emptied of better-educated, more venturesome young people as well as external costs on urban infrastructure and lost output. Relevant migration and employment policies include an emphasis on rural development, rural basic needs strategies, elimination of factor price distortions, and appropriate technology choice as well as appropriate education. Each is intended to increase the incentives for rural residents to remain in rural areas rather than migrate to cities.

Migrants tend to be younger and better educated than non-migrants, and come from all socioeconomic strata. Almost by definition they seem to show above-average entrepreneurial drive. Thus, paradoxically, migrants seem to have slightly better prospects in the rural areas than those who do not migrate.

India provides an interesting setting for a case study, because future urban migration is potentially so vast, and because a number of interesting studies have been undertaken there. Botswana offers a good counterpoint, because it has better published data and more advanced statistical analysis of that data has been undertaken there than for most developing regions.

One of the best detailed studies of the economics of rural-urban migration, providing some tests of the Todaro migration models and depicting the characteristics of migrants and the migration process, is Biswajit Banerjee's *Rural to Urban Migration and the Urban Labor Market: A Case Study of Delhi.*

Everyone who has been to a major city in a developing country has noticed the sharp inequality between those with modern sector jobs and those scratching out a living in the informal sector. But can the informal sector be seen as a temporary way station to the formal sector, or can the barriers between these sectors be explained by education and skill requirements that informal sector workers cannot hope to meet? Banerjee found that the idea of segmented formal-informal rural labor markets could be substantiated statistically. After carefully controlling for human capital variables, Banerjee was still left with earnings in the formal sector 9% higher than in the informal sector that were not explained by any standard economic factor.

We should not automatically assume that when we observe those with more schooling receiving higher earnings that this is a direct reflection of more skills learned in school. It may be that employers simply hire more educated workers as a way of selecting among their many job applicants. It should be noted that there are differences in wages across industries even in a developed country such as the United States. Even so, the earnings differences found in India were not nearly so dramatic as implied in some of the migration literature.

In the literature on urbanization, and in the anecdotes told about the informal sector by lecturers on development the world over, the typical laborer is characterized as self-employed or working on some type of piecework basis. But Banerjee found that only some 14% of his informal sector sample worked in nonwage employment. Interestingly, average monthly income of nonwage workers were some 47% higher than those of formal sector workers.

Banerjee argued that entry into nonwage employment was not easy in Delhi. Some activities required significant skills or capital. Those that did not were often controlled by cohesive "networks" of operators that controlled location of activities in various enterprises. Entry barriers to self-employment in petty services are probably lower in other Third World cities.

Consistent with these findings, Banerjee found that mobility from the informal to the formal sector was low: there was little evidence that more than a very small minority of informal sector workers were actively seeking jobs in the formal sectors; and only 5 to 15% of rural migrants into the informal sector had moved over to the formal sector within a year.

Moreover, the rate of entrants into the formal sector from the informal sector was just one-sixth to one-third that of the rate of direct entry to the urban formal sector from outside the area. Informal sector workers tended to work in the same job almost as long as those in the formal sector; the average informal sector worker had worked 1.67 jobs over a period of 61 months in the city, while formal sector workers averaged 1.24 jobs over an urban career of 67 months.

Banerjee's survey data suggested that a large number of informal sector workers had migrated to the city attracted by the informal rather than the formal sector, coming to work in such occupations as domestic servants, informal construction laborers, and sales workers. Of those who began nonwage employment upon their arrival, 71% had expected to do so. The fact that only a minority of informal sector workers continued to search for formal sector work was taken as further evidence that migrants had come to Delhi expressly to take up informal sector work.

One reason for this focus on the informal sector was concluded to be the lack of contacts of informal sector workers in the formal sector. About two-thirds of direct entrants into the formal sector and some 60% of those switching from the informal to the formal sector found their jobs through "contacts." This overwhelming importance of contacts was taken to explain why some 43% of Banerjee's sample migrated after receiving a suggestion from a contact, which suggests that job market information is often available to potential migrants without their being physically present in the city. An additional 10% of the sample had a prearranged job in the city prior to migration.

Finally, there is on average a very short spell of unemployment following migration. Within one week, 64% had found employment, and although a few were unemployed for a long period, even averaging these in, the average waiting time to obtain a first job was just 17 days.

Banerjee also found that migrants kept close ties to their rural roots. Some three-quarters of the migrants visited their villages of origin and about two-thirds were remitting part of their urban incomes, a substantial 23% of income on average. This indicates that concern for the whole family appeared to be a guiding force in migration. It also suggests a source of the rapid flow of job market information from urban to rural areas.

In a separate study, A. S. Oberai, Pradhan Prasad, and M. G. Sardana examined the determinants of migration in three states in India—Bihar, Kerala, and Uttar Pradesh. Their findings were consistent with the ideas that migrants often have a history of chronic underemployment before they migrate, migrate only as a measure of desperation, and with the expectation of participating in the informal urban sector even in the long run. Remittances were found to be substantial and considerable levels of return-migration were also documented, among other evidence of continued close ties of migrants to their home villages.

Of course, Delhi in particular and India in general may be different from other developing areas. As a whole, these two studies have been taken as a challenge to the applicability of Harris-Todaro or other "probabilistic migration models," at least in the case of India, and suggest that they need to be extended to accommodate the apparently common pattern of migrating with the ultimate aim of urban informal sector employment.

But Banerjee's findings, fascinating as they are, do not necessarily represent as strong a case against the Todaro migration models as some (including Banerjee) have made them out to be. As Ira Gang has noted, one can modify the model to include in the urban area not only a formal sector, but a high-paid informal sector, as well as a low-paid (or unemployed) sector. In this case, people will migrate looking for either a formal sector job or a high-paid informal sector job. This seems to be consistent with Banerjee's evidence. The assumption that keeps the essence of the Todaro models intact is that the wage of the formal urban sector exceeds the high-paid informal wage, which in turn exceeds the agricultural wage, and in turn exceeds the low-paid informal (or unemployed) wage. The particular formulations of the Todaro models are really no more than examples of a general principle—that migrants go where they expect in advance to do better, not where they do better after the fact. The essence of the ideas of the Todaro models do not depend on a particular notion of an informal or a formal sector.

Oded Stark's ideas on a family's use of migration can be a useful supplement to the Todaro models, and may apply to some of Banerjee's findings. In this view, a family will send members to different areas as a "portfolio diversification" strategy, to reduce the risk that the family will have no income. This approach is useful to explain any observed migration from higher- to lower-wage areas, and into higher-wage areas, but not necessarily the area with the highest expected wage. The basic idea of the Todaro models still applies, but this approach looks at families rather than individuals, and stresses risk aversion.

In other studies, the Todaro migration models have held up well without modification in other parts of the world. The survey by Dipak Mazumdar showed that the evidence is overwhelming that migration decisions are made according to rational economic motivations. But most of these have used macro-level data not really designed to address the Todaro hypotheses directly.

A recent study of migration behavior conducted by Robert E. B. Lucas in Botswana addressed such problems in the most economically and statistically sophisticated empirical study of migration in a developing country. His econometric model consisted of four groups of equations—for employment, earnings, internal migration, and migration to South Africa. Each group was estimated from microeconomic data on individual migrants and nonmigrants. Very detailed demographic information was available in the survey used.

Rural migrants in Botswana move to five urban centers (they would be called towns rather than cities in many parts of the world) as well as to neighboring South Africa. Lucas found that unadjusted urban earnings are much higher than rural earnings—68% higher for males—but these differences become much smaller when schooling and experience are controlled for.

Lucas' results confirm that the higher a person's expected earnings and the higher the estimated probability of employment given a move to an urban center, the greater the chances that the person will migrate. And the higher the estimated wage and probability of employment for a person in his or her home village, the lower the chances that the person will migrate. This result was very "robust"—not sensitive to which subgroups were examined or the way various factors were controlled for—and statistically significant. It represents clear evidence in support of Todaro's original hypothesis.

Moreover, Lucas estimated that at current pay differentials, the creation of one job in an urban center would draw more than one new migrant from the rural areas, thus confirming the Harris-Todaro effect. Earnings were also found to rise significantly the longer a migrant had been in an urban center, holding education and age constant. But the reason was because of increases in the rate of pay rather than in the probability of modern sector employment.

Taken together, the best-conducted studies of urbanization confirm the value of the Todaro migration models as the best place to start in seeking explanations of rural to urban migration in developing countries. But these studies underscore the need to expand these explanations of migration considering that many today migrate to participate in the informal rather than the formal urban sector.

Workers who appear underemployed may not consider themselves as such, may perceive no possibility of moving into the modern sector, may be unable to effectively search for modern sector work while busy employed in the informal sector, and thus do not create as much downward pressure on modern sector wages as it would first appear. This may be one factor keeping modern sector wages well above informal sector wages for indefinite periods of time despite high measured urban underemployment.

Sources

Banerjee, Biswajit. *Rural to Urban Migration and the Urban Labor Market: A Case Study of Delhi.* Bombay: Himalaya Publishing House, 1986.

Banerjee, Biswajit. "The Role of the Informal Sector in the Migration Process: A Test of Probabilistic Migration Models and Labour Market Segmentation for India." Oxford Economic Papers 35 (1983): 399–422.

Cole, William E., and Richard D. Sanders. "Internal migration and Urban Employment in the Third World." *American Economic Review 75* (1985): 481–94.

Corden, W. Max, and Ronald Findlay. "Urban Unemployment, Intersectoral Capital Mobility and Development Policy." *Economica 42* (1975): 37–78.

Gang, Ira N., and Shubhashis Gangopadhyay. "A Model of the Informal Sector in Development. *Journal of Economic Studies 17* (1990): 19–31.

Harris, John, and Michael P. Todaro. "Migration, Unemployment and Development: A Two-Sector Analysis." *American Economic Review 60* (1970): 126–42 .

Lucas, Robert E. B. "Emigration to South Africa's Mines." *American Economic Review 77* (1987): 313–30.

Lucas, Robert E. B. "Migration amongst the Batswana." *Economic Journal 95,* (1985): 358–82.

Mazumdar, Dipak. "Rural-Urban Migration in Developing Countries." *Handbook of Regional and Urban Economics, vol. 2.* New York: North Holland, 1987.

Oberai, A. S., Pradhan Prasad, and M. G. Sardana. *Determinants and Consequences of Internal Migration in India: Studies in Bihar, Kerala and Uttar Pradesh.* Delhi: Oxford University Press, 1989.

Oded, Stark. *The Migration of Labor.* Cambridge, MA: B. Blackwell, 1991.

Todaro, Michael P. "A Model of Labor Migration and Urban Unemployment in LDCs." *American Economic Review 59, no. 1* (1969): 138–48.

United Nations. *An Urbanizing World: Global Report on Human Settlements.* Report presented to the Habitat II conference, Istanbul, 1996.

12. Innovation in Rural Development or Land Reform in Reverse? Opening the Ejidal Sector to Private Investment in Mexico

Amy Grat Contributed to this Case Study

On New Year's Day in 1994, a dramatic peasant uprising in the Mexican State of Chiapas captured the world's attention. Chiapas is a very poor and strikingly unequal state on the Guatemalan border with a high percentage of indigenous Mayan peoples. Nearly three-quarters of the population is said to live below the national poverty level, with a fifth of the economically active population earning no cash income. Malnourishment among children is widespread, and nearly 30 percent do not attend school. Yet with about 4 percent of Mexico's population, Chiapas exports more coffee than any other state, and is among the top three exporters of corn, bananas, tobacco, and cacao. Leaders of the uprising demanded changes in the agrarian system and national trade policies that they argued would benefit impoverished peasants throughout the country. A closer look at Mexican agriculture reveals an extremely complex situation, where a history of social inequity, and serious but flawed attempts to redress these inequities, have led to continued poverty, inequality, and inefficiency of large and small farms alike. Current policy initiatives designed to improve efficiency may not achieve that goal unless they are supplemented with policies to achieve greater equity.

The "Zapatista" uprising in Chiapas was timed to coincide with the official beginning of NAFTA, the free trade agreement between the U.S., Canada, and Mexico (see Case 17), a crowning achievement in the Mexican government's drive toward a coveted status as a modern economy. But as many in the press interpreted the events of early 1994, the backward state of peasant agriculture in Mexico suggested that the country was "closer" to its Central American neighbors than its new NAFTA partners.

The uprising over land inequality and injustice were all the more striking as Mexico had burnished a reputation for decades as a government where enormous progress had been made in redressing the gross injustices—and inefficiencies—of the agrarian system established by the Spanish conquerors.

Latin America is well-known for its inordinately unequal agrarian system, in which large, paternalistic, often inefficient Latifundia exist side-by-side with tiny, labor-intensive, impoverished minifundia. Numerous studies have demonstrated that a system of family-size farms or medium corporate or cooperative farms are more efficient than the latifundia-minifundia system.

In Latin America, Mexico was one of the few countries where serious moves toward land reform were at least attempted. Land redistribution was a central legacy of the Mexican Revolution of 1910–1917, and was deeply etched into the Mexican consciousness. The 1917 Mexican Constitution instituted the process of land reform and sanctified the *ejido,* or commons, as a preferred form of peasant land tenure. Since then, more than one-half of Mexico's total land and roughly two-thirds of its cropland have been redistributed from larger estates to small farmers under the *ejido* system. In Chiapas, some 54 percent of the land is in the *ejido* sector.

But Mexico illustrates that the kind of land reform undertaken and the support given for small farmers can be just as important as the act of land reform itself. In Mexico, large landowners were very often able to reserve their holdings of the best land, while more marginal lands were slated for the *ejido* sector. Moreover, the *ejido* system was itself inefficiently designed, with overregulation providing poor incentives for farmers, while necessary support in training, credit facilities, and infrastructure was lacking. The cumulative effects on economic performance were very adverse.

In Mexico, the agricultural sector contains one-fourth of the labor force and nearly one-third of the population, yet it represents less than 8% of national income. In terms of poverty alleviation, the agricultural sector is a critical arena for action: as in many LDCs, some 70% of Mexico's poor live in rural areas. Mexico has made significant strides in improving the efficiency of vegetable and fruit production, with improved quality allowing increased exports to the U.S. However, the *ejido* sector and other poor farmers have traditionally concentrated production in staple crops, where efficiency is low compared with the U.S. Mexico averages about 1.7 tons of corn per hectare, compared with about 7 tons in the U.S. Moreover, one ton of corn produced in Mexico uses about 17.8 labor days, compared with a mere 1.2 *hours* in the U.S. Mexico requires over 50 labor days to produce a ton of beans, while the U.S. requires just over one-half day. Despite the wage differentials, the country currently does not appear to have a comparative advantage in corn and beans with its NAFTA trading partners. Yet Mexico's many rural peasants cannot hope to be absorbed into the modern sector for many years, probably decades. Unless the traditional agricultural sector in Mexico is modernized, there is no hope of improving rural living standards above the subsistence level.

In November 1991, Mexican President Carlos Salinas de Gotari declared his administration's intention to amend Article 27 of the Constitution so as to end the redistribution of land and to open the way for a "profound transformation" of the *ejidal* sector that would "sow a new seed of freedom and autonomy in the rural areas." The resulting legislation aimed to open up the land reform, or *ejidal* sector, to private investment. In

December 1992 the legislation was approved by the Chamber of Deputies, where Salinas' party, the Institutional Revolutionary Party (PRI), continued its sixty-year hold on power.

The *ejidal* sector comprises 28,058 *ejidos* on 250 million acres, employing 3.1 million *ejidatarios,* or *ejidos* workers, and helping provide for some 12 million of their dependents. The peak of land redistribution occurred under the Cardenas administration (1934–40) with 17,906,429 hectares given in land grants (9.1% of Mexico's surface). Under the de la Madrid administration (1982–88), land redistribution was declared ended. As a result of this program, Mexico's land distribution has become more equal than most other countries in Latin America, although still much more unequal than that of successful East Asian countries such as South Korea and Taiwan. Moreover, the best farmland often remained concentrated in large estates, while the more marginal lands typically became incorporated into the *ejidos* sector.

An *ejido* consists of twenty or more *campesinos,* or peasants, eligible for land grants. Under the previous Agrarian Reform Law, all members of an *ejido* must work the land personally. Land was not to be privately owned, but to belong ultimately to the nation. The ejidatario farmer was given usage rights, but could not sell, mortgage, sharecrop, or rent the property. *Ejidal* parcels could only be passed on intact to a single heir. In addition to usage rights over individual parcels, *ejidatarios* had access to communal grazing and forestry lands.

Although land redistribution covered 54% of the total national territory in 1988, much of this is marginal farmland, and only 12 to 13% of that land was under production during 1989. It is estimated that the maximum feasible area for crops is not more than 18% of the total land area. Thus the lack of productivity in the *ejidos* land now cultivated is seen as a constraint on additional agricultural growth.

Within the *ejidal* sector the levels of input use and technical efficiency are considered particularly low. According to 1988 *ejidal* census figures, only 17% of all arable *ejido* land was irrigated. Some 62.2% of all *ejidos* had no agricultural installations such as stables, silos, livestock dips, or hatcheries; 42% had no tractors; and 89.3% operate without agricultural equipment such as sawmills, dehydrating plants, and packaging plants. There is also a gap in public services, with 31.7% communities without electric lights, 51.9% without piped potable water, and 78.2% without paved roads.

Part of the reason for this low productivity is the paternal input and credit relationship between the government "parastatal" enterprises such as Productora Nacional de

Semillas (PRONASE) and Banco Nacional de Credito Rural (BANRURAL) and the *ejidal* sector. Without the ability to use their lands as collateral, *ejidos* have been reliant on government for sources of credit. Up until 1990, inputs had been provided in kind by BANRURAL, rather than allowing farmers to control their own purchases. Decisions about crop mixes and usage of inputs were instituted in a top-down fashion, by extending credit based on government subsidy policies. The result has been that *ejidatarios* have not responded to price changes quickly. Additionally, insufficient or late deliveries of inputs such as fertilizer or seed, and widespread corruption have led to inefficient allocation of resources.

Another economic rationale for a change in agrarian policy is the required opening of the agricultural sector under the North American Free Trade Agreement (NAFTA). This has resulted in the gradual elimination of government subsidies for fertilizer and seeds. It is the driving force behind a change in the national food policy from one of "self-sufficiency," represented by the program Sistema Alimentario Mexicano, to one of "food security," based on specializing according to comparative advantage.

The negotiations of NAFTA resulted in an agreement to eliminate corn subsidies over a 15-year period. Because two-thirds of all *ejidatarios* grow heavily subsidized corn, 90% under arid or semi-arid conditions, and produce at yield rates far below the U.S. average, it will benefit the government to reduce the number of people in that sector and move them into "crops more suitable to Mexico's terrain and market position." The opening up of the *ejidal* sector was part of a government plan to reduce by two-thirds the number of farmers who plant corn by 1996. This goal has not been achieved for many reasons, including the sharp recession of the mid-1990s.

Additionally, the *ejidos* system has been criticized as impeding new investment on the part of private landholders, due to fears of expropriation. Less than 1% of the total foreign investment flowing into Mexico in 1991 went to agriculture. The new law allows private landholdings to be improved through capital investments (such as irrigation) without being "reclassified" for redistribution.

Finally, there is the perceived need to legitimize what is already occurring in many parts of Mexico. Estimates for scope of "illegal" leasing of *ejidal* lands range from a rate of 35% to 50% in the Bajio to 50% to 90% in the irrigated districts of Sonora and Sinaloa. By bringing these arrangements into the open, better legal protection can be extended to both *ejidatarios* and private investors.

Tenure insecurity, the fear that peasants may lose title or the right to use their land, is a chronic problem, both in the *ejidal* sector and among large private landholders. Due to minimum holding size requirements for *ejido* registration and to the lack of a thorough survey, many *ejidatarios* are without usufruct titles.

Although earlier law permits *ejidos* to be farmed both individually and collectively, the vast majority of ejidos are "parceled," where each household is allocated its own tract of land and keeps the income that is generated. Collectively-farmed *ejidos* comprise only 3% of all *ejido* lands. The usufruct nature of the *ejidal* system has not kept the process of *minifundismo,* or subdivision into very small parcels, from occurring. The average parcel size in the *ejidal* sector is just 7.3 hectares, despite the ten hectare prescribed minimum for parcel registration. In states such as Mexico and Puebla with high population density, the average is 2.1 hectares. This can be compared with the average parcel size of private lands, 73.6 hectares in 1981. The size of parcels has had implications for household income generation. A 1960s study calculated that 84% of all *ejido* lands were insufficient to provide employment and adequate income for a peasant family—an insufficiency that is a basic definition of a minifundio. The limitations of parcel size, along with the unemployment problem that results from having only one child inherit the family parcel, have led to a high degree of reliance on off-farm work and outmigration.

This background helps explain some of the key provisions of the new law:

- **The constitutional obligation to redistribute land is removed.** (Repealed sections X–XIV.

- **Land ownership limits have been maintained and clarified, and "improved" lands will not be reclassified for expropriation.** (Title V; art. 117–121.)

- **An Agrarian Attorney General (PA) will be presidentially appointed and land disputes will be settled by autonomous Agrarian Tribunals.** (Title VII–X; art. 134–136.)

- *Ejidatarios* **may sell, rent, sharecrop, or mortgage their lands as collateral for loans. They will no longer be required to work their land personally.** (Chapt II, section VI, art. 78.)

- *Ejidatarios* **may enter into joint ventures with outside investors, may form associations among themselves, and may sign long-term production contracts with outsiders.** (Chapt II, section I, art. 46; title VI, art. 126, 127.)

- **Legal restrictions on foreign investment are lifted, but a foreign equity capital limit of 49% remains.** (Title VI, art. 130.)

Although aiming to open up opportunities for investment in the agricultural sector, the law still retains limitations on size of holdings. The most significant is the establishment of a 2,500 hectare ceiling on the area of prime irrigated land that may be controlled by associations of peasants or private companies. This clause, as well as another that prevents individuals from owning stock in several agricultural companies, is offered as a safeguard against extreme land reconcentration.

For an *ejido* to dissolve itself and convert into private property the Agrarian Attorney General must approve the initiation of the process, upon solicitation of the *ejido* members. Two-thirds of the *ejidal* assembly, with at least three-fourths attendance, must vote in favor of dissolution. If this proportion of assembly members is not present at the first call, then only a simple majority needs to be present upon the second call. A representative from the Agrarian Attorney General as well as a notary public must be in attendance.

Criticisms of the new changes in agrarian law stem from fears of reconcentration of land and of the unequal bargaining power of *ejidatarios* in relation to the more powerful landowners and private investors. Critics say the safeguards against reconcentration found in the law are not as foolproof as they appear to be. In practice, specifications such as those for dissolution of an *ejido* are highly subject to abuse. There are historical precedents for significant pressure being placed by local wealthy elites to call assemblies to achieve their own ends. It does not often happen in practice that an *ejidal* assembly would achieve the necessary 75% quorum to pass dissolution procedures on the first call, thus there is a possibility that some dissolutions may occur with as little as 33% of the total *ejido* represented on the second call.

In a 1991 survey taken before the law changed, two-thirds of ejidatarios interviewed indicated no willingness to sell their land. A "plurality" was in favor of production associations with private investors.

A final criticism of the changes in the agrarian reform law stems from the expectation of increasing social differentiation and inequality in the agricultural sector. This result is highly plausible. The flow of investment will be directed toward those *ejidal* operations that offer the best return. Estimates show that only about 10% of all *ejidos* have the necessary levels of organization, good quality land, and irrigation to be considered viable targets for outside investment. The regions of Mexico that are already highly commercialized and export oriented, such as the states of Coahuila, Sinaloa, Sonora, and Guanajuato, are best situated to benefit from the opening of the agricultural sector. By contrast, states such as Jalisco, Michoacan, and Zacatecas where much of the production is in subsistence crops such as corn and beans, the level of opportunity may be much less. Already, most of the existing joint ventures are found in the more developed northern states of Sonora, Sinaloa, and Nuevo Leon.

During 1991, under previous relaxations, and in anticipation of the new law, there were 80 joint venture projects formed between ejidatarios and private firms. As of late 1992, just over 100 new projects had been created, but according to government sources, commercial banks are considering between 800 and 1,000 joint venture credit requests. The hold-up in investment is blamed on lack of credit sources rather than the lack of initiative on the part of investors and ejidatarios.

Most investment is going into production agreements, in which private investors agree to purchase *ejidal* products, and agricultural processing operations. Examples are: Nutrimex purchases soybeans, Grupo Visa purchases barley, and Gamesa purchases wheat; while BIMBO sets up cacao processing plants, and AGROINSA processes *ejidal* wheat into flour.

A recent study by the National Foreign Trade Bank of Mexico (BANCOMEXT) identified the problems hampering the creation of joint ventures as "poor budgeting, underestimation of operational and supply costs, *ejido* members' lack of experience with crops and new technologies, an ignorance of soil differences, high transportation costs, and an excessive product loss due to the distances between *ejidos* and processing plants." Additional problems included "attempts to transplant unfamiliar business practices, delayed responses to credit requests, unclear lines of responsibility, and scant follow-up to actions taken."

Many of the problems result from insufficient technical training and infrastructure. *Ejidatarios* may require additional technical assistance before they are viable investment partners. The physical infrastructure in the ejidal sector must be revitalized. The commercial banks, recognizing these shortcomings, are hesitant to lend.

The sluggishness of land sales is in great part due to the lack of accurate titling (or land record) information on the *ejidos*. Even though the government has promised an aggressive policy of land titling and the government has mandated a thorough survey, only 3,000 of the 28,000 *ejidos* presently have *ejidal* certificates, which must be converted into titles. Even before titles are handed out, the titling agency must first contend with an enormous backlog of land petitions that legally must be processed. Estimates of these in-process petitions are as high as 32,000, involving over 3 million petitioners.

Previous attempts to modernize the agricultural sector through the expansion of irrigation infrastructure and the introduction of high-yield varieties resulted in regional polarization, with the irrigated districts of the north receiving the lion's share of benefits. The result has been an even greater concentration of production, where almost 50% of agricultural production comes from 23% of total cropland and is produced by 19% of the rural workforce. In addition to the concentration of production, there is also a concentration of land in the more modernized states. In Sonora, where 31% of the land is in the *ejidal* sector, the land gini coefficient, a measure of inequality in land distribution, was .79 in 1970. Even the states with lesser agricultural modernization and higher percentages of *ejidal* lands, such as Chiapas and Jalisco, land Gini coefficients are a still high .52 and .60. The current attempt at modernization may further exacerbate the efficiency problems in Chiapas if the unirrigated lands of the south are not seen as good investment possibilities by private investors. And without attention to social equity, any efficiency gains may prove ephemeral.

After the financial crisis in Mexico in late 1994 and early 1995, and the recession that ensued, most urban Mexican citizens seemed to become more concerned with their own survival than with injustices in the countryside. In an attempt to recapture public attention, the Zapatistas called a national consultative referendum on their political future on August 27, 1995. Despite a low turnout, most observers saw the Zapatistas moving toward the mainstream of the Mexican political process. But while the countryside seemed to quiet down, in mid 1996 there were renewed signs that the conditions that led to the Chiapas uprising were not improving, nor were they confined to that poor state. There was a more modest rebel uprising in the Pacific coast state of Guerrero, and though some observers thought the unrest was orchestrated by landowners favoring a crackdown on dissent, in either case the events pointed up that social tensions continue unabated. Evidence of discontent in other regions, coupled with data showing that rural incomes and living conditions are showing no overall improvement, suggest that Mexico will face problems in its rural areas for quite some time.

The changes in agrarian law, if they are to benefit everyone, and not just those communities that are already well-integrated into the international market, must be complemented by other government investments in agriculture. Although there is a significant role for private investment—especially in rural industries—initial infrastructure development must be provided by government. Provision of information and legal and technical assistance, development of appropriate infrastructure, and supplying investment guarantees could help.

The case of Mexico demonstrates that even a rapidly industrializing country cannot afford to ignore development of the rural areas and the agricultural sector, or to concentrate attention on agribusiness to the exclusion of the poor peasantry. As Albert Hirschman argued a quarter century ago, tolerance for inequality tends to fall as economic development proceeds. And rural poverty may present economic and social constraints on further development in unexpected ways. Mexico must modernize its agricultural sector, but it must do so with a carefully designed policy that considers equity as well as efficiency.

If the changes Mexico has been implementing in the agricultural sector are to truly achieve their promise of modernization, as well as equity, then the Mexican government must go further than simply "sowing a new seed" by opening the *ejidal* agricultural sector to investment. It must cultivate it as well.

Sources

Burbach, Roger, and Peter Rosset. *Chiapas and the Crisis of Mexican Agriculture.* Food First Policy Brief, Institute for Food and Development Policy, Dec. 1994.

Cornelius, Wayne A., "The Politics and Economics of Reforming the Ejido Sector in Mexico: An Overview and Research Agenda." *LASA Forum,* XXIII, no. 3, (fall 1992).

deJanvry, Alain, and Elisabeth Sadoulet. "Investment Strategies to Combat Rural Poverty: A Proposal for Latin America." *World Development 17,* no. 8 (1989): 1203–21

Dresser, Denise. "Neopopulist Solutions to Neoliberal Problems: Mexico's National Solidarity Program." *Current Issue Brief No. 3,* Center for U.S. Mexican Studies, University of California, San Diego, 1991.

El Financiero International, March 9, 1992; March 15, 1992; March 30, 1992.

Financial Times, various issues.

Heath, John Richard. "Enhancing the Contribution of Land Reform to Mexican Agricultural Development." *World Bank Working Paper #285,* 1990.

Heath, John Richard. "Evaluating the Impact of Mexico's Land Reform on Agricultural Productivity," *World Development 20,* no. 5 (May 1992): 695–711.

Heritage Foundation, *Backgrounder,* no. 914. Washington, DC.

Hirschman, Albert O. and Michael Rothschild. "The Changing Tolerance for Income Inequality in the Course of Economic Development. *Quarterly Journal of Economics* (Nov. 1973): 544–566.

Ireson, W. Randall. "Landholding, Agricultural Modernization, and Income Concentration: A Mexican Example." *Economic Development and Cultural Change 35* (1987): 351–66.

Los Angeles Times, October 22, 1991, November 26, 1990.

Villa-Issa, Manuel R. "Performance of Mexican Agriculture: The Effects of Economic and Agricultural Policies." *American Journal of Agricultural Economics* 72, no. 3 (1990): 744–48 and 758–60.

Washington Post, various issues.

13. Sharecropping and Constraints on Agrarian Reform: India

In developing countries, one of the most common forms of farm tenant contracts is sharecropping, in which the tenant farmer uses some of the landowner's farmland in exchange for a share of food output, such as half the rice grown. The landlord's share may vary from less than a third to more than two-thirds of output, depending on local labor availability, and the other inputs (such as seeds, hoes, or credit) that the landlord provides. In this case study, some of the principal economic perspectives on sharecropping will be reviewed; then the case of India, where sharecropping is widespread, will be examined. For convenience, in this case study, unless otherwise noted, we will assume that output is split 50-50 between landlord and sharecropper, the most common type of sharecropping in practice.

Sharecropping was long considered by economists to be economically inefficient. A century ago, Alfred Marshall observed that the farmer was in effect paid only part, rather than all, of his marginal product, and would rationally reduce work effort accordingly. With 50-50 sharing, the sharecropper has an incentive to work until only half of his marginal product of labor is equal to his alternative wage (or other opportunity cost of his time). But more recent work by Cheung, Newberry and Stiglitz, and other economic theorists has provided an understanding of significant scenarios under which sharecropping may be at least relatively efficient after all, because it makes the best out of an inherently uncertain and risky situation for both landlord and tenant.

In an influential analysis, S. N. S. Cheung argued that Marshall's pessimistic conclusion about sharecropping is flawed. First, Cheung noted that Marshall's model takes the share parameter as fixed when rationally it should be set as a result of negotiation. Second, Cheung noted that Marshall's model leaves the tenant free to decide on his level of effort, when rationally the landlord should demand and enforce a high effort. Cheung showed with a theoretical model that if the landlord can pick both share and effort, then a level of output can be induced that just equals the values that would result under a pure land rent contract, in which a fixed rent is paid for the use of the land regardless of how much is ultimately grown.

But Cheung's result has been widely doubted on the realistic grounds that landlords are almost never in a position to fully dictate effort levels of tenants, at least not without incurring substantial supervision costs. The landlord's farms are often widely dispersed across several tenants in many different locations some distance from the village. The landlord or a hired supervisor would have to visit various tenants on various farm plots to monitor their effort. Tenants would know they stand a good chance of not being monitored at any one time. Moreover, tenants often have advance notice that the landlord or supervisor is coming to their place of work—if only by the noise or dust cloud caused by an approaching wagon or motor vehicle—and it is simply too costly to have a supervisor watch a farmworker at all times. Finally, supervisors must themselves be monitored to make sure they are overseeing work as they are paid to, and though landlords will spend some time monitoring the work of supervisors and farmworkers, they often have too high an opportunity cost of time to spend very large amounts of their own time in supervision tasks.

But Cheung also noted that poor farmers were likely to be risk averse, and several studies, such as Fred Boadu's research on cocoa production in Ghana, have found some relation between the presence of share contracts and higher risk faced by farmers in output yields. This insight has enabled development economists to take the analysis one step further to the modern theory of sharecropping contracts.

It would be efficient for the landlord to pay the tenant a straight wage, if the tenant always gave his full effort and it didn't cost the landlord anything to make sure of this; but the tenant has an incentive to accept the money and not work hard. If the tenant pays a straight rent for the land, he faces the appalling risk that there will be a particularly lean year, such as caused by a drought, and there will not be enough food left over after the rent is paid up to prevent starvation. Sharecropping is now understood to represent a compromise between these two types of risk: the risk to the landlord that the tenant will not do much work, and the risk to the tenant that a fixed rent will in some years leave him no income. Given high unemployment risk, the tenant may also prefer the certainty of self-employment as a sharecropper. So even though sharecropping would be inefficient in a world of perfect certainty, in the real world it is "as efficient as we can get."

But the economic and social framework in which sharecropping takes place is one of extraordinary social inequality and far-reaching market failure. In many cases, when the peasant faces his landlord, he faces not only the individual whom he must persuade to rent him productive land, but at the same time he faces his prospective employer, his loan officer, and often his ultimate customer for any crops he wishes to sell. These are the conditions known as "interlocking factor markets," and they provide the rural landlord with abundant sources of monopoly and monopsony power, making traditional rural economic and social organization hardly resistant to efforts at reform. The consequences of this have been explored with economic theory and with case studies of agrarian regions.

Suppose a well-meaning government puts a cap on interest rates the landlord can charge. The landlord may simply respond by lowering any or all of the wage rate, the tenant's share of the crop, and the price the landlord pays for any crops the tenant seeks to sell; or he may raise the implicit price of seeds and tools advanced to the tenant. Under some conditions, in particular, because of the availability of a perfectly elastic supply of tenants and the ability of the landlord to subdivide his land into as many plots as he chooses, the peasant is forced to the same "reservation utility level," or next-best income opportunity, as before. One feature of this analysis, due to Avishay Braverman and T. N. Srinivasan, is that the peasant's effort per hectare increases with decreases in plot size. Interlinked factor market sharecropping does have the advantage that it is in the landlord's interest to see to it that his sharecropper receives credit from the lowest-cost source. Attempts to regulate several of these interlocked markets at once in an uncertain economy will generally lead to inefficiency—if not leave most tenants unemployed, as landlords switch to entirely different uses for their land. The Braverman and Srinivasan analysis concludes that "nothing short of land reform will affect the tenant's welfare."

As Yujiro Hayami and his collaborators, among others, have argued, well-meaning attempts to improve the lot of peasants by introducing piecemeal reforms, or by "negative" steps such as banning sharecropping, misunderstand the problems and choices facing farm laborers and have sometimes completely backfired in practice. Instead, land reform must not happen in a vacuum, but must first address the peasant's natural aversion to the extraordinary risks of rural poverty. It must offer some means of insurance against weather or price calamities; it must offer training in all aspects of economic life as a farm owner-operator, including not just modern cultivation methods but business, credit management, marketing, and other skills. Otherwise the resulting underuse of capital, fertilizer and similar inputs, and new varieties may result in an outcome much inferior even to sharecropping.

The teaching of basic literacy and numeracy may be a prerequisite for successful land reform. Steps to reduce monopolistic powers of landlords without destroying rural employment are needed. A progressive land tax discouraging speculative fallow land holdings, coupled with a ceiling on aggregate land owned, will reduce monopoly power; it will do so with a minimum of interventionist regulations that could backfire. Government will also need to help farmers obtain credit to buy land as it comes on the market. But otherwise, the less specific, discretionary, and interventionist activity of government, the less the actual opportunity for the landholding class to subvert land reform through corrupt practices.

Finally, policy must seek the right individual and group balance between assured family proprietorship on the one hand, and cooperation with other farmers, sometimes with public assistance, on the other. Thus land reform is not an event, but a process, one that may be expected to take up to a full generation.

Share tenancy continues to be extremely widespread in India despite numerous attempts by national and state governments to promote tiller-ownership and legally discourage, if not outlaw, traditional tenancy arrangements under many circumstances. Under 1952 legislation, a 30-acre limit was placed on traditional landlord landholdings. Tenants can request that land on which they labor be formally registered under the legislation and can eventually obtain title to it. The fact that tenants often do not take these steps lends support to theories that in a world of uncertainty, share tenancy brings clear benefits to laborers as well as owners.

On the other hand, the law limiting landholdings was not strictly enforced, nor was it well understood among peasants. There has been the real worry among peasants that until clear title is obtained one has to pay rent to the state—often viewed as operating under rigid and unfeeling bureaucratic rules—rather than a paternalistic landlord; and on net they may actually face greater risk of losing the land. A peasant may worry that if he sought tiller rights on one plot of land, landlords would never give him the opportunity to lease any other land in the future. Moreover, as Pranab Bardhan notes, a peasant is sometimes under "extraeconomic coercion" by landlords and may fear for his physical safety. Finally, a peasant may fear that success at gaining land will bring the opprobrium of all other landless farmers in the village who may (plausibly) consider their own future chance of renting land in the village threatened by the precedent.

Empirical evidence on sharecropping in India has been mixed. In *Land Labor and Rural Poverty,* Pranab Bardhan reported on a survey of over 300 villages in four Indian states. This survey confirmed that some form of sharecropping was the overwhelmingly predominant form of tenancy in India. It also showed that in practice, there are a very wide variety of forms of sharecropping contracts across regions in India. Within most villages, contracts were of a single type, but in a significant number of villages several contract types were found to coexist. Patterns were sometimes hard to discern, but some did emerge: high-yielding varieties were associated with higher tenant shares; in West Bengal, 50-50 sharecropping was much more common when fertilizer is *not* used than when it is used; and generally, the tenant's share tended to be higher when the landlord did not share in costs, while a very wide range of patterns of cost-sharing were observed.

Traditionally, the landlord pays land and irrigation taxes and the tenant supplies draft animal and plow. The cost of chemical fertilizer is commonly shared on a 50-50 basis. Close to half of the tenants in each region were found to have taken a production loan from the landlord, with a majority of these paying some form of interest. The tenant is occasionally obligated to perform other services for the landlord, at times without pay. Often this obligation is strictly outside the tenancy contract, and may represent extraeconomic coercion.

One of the most detailed single-village case studies of sharecropping and its connections to other village agricultural activities is C. J. Bliss and N. H. Stern's *Palanpur: The Economy of an Indian Village.* Palanpur has been widely studied by researchers, partly due to its convenient location near a railway stop. It is a village of mud and brick houses with a population of about 1,000 located in Western Uttar Pradesh. Some 22.8% of land in Palanpur is under tenancy; sharecropping, accounting for about 20% of cultivated land, is its usual form. Unlike the familiar overlord image, many of those renting out land or hiring farm labor own rather small quantities of land. This contrasts with assumptions in theoretical work such as that of Braverman and Srinivasan. Bliss and Stern infer from national statistics that overall some 14.2% of land is under tenancy in India, but there are some reasons to surmise that national statistics understate the actual extent of tenancy.

Most share contracts in Palanpur featured 50-50 output sharing and full tenant responsibility for traditional costs of seeds, draft animals, and cultivation labor, as well as of modern (or "discretionary") costs such as fertilizer and irrigation. This differs from studies of other parts of India that have found that 50-50 sharing of discretionary costs is common. These contract requirements mean that to be qualified as a tenant, a farmer must own or have access to draft animals. In practice, renting draft animal services is almost impossible. Thus a potential sharecropper will not typically be among the absolutely poor. This also helps explain why many less affluent peasants are at constant risk of becoming absolutely poor: a wealth "shock" represented by the death of a draft animal may easily have the effect of pushing a family below the absolute poverty line, even locking the family out of the sharecropper labor market.

For whatever reasons, the 50-50 output sharing rule has been in force in Palanpur for decades. This means that in Palanpur, market equilibration, or the equating of quantities of supply and demand in labor, land and input markets, has had to take place through mechanisms other than changes in the sharing rule. For example, Bliss and Stern suggest that disappointed would-be tenants will sell their draft animals or otherwise take themselves out of the market of potential renters—even though they might have been willing to work for a smaller output share if such a contract were available. Of course, many other prices and quantities of inputs may vary. In any case we must assume that for some reason landlords and tenants find the 50-50 output sharing rule very convenient. Certainly it is easy to calculate and carries the social advantage of sounding like a "fair deal."

Interestingly, modern or discretionary costs must be advanced by the tenant, and half reimbursed by the landlord only at harvest time. As Bliss and Stern note, this standard contract feature gives an incentive to a landowner to rent out land if he can find a tenant with cash or access to credit. At the time that a sharecropping arrangement is initiated, landlord and tenant also must reach agreement on which crops will be grown and which inputs will be used.

In the few exceptions to sharecropping tenancy in Palanpur, a landlord who is often absent from the village, say, to perform a salaried job outside of the village, will rent the land on a pure cash basis. This may be a relatively small rent because of the larger resulting risk that the tenant must bear. But this finding is consistent with the view that the landlord must play some, if a limited, monitoring role, under sharecropping as well as wage contracts.

Indeed, Bliss and Stern find that landlords regularly observe the progress of cultivation, and that tenants often complained that landlord interference was onerous. They also argue that legal restrictions on tenancy arrangements in which landlords also play a supervisory role may serve to encourage sharecropping, because it is easier for the landlord to claim he is cultivating the land himself and the tenant is a legal wage employee.

Although Palanpur contracts are for a duration of one season, in practice tenants have an incentive to work harder than this short-term horizon would suggest. In their interviews, Bliss and Stern were often told that landlords prefer a good farmer to a poor one, and surely a tenant's performance in previous seasons will be the key basis on which to judge a farmer's quality. Thus, we may judge that tenants will find it optimal to build up a reputation for quality work, although the reputation theory literature of industrial organization would also suggest that at some point in their working lives they will find it optimal to live on their past reputations and work less hard, thereby running their reputations down.

Bliss and Stern also examined efficiency across sharecropped and owner-farmed land. Overall, there is no difference in input use or output efficiency, which corresponds to Cheung's views. Surprisingly, in comparing lands on which a farmer works as a share-cropper on some land as well as farms some land he owns himself, sharecropped lands show somewhat greater efficiency. This is a direct test that holds constant the attributes of the cultivator. Bliss and Stern suggest that the sharecropped lands may be of higher quality than lands individually owned by these sharecroppers. They deemed this plausible because owners are of higher caste than sharecroppers. In any case, little evidence emerged in their study that sharecropping is truly inefficient, as Marshall had expected. But other studies had previously concluded otherwise. For example, comparing share-cropped and other land in northeast India tilled by the same farmer, Clive Bell found that the sharecropped land had lower yields, although this difference was generally not statistically significant.

Sheila Bhalla found some evidence in support of the idea that landlords manipulate contract terms to push laborers to their reservation utility. She found large variations in the terms of the sharecropping contract, including the output shares themselves.

One of the most advanced multi-village econometric studies of sharecropping was recently conducted by Radwan Ali Shaban using data from four districts in semi-arid tropical parts of India: Mahbubnagar in Andhra Pradesh, Sholapur and Akola in Maharashtra, and Sabarkantha in Gujarat. Most tenants cultivated at least some land they owned. This study found that both inputs and outputs per unit of land were greater for these tenants on land they owned than on land they sharecropped. Output was almost a third higher on the farmer-owned plots, and even after controlling for irrigation, plot value and soil quality output per acre was over 16% higher. With similar controls, family male labor was about 21% higher, family female labor 47% higher, and draft animal (bullock) inputs 17% higher on the owned plots. But no statistically significant differences were found in comparing plots that were owned with those that were leased on a fixed-rent basis. And while offering a careful statistical analysis involving more villages and offering more definitive statistical tests, the study did miss some of the detailed observations of peasant behavior that were an important part of the Palanpur study. Moreover, these findings do not prove that sharecroppers would be better off if they could own or lease on a fixed-rent basis, if they are averse to risk. For now, though, the study must shift the weight of evidence in favor of lower technical efficiency on share-cropped land.

The theory and evidence considered in this case study suggests that sharecropping is less technically efficient than owner-farming or fix-rent farming in many, but not all cases. But risk-averse sharecroppers may be better off than if they had to pay a fixed rent or mortgage. There is some evidence that the more backward areas of India, such as Bihar, conform to the picture of high landlord bargaining power, interlinked contracts, and high tenant indebtedness to the landlord. At the same time, more advanced areas, such as Punjab and Haryana, show essentially modern landlord-tenant relationships. Landless laborers are finding it harder to obtain the use of land on the basis of share tenancy.

In any case, the complexity of the issues and the lack of consistency in the data suggest that the case for land reform is on more solid ground if it rests on inefficiencies of very small farms and perhaps of very large ones—and on its anti-poverty and distributional advantages, making the use of land possible for landless laborers—rather than the inefficiency of sharecropping contracts themselves. Given the tenacity of landlord power and traditional contract practices, and the natural risk aversion of poor peasants, outlawing particular forms of tenancy such as sharecropping as a response to efficiency and equity problems is likely to be counterproductive as a policy for alleviating poverty.

Sources

Bardhan, Pranab K. *Land Labor and Rural Poverty.* New Delhi: Oxford, 1984.

Bell, Clive. "Alternative Theories of Sharecropping: Some Tests using Evidence from Northeast India." *Journal of Development Studies* (July, 1977): 317–346.

Bhalla, Sheila. Articles in *Economic and Political Weekly,* 1976 and 1983.

Bliss, C. J. and N. H. Stern. *Palanpur: The Economy of an Indian Village.* New Delhi: Oxford, 1982.

Boadu, Fred O. "The Efficiency of Share Contracts in Ghana's Cocoa Industry." *Journal of Development Studies 29,* no. 1, (Oct. 1992): 108–120.

Braverman, Avishay, and T. N. Srinivasan. "Agrarian Reforms in Developing Rural Economies Characterized by Interlinked Credit and Tenancy Markets." In Hans Binswanger and Mark Rosenzweig, eds., *Contractual Arrangements, Employment and Wages in Rural Labor Markets in Asia.* New Haven: Yale, 1984.

Cheung, S. N. S. *The Theory of Share Tenancy.* Chicago: University of Chicago Press, 1969.

Dreze, Jean P., and Anandita Mukherjee. "Labor Contracts in Rural India: Theory and Evidence." In S. Chakravarty, ed. *The Balance Between Industry and Agriculture in Economic Development,* vol. III. New York: St. Martin's, 1988.

Hayami, Yujiro, et al. *Toward an Alternative Land Reform Paradigm, A Philippine Perspective.* Manila: Ateneo de Manila University Press, 1990.

Newberry, D. M. G., and J. E. Stiglitz. "Risk-sharing, Sharecropping and Uncertain Labor Markets." *Review of Economic Studies,* Oct. 1977.

Shaban, Radwan Ali. "Testing between Alternative Models of Sharecropping." *Journal of Political Economy 95,* no. 5 (1987): 893–920.

Stiglitz, J. E. "Incentives and Risk Sharing in Sharecropping." *Review of Economic Studies.* April 1974.

14. Environment, Debt, and Development: Deforestation in the Brazilian Amazon Rain Forest

In recent years development specialists have made a major shift of focus toward problems of environment and development. Out of this, the theme of "sustainable development" emerged as a rallying point. It has been defined as "meeting needs of the present generation without compromising the needs of future generations," or as "development with respect for the natural world on which society and economy depend."

The idea of sustainable development may not offer anything qualitatively new to economic development analysis, but it does help ensure that important existing ideas will be brought to the fore. Sustainable development is partly embodied in previously available economic concepts, especially using an appropriate social discount rate, a correct valuation of the environment as a capital stock rather than a free flow of consumption, and the proper internalization of negative environment and health externalities of projects.

But sustainability offers a clearer definition of development, in which future as well as current welfare and its distribution across generations is stressed. Now the value of the idea is shown by the term's non-environmental uses, such as whether a project can be financially self-supporting after foreign aid ends, and the extent of actual technology transfer including innovative capacity. Further, the term "sustainable development" has served to coalesce a research agenda and concentrate policy makers' agendas. Even if it is no more than a glorified "bumper sticker," the concept of sustainable development is useful for these purposes alone.

There is a close connection between poverty and environmental degradation. This comes as a surprise to many students and, in fact, it was perhaps initially unexpected by much of the profession. It is a commonly made conjecture that the richest billion and poorest billion people do the most environmental damage; the poorest billion perhaps do more damage than the middle 4 billion together.

There are at least five important aspects of this poverty-environmental damage connection:

1. The absolutely poor have a high rate of fertility, and high population growth poses a threat to the environment.

2. When a person will starve if he or she does not use savings, there is no finite discount rate. The poorest are known to eat their next year's seed corn to avoid starvation now—this is a metaphor for the general problem.

3. Even if survival is not at stake, when a person has insecure land tenure rights as the relatively poor often do, there is an incentive to treat land as a short-term resource. Lack of access to credit can have the same effect.

4. In Latin America especially (also in the Philippines and elsewhere) inefficiently unequal land distribution produces political incentives to encourage poor farmers to establish inefficient rain forest settlements.

5. Poverty is closely linked with the low status of women, who often have roles as guardians of natural resources, such as water supplies; are responsible for agriculture, especially marginal agriculture; and generally play a larger role fertility choice than men.

At the macro level, there is also a close connection between the debt crisis and environmental degradation. The debt crisis (1) means LDCs cannot afford to import cleaner technologies, (2) creates a force for very high discount rates, and (3) this in turn encourages a shift from manufactures diversification to intensive natural resource extraction, which is often worse in total environmental impact than industry, especially when it degrades rainforests.

There is an important case to be made for new environment-oriented foreign aid, as benefits of maintaining rainforests—in particular to alleviate the greenhouse effect and preserve biodiversity—go in large part to the developed world.

In a real sense, environmental degradation is like consumption out of the nation's capital stock. Increases in physical capital that may accompany destruction of environmental capital often less than compensate for its loss. One important outcome of sustainable development research is the extension by Robert Repetto and others of social accounting analysis to include environmental accounting. But it must be said that our ability to put a precise valuation on the loss of rain forest, for example, is still very primitive. There are no markets for the public goods and values for future generations that are at the source of the controversy over deforestation. Values must be imputed, and differing conclusions are inevitable.

Deforestation of the Brazilian Amazon rain forest shows many of the conflicts between short- and long-term development goals. Deforestation has often represented nonrenewable resource extraction without attention to negative externalities and often benefitted from ill-conceived subsidies for grandiose showcase development projects (such as "Plan 2010") that often lacked economic justification but were supported by international development agencies such as the World Bank. The encouragement of low-income farmers to move in this case to Rondonia, seemed to be a politically inexpensive—but ecologically disastrous—alternative to land reform. In the end, it was no alternative at all, as the best land once again became concentrated in the hands of large, powerful farmers who kept control of these lands through extraeconomic coercion, including brutal atrocities.

Some of the perverse government incentives of this period have now been well-publicized. Land titles were awarded to settlers on the basis of forest area cleared; this provided incentives for rain forest burning even when no economic use was planned. Furthermore, tax breaks were given for using Amazon land for ranches, which led the wealthy to develop the region to save taxes rather than on the basis of economic merits. Thus, cattle ranching activities for which there was a negative real rate of return, before the value of ecological damage was even considered, became viable to investors on tax-saving grounds alone.

Hans Binswanger of the World Bank has analyzed several other Brazilian policies that encourage deforestation in the Amazon, including a land tax that gives benefits for converting forest to pasture and the availability of subsidized credit for ranching. The disastrous economic and social, as well as ecological, effects of the conversion of tropical forest to pasture in Brazil—and the fact that sound alternatives to using this land for pasture do exist—have been abundantly demonstrated in a recent volume of two dozen studies edited by Theodore Downing and his colleagues.

The case of deforestation and ecological devastation of Brazil's Amazon rain forest exemplifies these points. Rain forest loss is having negative consequences for long-term development goals of Brazil, as well as for world environment goals like reduction of global warming and preservation of biodiversity. Rain forest loss represents one of the most serious environment issues of the developing world. It is also a case that illustrates problems of sustainable development. Two charts comparing deforestation in Brazil with that in other countries are found at the end of this case study.

Economic activities in the Amazon have been based on nonrenewable resource extraction without attention to negative externalities, and often benefitted from ill-conceived subsidies. Grandiose showcase development projects and schemes were the order of the day, such as "Plan 2010" with its hydrodams and subsidized ore mining. Such projects often lacked economic justification but were all too quickly supported by development agencies. But today, Brazil and the development agencies are finally beginning to take a new approach toward Amazon development.

The Amazon tropical rain forest is the world's largest rain forest, covering approximately 5 million square kilometers of land. The Amazon River basin covers 7 million square kilometers, making it the largest river drainage system on earth. Its diversity of plant and animal life is unmatched anywhere in the world. Almost three quarters of the Amazon rain forest is located in Brazil; about 1.3 million kilometers of the rain forest are located in Peru, Venezuela, Colombia, and Ecuador.

Deforestation in the Amazon had not represented a significant problem prior to the 1980s. But most estimates show the total of deforested Amazon lands having grown dramatically from 3 million hectares in 1975 to 60 million hectares in 1988—an area larger than France. Estimates of deforestation by the mid-1990s ranged up to 100 million hectares, though one recent NASA study suggested that the annual rate of deforestation might be as little as one-third of previous estimates, with the loss of biodiversity much higher than previously estimated.

In one important study, Anthony Anderson examined the rush to establish charcoal-consuming industries in the Amazon supplied primarily by local rain forests. He found that this expansion has been driven by generous government incentives, that prospects for effective forest management looked weak, and he projected that over 1500 square kilometers of rain forest were likely to be destroyed each year as a result.

The northwest state of Rondonia has experienced the most devastation, beginning with the 1970s construction of roads to the area and the encouragement of low-income farmers to move there as a way of removing pressure for land reform. The results were disastrous. The settlers logged, and more often burned the forests; the wealthy grazed cattle and the poor planted crops.

Rain forest soils are well known to be fragile. Most nutrients in rain forest ecologies are in the biomass itself, and are lost when a rainforest is burned. As the soils became quickly depleted, new forests were cleared, in a form of nonrenewable slash-and-burn agriculture. The use of tree crops rather than annual crops was not encouraged in the tax code, despite its positive externalities and sustainability benefits, so soils were depleted all the faster.

In addition to rain forest loss, water resources were contaminated on a vast scale for downstream users, including erosion and siltation, and the spread of waterborne disease. Most egregiously, rights of indigenous peoples were flagrantly violated, with terrible atrocities committed by settlers. Ecological campaigners and activists among rubber-tappers whose livelihoods were threatened were attacked and sometimes murdered, as Francisco "Chico" Mendes was in 1988.

The World Bank was partly responsible for this calamity. For example, it funded the paved, all-weather highway from the region to Porto Velho and other Rondonia projects. This facilitated haphazard settlement of the area, including agriculture on fragile lands that quickly went barren. As Brent Millikan has described, some of the projects had nominal environmental protection components, but they were not enforced.

After intense pressure from environmental groups and concerned donor governments, the Bank stopped direct-lending support for these ill-conceived Rondonian settlements. The Bank also funded the vast Carajas Iron Ore project, which led to the environmental devastation of Para State, the costs of which were barely taken into account in project calculations and the balance sheets of participating companies.

These Amazon experiences and the resulting public outcry were also largely responsible for the establishment of the Environment Division of the World Bank and other reforms announced in 1987. The World Bank has steadily increased its financial and research support for environmental protection in the Amazon and elsewhere through the mid-1990s.

In the late 1980s, Brazil began to reverse its perverse Amazon incentives. Incentives for clearing Amazon land were sharply reduced. Publicly funded road building in ecologically fragile regions was greatly scaled back. After some pressure on Brazil, in 1992 the Rondonia Natural Resources Management Project (RNRMP) was introduced in an attempt to rectify these problems. The environmentally conscious RNRMP has earned high marks from environment and development specialists. As part of the plan, Indian reservations have been increased in size. Land titles are denied to settlers in prohibited zones. Several nature parks and biological reserves have been established. Land use planning has been rationalized through the use of in-depth satellite imaging, financed by the World Bank. The results confirmed that only a little over 10% of Rondonia's area (about 2.6 out of 24.3 million hectares) could support sustainable annual crop use. An additional 6.4 million hectares was determined to be capable of sustainable tree crop use (notably rubber, coffee, and fruit).

Avenues for public participation in land use decisions have been created in Brazil. The World Bank has increasingly demanded better legal protection for Indian rights. Certain "extractive reserves" have been established, like a 1.1 million acre reserve in Jari State established in 1990, on which 2,500 families live and engage in practices such as rubber tapping.

All of these changes have been helpful. But enforcement of the new rules has been difficult and poachers have continued their activities. Some of the loss of vital rain forest lands and other ecological damage may prove irreversible. In a sense, deforestation has gathered a momentum of its own. Now that critical initial investments have been made and economic activities have reached significant returns to scale, the once-crucial public subsidies are no longer needed for various activities, and the private sector has found it can operate profitably on its own—provided investors do not have to pay for the environmental damage they cause. For example, as Anthony Anderson reports, ranchers in the state of Para are constructing their own private road to the adjacent state of Marahao, to extract timber.

It is essential that more be done. The first need is for more research. Further attention to alternative uses, such as "eco-tourism," should be given. Forest management in other tropical rain forests has led to extremely high, profitable—and sustainable—fruit yields. Products that can be harvested without serious ecological disruption include fibers, latex, resins, gums, medicines, and game.

Some environmental advocates seem to have implied that people should continue practicing low-productivity, low-income traditional gathering activities indefinitely. But research can yield newer techniques and products that will support use of the rain forest in an ecologically sustainable manner. Another recent collection of studies edited by Anthony Anderson, *Alternatives to Deforestation,* has demonstrated that higher productivity practices are feasible—and sustainable. Support to further such research should be given a high priority.

Poor peasants are often blamed for a significant part of deforestation because of their slash-and-burn agricultural practices. This is a major proximate cause of the problem, but this is more like blaming the victim than a useful basis for policy. The poor move to the Amazon and practice ecologically harmful agriculture once they get there because they are lacking in resources. Land reform benefiting poor farmers and financial credit, extension, and other services for the poor once they get access to land should be a top priority.

Finally, because the rest of the world benefits from Brazil's rain forests through prevention of global warming, ecological cleansing, and irreplaceable biodiversity needed for future antibiotics other medicines and goods, the international community should be prepared to pay something to ensure its continuation. Financial support as well as political pressure for land reform is one clear direction. Debt for nature swaps would seem an important avenue for this, but unlike some other Amazon countries such as Bolivia (see Case 15), Brazil has traditionally resisted these swaps on the grounds that they infringe on sovereignty. Yet with imagination there must be some way to accomplish the same end. Recently Brazil has been participating in talks designed to achieve this delicate balance.

Deforestation

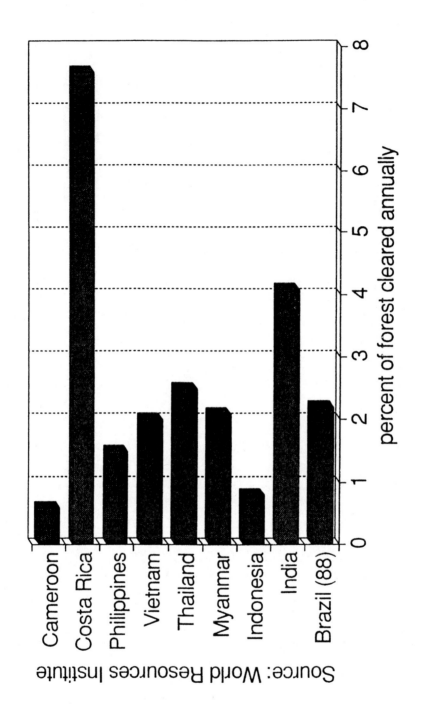

percent of forest cleared annually

■ avg. 1975-88

Source: World Resources Institute

Cameroon
Costa Rica
Philippines
Vietnam
Thailand
Myanmar
Indonesia
India
Brazil (88)

Deforestation

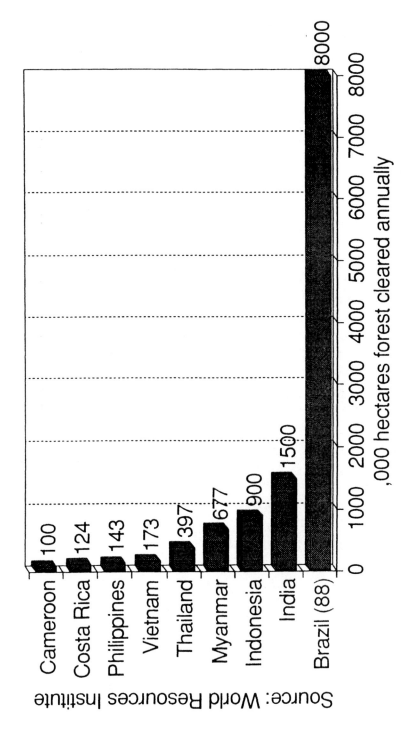

,000 hectares forest cleared annually

■ avg. 1975-88

Cameroon	100
Costa Rica	124
Philippines	143
Vietnam	173
Thailand	397
Myanmar	677
Indonesia	900
India	1500
Brazil (88)	8000

Source: World Resources Institute

Sources

Anderson, Anthony B., ed. *Alternatives to Deforestation.* New York: Columbia, 1990.

Anderson, Anthony B. "Smokestacks in the Rainforest: Industrial Development and Deforestation in the Amazon Basin." *World Development 18,* no. 9 (1990): 1191–1205.

Bank Information Center. *Funding Ecological and Social Destruction: The World Bank and The IMF.* Washington, DC, 1990.

Binswanger, Hans P. "Brazilian Policies that Encourage Deforestation in the Amazon." World Development 19, no. 7 (1991): 821–829.

Downing, Theodore E. et al, eds. *Development or Destruction: The Conversion of Tropical Forest to Pasture in Latin America.* Boulder, CO: Westview, 1992.

Goodman, David, and Anthony Hall, eds. *The Future of Amazonia.* New York: St. Martins, 1990.

Millikan, Brent. "Land Degradation, Deforestation, and Society." *Latin American Perspectives 19,* no. 1, (1992): 45–72.

Nature, "Mining in the Amazonian Rainforests" Feb. 1992, pp. 593–594.

Repetto, Robert, et al. *Wasting Assets, Natural Resources in the National Income Accounts.* Washington, DC: World Resources Institute, 1989.

Washington Post, May 31, 1992; June 25, 1993.

World Bank, "Development and the Environment," *World Development Report.* New York: Oxford, 1992.

World Bank. *Environment and Development in Latin America and the Caribbean: The Role of the World Bank,* Washington, DC: World Bank, 1992.

15. How Has a Debt-for-Nature Swap Worked in Practice?: Bolivia

Eva Canoutas contributed to this case study

Introduction

In recent years concern over the growing environmental problems of developing countries has intensified. At the same time, the international debt crisis has captured the world's attention, although in many countries the crisis has receded for now. These two developments have been argued to have three main interconnections. The debt crisis (1) means LDCs cannot afford to import cleaner technologies, (2) creates a force for very high discount rates, or a very short term time horizon, as foreign exchange earnings must be raised quickly to service debts, and (3) this in turn encourages a shift from manufactures diversification to intensive natural resource extraction, which is often worse in total environmental impact than industry, especially when it degrades rain forests.

A Debt-for-Nature Swap is intended to address both problems simultaneously, by reducing debt in exchange for ensuring greater protection of valuable environmental assets, usually rain forests. Bolivia's 1987 Debt-for-Nature Swap agreement was the pioneer in this mechanism, and enough time has now elapsed to begin an assessment of its impact in this case study.

The Debt-for-Nature Swap is a financial mechanism first created by international conservationists to protect endangered rain forest areas in a manner consistent with development goals. A conservation group is responsible for purchasing and retiring a portion of a country's international debt, thus contributing to the country's development. In exchange, the LDC government agrees to allocate local monies, usually by issuing conservation bonds, for local conservation activities, such as to maintain a preserve purchased by the conservation group. Thus, the exchange is analogous with debt-for-equity swaps because the LDC is able to exchange debt denominated in foreign exchange (that it does not control) for obligations denominated in local currency. (For more information on debt-for-equity swaps, see Case 19.) Thus, from the debtor country's point of view, the swap represents a much greater improvement than switching one form of debt for another might first suggest. Conservation bonds are financial instruments designed to ensure that the commitment of national currency does not cause inflation in the debtor country. Usually, care is taken to ensure that indigenous peoples using the designated areas for economic activities have their livelihoods protected.

The 1987 Bolivia Debt-for-Nature Swap

In July 1987, Conservation International (CI), originally an offshoot of the World Wildlife Fund, made headlines when it announced the first Debt-for-Nature Swap. A $100,000 grant donated to CI enabled them to purchase $650,000 of Bolivia's debt on the secondary market, offered at a huge—approximately 85%—discount at the time. (Note that most discounts on international debt instruments are no longer nearly this large.) CI then canceled this debt in exchange for the Bolivian government's agreement to raise legal protection on the Beni biosphere reserve to the maximum extent allowed by Bolivian law. In addition, Bolivia was to establish a multiple use conservation buffer zone around the reserve, together totaling 2.7 million acres. In addition, the government established an endowment fund in the amount of $250,000 worth of local currency to cover operating costs of managing the reserve.

Clearly, Bolivia gains by the greater environmental enforcement, and to the extent that environmental problems, such as global warming and loss of biodiversity, spill over international boundaries, so do other countries. Economic benefits to Bolivia include the cancellation of $650,000 of hard currency debt.

The Beni biosphere reserve encompasses a large part of the Amazonian region in northern Bolivia. With approximately 330,000 acres at the headwaters of the Amazon, the reserve was set up by the National Academy of Sciences in 1982 as a model sanctuary to protect the region's unique flora and fauna, as well as its native peoples. It supports 13 of Bolivia's 18 designated endangered species and is believed to harbor more species of birds than all of North America.

The buffer zone stipulated by the agreement, the Chimane Forest Reserve, is an area of 2,870,651 acres that will be available for environmentally sustainable economic use by local populations, including the Chimane Indians, as well as for carefully managed agricultural and forestry development. The approximately 250 families of the nomadic Chimane Indians will retain rights to their traditional hunting and fishing grounds. Approximately 800,000 acres of this area is also devoted to the Yacuma Regional Park, which includes ranches and natural habitat, and the CORDEBENI Hydrological Basin, a watershed that is the source of major rivers in the area. Unlike the remainder of the Chimane Forest reserve, the Beni reserve area at the core will be maintained undisturbed for research, and the Hydrological Basin is to be protected from logging to prevent erosion.

This case study will examine the motives and actions of the major parties to the agreement, and factors that might affect the direct and indirect, or transaction, costs of their participation.

Conservation International

The debt-for-nature swap contract stipulated that CI would serve as an official advisor to the Bolivian government in the design and planning of the Beni biosphere region, as well as work with wildlife management and the monitoring of the protected areas. In 1987, CI was responsible for providing technical, financial, scientific, and administrative support to the area. This role included start-up funding, institutional development, training, and the coordination of international assistance for the protected areas.

During the first stages of the project, Maria Teresa Ortiz, the principal architect behind CI conservation efforts in the area, set up the Bolivian Interinstitutional Technical Commission. This committee was composed of regional and national government and nongovernmental organizations (NGOs). The Commission was responsible for local programs for environmental education, termed sustainable socioeconomic systems, as well as wildlife and forestry management. In addition to regional planning, CI planned to involve government and nongovernmental agencies at the national level in such areas as environmental law, technical training, institution building, and conservation planning. Representatives of the different organizations were to meet every two months to discuss the project's progress. CI worked with an impressive array of experts including individual organizations (The Nature Conservancy, WWF), government agencies (the Ministry of Agricultural and Peasant Affairs, USAID), the Environmental League (LIDEMA), the Beni Forestry Service, the National Conservation Data Center, the National Institute of Ecology, and other scientific and academic organizations, including the National Academy of Sciences, the International Tropical Timber Organization (ITTO), and Stanford University Center for Conservation. Although their input was initially through the medium of CI, many of these groups later played a more direct role in sustaining the agreement.

Among other things, CI helped develop forest inventories, prepare operations manuals, and recruit and train personnel for the Beni Forestry Service. CI also used funds to leverage financial support for ITTO, which granted $1.2 million to the government of Bolivia to continue forestry work with CI. CI asked loggers to use only 10% of the area per year. The forest management system of logging with replanting, called "permanent production," was introduced.

Biological research was also part of the program. Funds for research and training scholarships for scientists were provided by CI, and the group further implemented six research projects concerning resource use by the Chimane Indians, primate biology, and soil classification and use. CI also played a role in general environmental education, establishing training models for rural communities on environmental education that included workshops on health, horticulture, and the conservation of resources. They helped LIDEMA sponsor a journalists' seminar to communicate the importance of conservation and development.

The benefits to CI in deciding to enter the agreement are clear. Perhaps most important, it received a direct role in administering some of the natural systems over which it was most concerned. Certainly, it acquired more funding than it otherwise would have, and strongly raised its profile in the international environmental community. It is not clear, however, that CI fully appreciated the logistical difficulties of implementing and maintaining the program, including problems of how to respond when parts of the agreement were not honored by either private and public sectors.

The Bolivian Government

In contrast to CI, the Bolivian government played a minimal role in the first few years following the swap. The government's initial task was to agree to the implementation of the exchange and to issue bonds in the amount of $250,000 to cover costs of protecting the Beni area. The bonds are held by the Central Bank of Bolivia, and are set up as an endowment; some $25,000 to $30,000 per year is allocated for administrative costs. Victor Paz Estenssoro, the Bolivian president in 1987, agreed to implement CI's idea and authorized the Ministry of Agricultural and Peasant Affairs, along with CI's national affiliate, to administer the funds.

Secondly, the original contract specified that the government would establish and recognize the Chimane Forest of Permanent Production, the Yacuma Regional Park, and the CORDEBENI Hydrological Basin watershed area. The contract also stipulated that the Bolivian government was to establish appropriate legal mechanisms needed to administer the Debt-for-Nature transaction. All new projects and programs required the approval of Bolivia's Ministry of Planning and Coordination as well as the Ministry of Agricultural and Peasant Affairs.

The decision to enter into this agreement could not have been an easy one for the Bolivian government, or any sovereign state, even one very committed to environmental protection. There is the danger that the government could appear to be surrendering its sovereignty and prerogatives to foreigners, even though CI had a local affiliate and was largely staffed by Latin Americans. As a result, many governments may enter these agreements only under the duress of large debt burdens. Once the debt is retired, there is some incentive to renege on the agreement, at least on the part of later governments that may come to power, in part, on the argument that sovereignty has been compromised.

Private Logging Companies

Although the dominant economic activity in the area is cattle ranching, the mahogany lumber business provides a lucrative alternative for the local population; thus lumber companies are directly involved in the Beni project. In order to manage the reserve forest in a sustainable way, the Bolivian government has attempted to curb logging activity by allocating forest concessions to certain companies. Because lumbering in Bolivia traditionally included very little replanting, companies have seen uncontrolled deforestation due to increasing logging activity. This may benefit some individual companies but is inefficient from the standpoint of the logging industry as a whole. This provides an incentive for the loggers to participate as a group. There may also be concern that an alternative plan might be even more restrictive.

Indigenous Population

Some 80 Indian communities are found in the Beni area, including the Chimane. They have claimed the land for centuries and have managed to maintain their homes despite their vulnerability to exploitation. The agreement had intended to safeguard their traditional territories from logging and colonization already threatening their way of life. CI initially underestimated the extent of their involvement, but the indigenous population has clearly come to play an important role. The consent of the Chimanes, along with the other tribes, is an integral factor in the sustainability and success of project implementation. Their interest in participation is very strong. Although they may not like outside interference in the management of their lands, they clearly realize that the arrangement is far better for them than any other conceivable outcome. By participating, they also raise their profile internationally, giving them some added measure of protection from the abuses often experienced by indigenous peoples.

Recent Developments

Organizations such as CI have a much smaller direct role in recent debt for nature swaps than before. Independent, national trust funds are now typically established, with representatives from government, the private sector, and often international donors. These funds are channeled to qualified local private and public conservation organizations; the setting of priorities and financial decision making is localized. Many accept funds from other sources in addition to debt-for-nature swaps.

Accordingly, in Bolivia, although the goals of the program have not changed, the institutions involved have changed significantly since the original agreement. In recent years, the institutions of the Bolivian government have become more formalized, and consequently, so has the agreement itself.

In 1990, with the support from the Nature Conservancy, Bolivia established a precedent setting trust fund called the National Fund for the Environment (FONAMA). The fund will guarantee the regular infusion of capital to carry out projects of a growing community of local NGOs and the newly created General Secretariat of the Environment (SENMA). The Fund's administering board consists of the new Special Minister of the Environment, the National Counsel for the Protection of Biodiversity, and three NGOs, including the Bolivian Indigenous Peoples Federation.

In 1987, CI was responsible for funding as well as providing technical, scientific, and administrative support. Now that FONAMA has taken the lead financial role, CI is still a source of funding, but their involvement has been limited to technical training in the field. Funding now goes through FONAMA, and SENMA and local NGOs allocate the resources according to their priorities.

Thus, at least one enduring achievement of the agreement is the regular infusion of financial resources to the Beni region. The creation of FONAMA has helped institutionalize environmental activities in Bolivia and has helped attract larger funds from environmental organizations as well as commercial banks such as J. P. Morgan. But enforcement problems have not been solved.

Unresolved Problems

Despite improvements, problems continue to prevent full implementation of the agreement. Local logging companies still have failed to comply with the rules set by the agreement, and the majority of replanting has not succeeded. Because most companies have not improved their technology, methods of extraction continue to be very inefficient and wasteful. Most companies operating in the Chimane have not fulfilled the legal requirements that allows their work in the area, such as reporting on inventories and management plans.

The Debt-for-Nature Swap has been very costly to negotiate. Considerable human resources went into both sides of the negotiations, and have not been calculated in the costs of the project. In the future, agreements will have to be arrived at that are less costly in government, environmental staff, and paid legal time. Moreover, monitoring and enforcement have been expensive, and not cost effective. Little has been known about the regions affected, and thus information costs have contributed to the high costs for all parties involved. Finally, training of those who will work in the new institutions can also be expensive. Some way will have to be found to reduce these very substantial transaction costs if the Debt-for-Nature Swap is to prove an enduring institution.

The contract also stipulated that CI, with the approval of the Ministry of Agricultural and Peasant Affairs, name a local institution as a counterpart in order to facilitate the project's programs and represent CI's interests in the region. This, however, has not been implemented.

Forestry officials are trying to address some of the remaining problems. Timber companies will have to submit forestry plans before new contracts are approved. Trees that may or may not be cut down are to be marked. But again, the Chimane Permanent Production Region is a large, remote forest. It is not yet clear that forestry officials can do a better job of enforcement under the new rules than the old. Even if the logging industry associations agree to rules, there is the potential for free riding by companies that benefit by others' compliance, but do not comply themselves. Moreover, as in most developing countries, corruption remains a serious problem in Bolivia. Policemen and officials are said to be easily coerced, and bribes are still considered an integral part of business practice.

We have seen that there have been very large costs associated with setting up the Debt-For-Nature Swap, including legal fees, negotiating time, enforcement expenditures, and other such transaction costs. One key to expanding and maintaining these agreements will be to create institutions capable of lowering these costs and helping to close the gap between policy and performance.

The increasing organization and assertiveness of the indigenous peoples of the area is in some ways the most encouraging development. These residents have a vested interest in maintaining the ecological integrity of the region. Moreover, although they have not systematized their information scientifically, in many cases residents have the practical knowledge of the workings of the ecology of the area that other parties lack. Thus, involving indigenous peoples, in addition to its inherent fairness, may be an effective means of lowering the full costs of effectively negotiating and implementing such agreements. Perhaps this is the development worth watching most carefully in this and other debt-for-nature agreements in coming years.

Sources

The case study is largely based on interviews in the field in Bolivia and with Conservation International officials in Washington, DC, conducted by Eva Canoutas.

Conservation International. *The Debt for Nature Exchange: A Tool for International Conservation.* Washington, DC, 1991.

Forsyth, Adrian. *The Beni: Impressions from the Field.* Washington, DC: Conservation International, undated.

New York Times, various issues.

North, Douglas. *Institutions, Institutional Change and Economic Performance.* New York: Cambridge, 1990.

Ortiz, Maria. *The Road to El Porvenir.* Washington, DC: Conservation International, undated.

Science. "Bolivia Swaps Debt for Conservation." Aug. 7, 1987.

South. "Unpaid Debt to Nature," August 1989.

16. The Many Development Benefits of Educating Girls: Pakistan

In the 1992 Quad-i-Azam lecture to the Pakistan Society of Development Economists, Larry Summers, then chief economist of the World Bank, argued that giving 100 girls one additional year of primary education would prevent roughly 60 infant deaths and three maternal deaths, while averting some 500 births. Drawing on earlier World Bank-sponsored research, he argued that programs to increase female education are less expensive than other development investments, at a cost of some $30,000 for 100 girls. This is actually a conservative estimate because it is based on secondary school cost, and primary school costs are lower. Summers concluded that the social benefits alone of increased education of girls is more than sufficient to cover its costs—even before considering the added earnings power this education would bring.

The World Bank's growing focus on girls' education is part of a broad evolution of attitudes about the role of women in development, and the unacceptability of continuing to treat educational discrimination against females as a sovereign cultural matter outside of the purview of development agencies. In this study we look more deeply at the case of Pakistan, to better appreciate the reasons for this.

Girls receive significantly less education, health care, and other resources needed for a productive and successful life than do boys. This pattern repeats itself generation after generation. Of course, this is patently unfair. It is hard to see how apologetics by cultural relativists who say Western values of gender equality should not be imposed on Third World societies are ultimately meaningful in cases such as this. But the repercussions from the efficiency point of view are as serious as the equity repercussions, and this case study is about the economic rather than the social development implications of gender inequality.

In Pakistan, girls face perhaps more relative deprivation in comparison to boys than any other Asian country, and possibly as much as anywhere else in the world. It has been found to be one of the countries in which boys are most favored by parents over girls, along with Bangladesh, Jordan, Nepal, South Korea, and Syria.

In Africa, women are often seriously disadvantaged relative to men, but both men and women are more often in absolute poverty. Pakistan is thus a case in which the "gender gap" as a *relative* hardship can be seen very vividly.

Based on a 1981 census, the government of Pakistan acknowledges that just 16% of women are literate (and 26% of the total population including men and women). Recently published statistics show that these numbers have barely moved to 19% and 30% respectively after 15 years of efforts. Far too few of the young are receiving an education sufficient to pull up this figure any faster. UNESCO data show that only one-third of primary school-age children and an even smaller percentage of girls in Pakistan are enrolled in school.

Just 1.7% of Pakistan's GNP is allocated to education, and this small allocation is extremely inequitable. Thirty times as many public education dollars are spent per pupil for university education as for primary school education—and that is an average. Primary school expenditures are extremely unequal, with the lion's share of funds going to schools that more often train the few students who will eventually go on to universities. Discrimination and limited opportunities affect the poorest rural Pakistani girls the most and seem to affect the daughters of the urban elite little, if at all. Poor girls lack the political voice to demand action for their problems.

While Pakistan has been receiving more than $1 billion annually in development assistance for its primary schools, only a fraction actually reaches the rural schools where it could make the most difference. As in most developing countries, poverty in Pakistan is concentrated in rural areas. Over two-thirds of Pakistan's population is still rural, and this is where problems of undereducation, especially for girls, are overwhelmingly concentrated. By the mid-1990s, while 55.3% of urban males are literate, the corresponding share of rural females is just 7.3%. Women also often have greater difficulty in practicing and maintaining their hard-won literacy skills than men. Reading materials are generally not designed for the interests or needs of women, when they are available to them at all.

Problems for poor girls in rural areas do not begin or end with undereducation, though most other problems are closely related to it. One of the most serious problems afflicting poor children is diarrhea. It accounts for a large percentage of deaths before age five. Even with good food availability, chronic childhood diarrhea leads to malnutrition and long-term health problems even where it is not fatal in the short run. Girls are differentially affected because studies show they are less likely to receive medical attention than boys.

Inferior health care access for girls shows the interlinked nature of economic incentives and the cultural setting. The parents may be perceived as behaving rationally according to the economic incentives and constraints they face. A boy provides future economic benefits, such as support in old age, receipt of a dowry upon marriage, and often continues work on the farm into adulthood. A girl, in contrast, will require a dowry upon marriage, often at a young age, and will then move to the village of the husband's family, becoming responsible for the welfare of the husband's parents. A girl from a poor rural Pakistani family will perceive no suitable alternatives in life to serving a husband and his family.

To a poor family, the income value of a boy is substantial and consequential. Treatment of disease may be expensive and may require several days lost from work to go to the town. Empirical studies demonstrate what we might guess from these perverse incentives: much more strenuous efforts are made to save the life of a son than a daughter.

It is well known that fertility is inversely related to years of mothers' schooling. The usual interpretation is that mothers with more schooling have a higher opportunity cost of childrearing, or higher potential wages that they would have to give up to devote time to bearing another child. Poverty encourages high fertility, and high population growth hinders development in an endogenous vicious circle. Evidence suggests that despite discrimination and frequently lower wages for women who do work comparable to men, the percentage returns to additional schooling is similar for males and females in developing countries. These returns are between 10 and 25% in most developing countries, and by most estimates are in the high part of this range in Pakistan. These impressive returns alone justify expanding educational opportunities.

There is some limited evidence that population growth may actually increase up to the first approximately four years of a woman's education. The explanation is that a woman has learned enough in school to take better care of basic nutrition and health, so that the number of surviving children will rise to its higher, desired level. In any case, after four years of schooling, the desired level itself seems to fall. Recently, the United Nations has begun to push for a minimum of six years of schooling for all children.

Returns are generally highest at the earliest years of schooling. The explanation is found in a simple application of the law of diminishing returns. Because girls receive less education than boys, if any at all, taken together this makes the case for special emphasis on increasing years of schooling for girls. Yet more than two-thirds of primary school dropouts in Pakistan are girls. Keep in mind that these wage benefits are not even part of the calculations of health and other social benefits considered earlier.

For a given family income, the smaller the family, the more resources each child receives on average. And in most countries at most points in economic history, rapid population growth hinders development. In virtually all plausible scenarios, lower population growth rates would lead to higher growth of per capita income. Education of girls is one of the most effective ways to achieve these objectives.

Greater mothers' education might improve prospects for the daughter's welfare. Studies show that mothers' education plays a decisive role in raising nutritional levels in rural areas. The level of child stunting, a valid indicator of child undernutrition, is much lower with higher education attainment of the mother, at any given income level. Harold Alderman and Marito Garcia report evidence that projects that the incidence of child stunting would be reduced by a quarter of current levels (from 63.6 to 47.1%) if women were to attain a primary-level education. They note that this is almost ten times the projected impact of a 10% increase in per capita income. Coupled with the result that in many countries mothers education tends to makes a disproportionately larger health difference toward daughters than sons, as Duncan Thomas has reported, we can expect major benefits for girls.

The bias toward boys helps explain the "missing women mystery." In Asia, the United Nations has found that there are far fewer females as a share of the population than would be predicted by demographic norms. In developed countries there are about 105 girls for every 100 boys. Worldwide as many as 100 million women are "missing." But in Asia there are about 110 boys for every 100 girls, an average pulled up by the infamous case of China, where the rate is about 115 to 100. In Pakistan, the rate is about 109 to 100. Reasons include female infanticide and selective abortion, but a larger part of the explanation is poorer treatment of girls.

What can be done? Some small steps are easy. Increasing the available information on gender discrimination will have direct and indirect effects. Development professionals need to begin to collect information on gender differences in development much more systematically, and to warn health and social workers to be alert for effects of gender discrimination.

Some programs have had some success. Literacy programs in Pakistan's province of Baluchistan have been hampered by the wide distances between villages—about 50 miles on average. Only about 2,600 of the 5,800 villages in the region even have a primary school.

In many areas it is considered improper for a male teacher to teach female students. On the other hand, due to the lack of schooling opportunities the rate of female literacy is so low it can be hard to find qualified female teachers. This classic catch-22 will be a difficult paradox to resolve.

In addition to the need for female teachers, there is a related shortage of female agricultural extension workers. In rural Pakistan, women are often actively involved in farming, but almost all extension agents are male, who for cultural reasons are often unable or unwilling to train women. Female agents must be trained, but even assuming the government has the will to address this problem, literate women capable of filling this role can be hard to find. There is a stigma in rural Pakistan against women working in the fields, and many poorer families simply deny that women and girls are working at all. Again, we seem confronted with a catch-22.

Other goals will be even harder to attain. It would certainly help to abolish dowries and other practices that unnecessarily increase the cost of raising girls. But this is much easier to legislate than to enforce. The creation of a viable pension system, such as South Korea has established, would help to change the perception that sons are much more worthwhile because they alone can provide financially for parents in old age.

In recent years the government of Pakistan has made some efforts to promote female literacy. But despite all the attention and pressure on the issue, progress continues to be painfully slow. In the 1990s, the Bhutto government decided that it had to back down from its earlier lofty goal of attaining 90% literacy to providing educational infrastructure that could serve all children age 5 to 9. This was intended to reduce urban bias as well as lower barriers to girls' education. The achievement of this goal remains far in the future. The government is also trying to get the private sector involved, but this too will have small impact on rural areas.

The case for stressing girls' education is so strong it may be hard to see why action is not forthcoming, especially now that top government leaders are at least paying lip service to the problem. One reason is that while girls' education is a boon for development as a whole, it is not necessarily in the economic and political interests of some of those now in powerful positions, especially at a more local or regional level.

In rural areas of Pakistan, as elsewhere in South Asia and the Middle East, landlords gain from peasants from "extraeconomic coercion" as well as from free and honest exchange. In sweatshops, laws on such matters as child labor and fire safety are regularly disregarded. Workplace rights problems in the U.S. on such matters as sexual harassment and the right to unionize seem very mild compared to the abuses that go on in fields and workplaces in this part of the world.

With education, as some landlords and industrialists know well, workers, especially women, may finally demand that laws already in place to protect them be enforced. It is sometimes in their business interest—as well as in their self-interest more generally—to see that this does not happen.

In this the landlords and industrialists often have allies in groups, such as local religious leaders, who view women's education as a cultural threat. Seclusion of girls and women remains widespread in rural areas. Many male heads of household will prevent their daughters from becoming educated or their wives from gaining literacy because they fear their loss of power at home, or fear ostracization by peers who feel more threatened than they. Rural girls see that women reaching marriage age often have difficulty finding a husband if they are literate—a powerful disincentive to education. The ongoing "Islamization" movement, as it has unfolded so far, is viewed by United Nations observers as not helpful to the advancement of education of girls.

Not surprisingly in this climate, a women's rights movement has been growing in Pakistan. There is an active debate over whether Islamic fundamentalists' position on women represents a "biased" reading of the Koran. The growth of a women's movement must be treated as a good sign, because without the kind of political pressure such a movement can create, it is doubtful whether the harder steps will be taken any time soon. Even so, the huge gulf between urban and rural Pakistan will be difficult to cross.

Sources

Alderman, Harold, and Marito Garcia. "Food Security and Health Security: Explaining the Levels of Nutrition in Pakistan." *World Bank Working Paper PRE 865,* 1992.

Christian Science Monitor, Oct. 28, 1991.

Courtney, Hugh, and Stephen C. Smith. "Growth and the Distribution of Human Capital Investment: Theory and Cross-National Evidence." *George Washington University Economics Discussion Paper 9314,* 1993.

Hussain, Neelam. "Women and Literacy Development in Pakistan." Undated working paper.

Lind, Agneta. "The Gender Gap. Women: One Billion Illiterates." *UNESCO Courier,* 1990.

Ravindran, Sundari. *Health Implications of Sex Discrimination in Childhood.* Netherlands: International Statistical Institute.

Saito, Katrin. "Extending Help to Women Farmers in LDCs." *Finance and Development,* Sept. 1991.

Summers, Larry. "Investing in All the People." *World Bank Working Paper PRE 905,* 1992.

Thomas, Duncan. "Gender Differences in Household Resource Allocations." *World Bank Living Standards Measurement Study Paper 79,* 1991.

World Health, "Daughters are Disadvantaged from Birth." June 1986.

17. NAFTA and Beyond: Impact on Mexico and Latin America

In mid-1990, President Carlos Salinas de Gotari of Mexico and then-U.S. President George Bush began negotiations toward a North American Free Trade Agreement (NAFTA). Negotiations proceeded quickly and at the end of 1992, the U.S., Canada, and Mexico signed a draft NAFTA accord, which became law on January 1, 1994, after it was ratified by each country's legislature and side agreements on labor and environmental standards were worked out.

NAFTA is of great significance not only for Mexico, the second-largest Latin American economy, but in the precedent it sets for development opportunities and dilemmas throughout the developing world. NAFTA is the first free trade agreement between developed and developing countries of significance, and has already played a major role in defining the future policy debate on trade and the developing countries.

Other Latin American countries, led by Chile, seem eager to join in a broader regional free trade agreement as soon as possible. However, Chile's application has been put on hold in a climate of growing protectionism in the U.S., and in the meantime, Chile has decided to join with other South American countries in the expanding MERCOSUR free trade area.

NAFTA eliminates all tariff barriers and most nontariff barriers between the three countries within ten years, though a few products would be given a 15-year transition period. It includes free trade in agricultural products, a frequent stumbling block in trade accords. Mexico will be able to export textiles and apparel to the U.S. and Canada without the protectionist restrictions of the multifiber agreement that limits textile exports from many other developing countries. NAFTA will largely open up financial services markets, as well as telecommunications and transportation services markets. Foreign investors from the three signing countries investing in other NAFTA countries would receive legal treatment equal to that of local investors in each country.

The debate in the lead-up to NAFTA and the subsequent turbulent period in Mexico mirrors the longstanding debate about advantages and disadvantages of openness to direct foreign investment and free trade more generally with developed countries for developing countries' economic prospects. Free trade critics have doubted expected growth for primary exports because of low income elasticities of these static comparative advantage goods, also associated with secular deterioration of terms of trade. They equate modern economies and modern economic growth with industrialization, and fear that free trade would induce them to specialize in goods with low long-term productivity growth. However, the objection to free trade that first world protectionism is substantial and appears to be on the rise would appear to be obviated by a genuine free trade pact. (For a review of developing country criticisms of direct foreign investment, see Case 20.)

Free trade proponents expect exports to grow and lead economic growth, arguing that free trade improves resource allocation, eliminates distortions, promotes efficiency, raises domestic and foreign savings, and generates foreign exchange. Certainly, neither side is always correct; the answer depends on prevailing world economic conditions such as protectionism, and on the ability of a developing country to carry out an efficient industrialization strategy.

To date, the development literature specifically on economic integration, as opposed to free trade generally, has concentrated on free trade areas among developing countries. There is also a large general literature on integration and on common markets among developed countries. Proponents argue that free trade areas provide dynamic creation of new industries, economies of scale, and possibilities of coordinated industrial policy as well as static trade creation. Many analysts argue that free trade areas are beneficial to the extent that they "create" trade, but detrimental to the extent that they "divert" trade that would have taken place with other countries that might have a more appropriate comparative advantage.

For example, the NAFTA rules are expected to lead to a diversion of trade in textiles to Mexico and away from other developing countries. However, some analysts argue that even trade diversion may provide development benefits when seen in a dynamic perspective, along the lines of the "infant industry argument" that developing countries just need some time to get efficient industries established.

A desire to lower debt burdens was an important impulse for Mexico and other LDCs to join the free trade agreement (FTA) bandwagon. FTAs will attract direct foreign investment, or at least keep it from getting diverted to other countries that do set up such agreements. NAFTA may be perceived as a kind of insurance against the United States setting up new trade restrictions. The United States was already by far the largest importer of Mexican goods prior to NAFTA, and Mexican business and political leaders hope that NAFTA will continue to build on this base.

Due largely to a misguided policy of overvalued exchange rates, Mexico ran large trade deficits with the U.S. in the run up to NAFTA and 1994. After the drastic declines in the value of the peso in late 1994 and early 1995, and the sharp recession that followed, the Mexican balance of trade has improved markedly.

Perhaps most important, the Mexican government saw NAFTA as a means of attracting more U.S. direct foreign investment. That is, as the recent collection of essays, NAFTA as a Model of Development, edited by Richard Belous and Jonathan Lemco, makes clear, in the view of many Mexican policymakers, the prospect of increased investment was more important than the prospect of increased exports. The agreement provided guarantees for direct foreign investment (DFI) that held the status of an international treaty. Equity investment is a substitute for debt, so the investment aspect of NAFTA was consistent with the goal of lowering debt burdens. However, some Mexicans, critical of the role of multinational corporations (MNCs) in economic development, saw the investment provisions as a major drawback of NAFTA (see Case 20).

Despite disclaimers, the Mexican government would like nothing more than to hear the sweet sound of Ross Perot's "giant sucking machine," transporting formerly American jobs to Mexico—that is their job. Other Latin American countries will try to enter NAFTA, in part out of fear of losing diverted trade to Mexico. But even if all of Latin America were to set up free trade agreements with the U.S., most of the benefits would probably still go to Mexico, at least until Mexican wages rose substantially, due primarily to its location on the U.S. border. A comparison of labor costs in 16 countries, including the United States and Mexico, is found at the end of this case study. As most economists emphasized prior to NAFTA, the effects on the U.S. economy have been small. In 1992, Mexico's GDP was just 5% of that of the U.S. Effects on Mexico have been much larger, but so far overshadowed by the effect of the financial crash and deep recession of 1994–1996.

Investment began pouring into Mexico since negotiations on the treaty began, anticipating a January 1, 1994 free trade area—just as investments increased in European Union countries leading up to the more ambitious January 1, 1993 completion of the single internal European market. Depending on how they are measured, inflows of capital to Mexico amounted to about 8.5% of GDP in 1992, or over $20 billion. But just as cross-border investments slowed after the single European market became law, investments slowed after NAFTA took effect.

Before it took effect, some studies were very optimistic about the impact of NAFTA on Mexico. An Institute for International Economics analysis projected that NAFTA would create some 600,000 jobs in Mexico. Unemployment was very high in Mexico in the mid-1980s, reaching about 18% in 1986–87. By 1991, the official figure had fallen to just 2.7%. As usual, it is hard to interpret LDC unemployment figures. Underemployment is generally much higher than unemployment, and Mexican underemployment rates have been estimated at 25 to 40%. This latter figure underscores the concern over jobs in Mexico. Moreover, Mexico has a dramatic age pyramid, with some ten times the number of young workers entering the labor force as old workers retiring. By the mid-1990s, unemployment was on the rise again in Mexico, though probably a temporary result of the financial crisis and recession.

Most developing countries, including those in Latin America, tend to view Mexico's open access to the world's largest economy with envy. Some economies, such as Taiwan whose development has been fueled by exports to the United States, have been extremely concerned about the potential loss of business to Mexico.

One concern that Mexicans have is the possible erosion of import substitution firms that may not be able to stand up to U.S. competition. Studies by Michael Porter and others strongly suggest that the presence of domestic-owned and -based firms is very important in securing long-term economic development. Free trade agreements can inhibit rather than encourage the development of indigenous industrial capacities. For this reason, critics Robert Pastor and Jorje Castenada have raised the specter of Mexico becoming "a nation of *maquiladoras,* dishwashers, U.S. welfare recipients, and hotel help, condemned to produce the few goods for which it has a significant comparative advantage."

The history of NAFTA does begin in 1965 with the *maquiladoras* assembly industries on the U.S. border. In the last half of the 1980s, maquiladoras industries have been estimated to be responsible for some 84% of Mexico's economic growth. By the time NAFTA was ratified, over 2000 maquiladoras plants, most located in the Mexican border states, employed over 500,000 workers. The late 1980s also saw the beginnings of upgrading the types of labor performed there. Still, no more than 20% of the maquiladoras' chief executive officer positions are filled by Mexican nationals. Most of the rest are Americans, many of whom live north of the border. But while some 87% of maquiladoras are on border states, those that are located further south tend to have Mexican CEOs, and the prospect of this becoming more the norm was clearly one selling point of NAFTA to the Mexican government.

Mexico has traditionally wished to avoid dependence on the United States for its development. There have been nationalist tensions between the two countries since the U.S.–Mexican war a century and a half ago.

Mexico's highly protectionist development strategy with its active use of state owned enterprises (SOEs) throughout most of this century evolved in significant part to assure economic independence from the enormous U.S. economy to the North. Industrialization was always seen as the key to economic autonomy. But industrialization requires industrial know-how and capital. Earlier, the intention was for these to be accumulated internally through learning by doing and savings generated through taxes and profits of state-owned enterprises.

Despite the disappointments of SOE inefficiency, this stress on autonomy was reinforced when large new oil reserves were proven. But the overhang of the debt crisis, continued inefficiency, and falling oil prices in the 1980s showed that a role for foreign capital would be needed. Before NAFTA, Mexico went to some lengths to push for expanded Japanese and European investment, including major promotional tours of Japan and the European Community in 1990 by President Salinas. But with the world seemingly coalescing into regional trading groups, and great doubts about the plausibility of large-scale European and Japanese investments in Mexico, it became clear that an arrangement would first have to be reached with the U.S.

Even so, in some ways NAFTA represents a change in Mexican industrialization tactics more than in development strategy. The goal is still to make Mexico an important industrial power. In abandoning the Latin American inward-looking development model, Mexico seems to wish to copy the state-led development strategy of East Asia rather than the pure free market model. As in East Asia, the state is getting out of productive activity, but retains a strong hand in guiding that activity toward a more sophisticated skill and technology content.

While Mexico's leaders realized that investments would have to come first from the U.S., they have not given up on special arrangements with Europe and Japan. Mexican foreign minister Fernando Solana said in Europe in April 1993 that after NAFTA is ratified Mexico will seek a special trade accord with the European Community. Such goals were put on hold by the Mexican financial crisis.

Issues of labor rights and environmental protection have been at the center of disputes over NAFTA. Mexico and the United States negotiated "side accords" to the agreement intended to ensure that firms do not move to Mexico only to avoid environmental or job safety responsibility and that Mexican labor and environmental laws are enforced. In principle, such side accords should benefit the public interest in both countries.

Gene Grossman and Alan Krueger have suggested that Mexico's environment will be helped by NAFTA. They have found some evidence for an "inverted U" relationship between income per capita and pollution. As income rises, pollution rises until upper middle-income levels are reached; then it begins to fall as societies become willing and able to pay for environmental protection. Grossman and Krueger argue that NAFTA will increase income in Mexico so much that Mexico will start to pay for pollution clean-up without outside prompting (or, in other words, move to the downward-sloping side of this curve). But incomes have been stagnant in Mexico in the mid-1990s.

Part of the motivation for Mexican leaders is to keep Mexico committed to the free market, liberalization strategy they have been pursuing since the mid-1980s. NAFTA codifies many of the liberalization measures undertaken by Salinas. As an international treaty, NAFTA would be hard for a subsequent administration to overturn.

Mexican officials hope that NAFTA will result in higher Mexican wages, and economic theory offers support for this idea. The factor price equalization theorem predicts that free trade will equalize wages of the various skill types across two free-trading regions. Evidence for this is mixed, partly because it is not clear how close conditions have to be to free trade for this to occur at any given speed. Given Mexico's large and growing, often underemployed unskilled workforce—some two-thirds of the total—it is hard to believe unskilled workers' wages can rise quickly. Unskilled wages in America, on the other hand, may more likely continue to fall.

The case of Puerto Rico, which has had effective free trade with the U.S. for decades, provides limited support for both supporters' and critics' concerns. Certainly wages have risen more rapidly in Puerto Rico than elsewhere in Latin America, but as noted by Gary Hufbauer and Jeffery Schott, wages remain at about half U.S. levels. There has been no flood of investment from the U.S. or other countries; unemployment in Puerto Rico remains extremely high even by Latin American standards, and less than 15% of the workforce have manufacturing jobs, fewer than 20 years ago. Moreover, dependence on U.S. companies and investments is almost total, and indigenous Puerto Rican corporations have not become even a tiny factor in the world economy. Nor has Puerto Rico's innovation capacity grown much. Puerto Rico may have benefitted from short-run income gains at the expense of long-run development.

But Puerto Rico's true alternative might have been much worse. Without its close ties to the American economy, the island of Puerto Rico might well have been more a Dominican Republic than a Japan. Its per capita GNP ranks in the upper middle-income range. One must always evaluate a policy against the true next-best alternative, not against an imagined ideal. More than anything Puerto Rico seems to suggest the unspectacular nature of free-trade agreements. The impact, whether more a long-run spur or hindrance to true development, is likely to be modest in size.

Finally, we have the vexing question of whether NAFTA would strengthen or weaken the world trading system. If regional free trade agreements are just a more realistic stepping stone toward an ultimately freer world trade regime, NAFTA will help. But if it is seen as an end in itself and an alternative to trade with other regions, NAFTA could do much to speed the trend toward a system of trading blocks. The Institute for International Economics has concluded that without strong GATT reforms, NAFTA could be trade diverting rather than trade creating. If some developing countries end up privileged by the new system and others are left out in the cold, the results could be a net negative for development prospects.

In sum, we can be sure that NAFTA offers Mexico the opportunity for employment creation in the long run, provided that it is complemented with sound macroeconomic policies. The greatest employment effects may be found in the potential expansion of the modern sector through the encouragement of direct foreign investment, rather than through expanded exports per se. Whether NAFTA carries risks of restraints on future development, either for Mexico or for developing countries left out of such special arrangements, still remains to be seen.

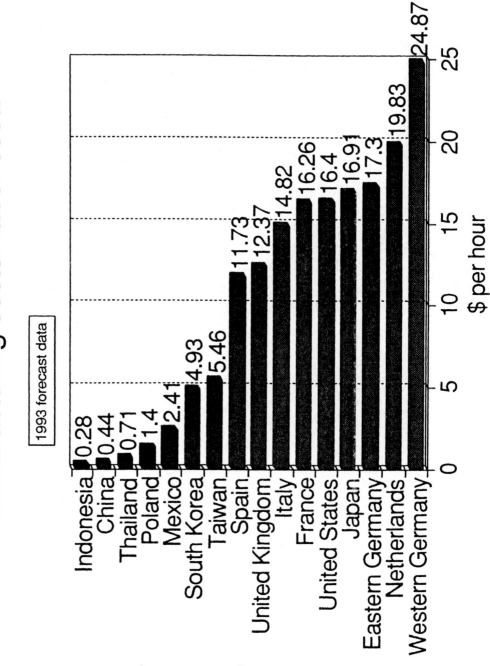

Labor costs
Manufacturing sector labor costs

1993 forecast data

Country	$ per hour
Indonesia	0.28
China	0.44
Thailand	0.71
Poland	1.4
Mexico	2.41
South Korea	4.93
Taiwan	5.46
Spain	11.73
United Kingdom	12.37
Italy	14.82
France	16.26
United States	16.4
Japan	16.91
Eastern Germany	17.3
Netherlands	19.83
Western Germany	24.87

Source: Morgan Stanley

Sources

Belous, Richard S., and Jonathan Lemco. *NAFTA as a Model of Development*. Albany: SUNY Press, 1995.

Business Week, "The Mexican Worker," April 19, 1993.

Erzan, Refik. "Free Trade Agreements with the United States: What's In It for Latin America?" *World Bank Policy Research Working Paper 827,* 1992.

Fatem, Khosrow. *The Maquiladora Industry: Economic Solution or Problem*. New York: Praeger, 1990.

Hufbauer, Gary C., and Jeffrey J. Schott. *NAFTA: An Assessment*. Washington, DC: Institute for International Economics, 1993.

Hufbauer, Gary C., and Jeffrey J. Schott. *North American Free Trade: Issues and Recommendations*. Washington, DC: Institute for International Economics, 1992.

Meade, James Russell. *The Low-Wage Challenge to Global Growth: The Labor Cost-Productivity Imbalance in Newly Industrialized Countries*. Washington, DC: Economic Policy Institute, 1991.

Pastor, Robert F. and Jorje G. Castenada. *Limits to Friendship: The United States and Mexico*. New York: Vintage, 1988.

Porter, Michael. *The Competitive Advantage of Nations,* New York: Free Press, 1990.

Prestowitz, Clyde et al. *The New North American Order: A Win-Win Strategy for US–Mexico Trade*. Washington, DC: Economic Strategy Inst., 1991.

U.S. Dept. of Labor Bureau of International Labor Affairs. *Foreign Labor Trends,* various issues.

Whiting, Van R. *The Political Economy of Foreign Investment in Mexico: Nationalism, Liberalism and Constraints on Choice*. Baltimore: Johns Hopkins University Press, 1992.

18. Industrial and Export Policy in South Korea

Many developing countries have conducted active industrial policies. Those of some countries have clearly been failures, such as India and Argentina. But industrial policy has not failed everywhere, and South Korea appears to be a good example of success. Exports, particularly manufactured exports, including such key sectors as motor vehicles, have grown at an extraordinary rate in Korea, as summarized by three charts at the end of this case study.

While one can never absolutely prove cause and effect, one of the most important reasons for South Korea's remarkable industrial achievements appears to be the orientation of its industrial policy toward promotion of exports of increasingly sophisticated skill and technology content. Strong financial incentives for industrial firms to move up the ladder of skills and technology have been present in most of its policies.

There appear to be market failures in the transfer of technology from developing countries similar to those in innovation of original technology in developed countries. Policies that reward success in the export of goods a step up in technology and skill content provide a good match between policy goals, incentives to firms to meet those goals, and monitoring to make sure goals are really met before rewards are received—or are "incentive compatible." Specifically, firms get efficient feedback on whether their goods meet world price and quality standards by competing on world export markets; and governments can more easily ensure that rewards go to firms that really make and sell the intended number and quality of the required products (exports can be "counted on the dock," or are otherwise more observable than goods for the home market). These points are brought out with a close examination of the case of South Korea.

There have been at least 21 major types of export promotion-oriented industrial policy interventions in South Korea. Only some of these policies have been in effect in any one industry and at any one time, and in the most recent years, effective subsidies have been considerably scaled back but not eliminated. These are:

1. Currency undervaluation. The effective exchange rate (EER) for exporters was kept *higher* than that for importers. As early as 1964, South Korea's EER for exports was 281 and its EER for imports was 247—not trade neutrality but a pro-export bias.

2. Preferential access to imported intermediate inputs needed for producing exports, with strict controls to prevent abuse. Since 1975, rebates are only received after documenting the completion of the exports.

3. Targeted infant industry protection as a first stage before launching an export drive. South Korea has had high dispersion of effective rates of protection even with a relatively low average.

4. Tariff exemptions on inputs of capital goods needed in exporting activities. (This is a price incentive, while preferential access (#2) is based on quantity restriction.)

5. Tax breaks for domestic suppliers of inputs to exporting firms, which constitute a domestic content incentive.

6. Domestic indirect tax exemptions for successful exporters.

7. Lower direct tax on income earned from exports.

8. Accelerated depreciation for exporters.

9. Import entitlement certificates (exemptions from import restrictions) linked directly to export levels. Korea has long maintained an extensive list of items generally prohibited for import, including both luxury goods and import substitution targets. Profitable exemptions from this prohibition have often been available for firms exporting specified goods having low profit margins.

10. Direct export subsidies for selected industries (no longer in use).

11. Monopoly rights granted to the firm first to achieve exports in targeted industries.

12. Subsidized interest rates for exporters.

13. Preferential credit access for exporters in selected industries, including automatic access to bank loans for the working capital needed for all export activities. Medium- and long-term loans for investment are rationed and often available only to firms meeting government export targets and pursuing other requested activities.

14. Reduced public utility taxes and rail rates for exporters.

15. A system of export credit insurance and guarantees, as well as tax incentives for overseas marketing and postshipment export loans by the Korean Export-Import Bank.

16. The creation of free trade zones, industrial parks, and export-oriented infrastructure.

17. The creation of public enterprises to lead the way in establishing a new industry. As Alice Amsden documents, public enterprises produced the first Korean output of ships and refined petroleum products and petrochemicals. Howard Pack and Larry Westphal found that "the share of public enterprises in Korea's nonagricultural output is comparatively high, being similar to India's."

18. Activities of the Korean Traders Association and the Korea Trade Promotion Corporation to promote Korean exports on behalf of Korean firms worldwide.

19. General orchestration of sector-wide efforts to upgrade the average technological level, through use of a new generation of machinery.

20. Government coordination of foreign technology licensing agreements, using national bargaining power to secure the best possible terms for the private sector in utilizing proprietary foreign technology.

21. The setting of export targets for firms (since the early 1960s.) Firms set their own targets, which may be adjusted by the government.

The use of manufacturing exports of growing technological content as a yardstick of performance automatically emphasizes targets with very strong development benefits. In addition, the world export market is an arena in which performance is clearly, quickly, and rigorously tested, while keeping the development ministries, whose resources and information capacities are inherently limited, tightly focused on relevant and manageable problems.

In this regard, export targets as a development policy mechanism hold the distinct advantage over general output targets in that they are easily observable. This fact has long been understood by LDC fiscal authorities who have taxed exports precisely because they are observable and therefore not subject to the tax evasion that is so rampant in the developing world. This distortion has a well-publicized (if not self-evident) anti-export bias effect. South Korea puts this "fiscal observability" to use as the centerpiece of its industrial policy system, in a way that reverses by 180 degrees the negative incentive effects of export taxes.

Enforcement of export targets in the case of Korea is mostly moral or "cultural" in nature, but the evidence seems persuasive that in Korea these have been among the most powerful incentives. South Korea as a whole has an extensive pattern of "rituals" reinforcing these economic incentives with cultural ones. A key ritual in Korean economic life is the Monthly National Trade Promotion Meeting. According to Yung Whee Rhee, Bruce Ross-Larson, and Gary Pursell,

"Chaired by the president, the monthly trade promotion meetings are select gatherings of the ministers and top bureaucrats responsible for trade and the economy; the chief executives of export associations, research organizations, and educational institutions; and the heads of a few firms, mainly the general trading companies and other large firms. The prominence of those attending shows that the monthly meetings are far more than perfunctory meetings to improve coordination between the private and public sectors."

Firms in the sample were either represented by their particular export association or, in many cases for large firms, represented directly. After briefings, awards are typically presented for excellent export performance. On a more national scale, one of the major national holidays in South Korea is called "Export Day," which has been held on November 30 since 1964, when exports first topped $100 million. As Rhee, Ross-Larson, and Pursell describe,

"The focus of the celebration is the award of prizes at a large public gathering, prizes that the heads of firms take seriously. There are President's prizes for being the number one exporter in an industry, for export merit as a small or medium-sized firm, for exceeding a target by more than 50 percent. There are Prime Minister's prizes for inventions, for excellence in design, for having a high reputation in exhibitions overseas, or for developing an export product of high quality. And there are prizes for reaching a certain level of exports. There are in addition industry medals and prizes awarded by various ministries. The award of these prizes is akin to the pinning of medals on officers—with salutes, solemnity and sharp strides. The heads of firms typically display the awards in their offices—along with a picture of the president and calligraphy inscribed to the head of the firm and carrying messages on the importance of exporting."

To what extent is this cultural aspect of the Korean export experience transferable to other countries? There is no obvious connection between Export Day and Confucianism. The love of public recognition through contests and competitions, medals and prizes seems to be a universal human trait. Recently, such an approach has been adopted successfully by the United States, in the popular Malcolm Baldridge awards. Most likely, the idea could be successfully adopted by other developing countries. In fact, this approach has recently been adopted by Thailand. On the other hand, one may reasonably doubt its effectiveness in the absence of reinforcing economic policies.

Import substitution often precedes, logically and empirically, export promotion. The influential study of Hollis Chenery, Sherwin Robinson, and Moses Syrquin concludes that "periods of significant export expansion are almost always preceded by periods of strong import substitution." Strong support for the implication that this import substitution phase had something to do with the export success that followed comes from the observations that after the switch to export promotion the leading industrial sectors did not change.

In the South Korean case, industrialization began with an import substitution phase in the 1950s and early 1960s. After the country's switch to an export-led growth strategy in the 1960s, selective protection of industry continued to play a very important role in industrial development.

In addition to many domestic content regulations, Richard Luedde-Neurath has described how South Korea maintained a very extensive system of import controls well into the 1980s. What he terms the "Korean Kaleidoscope" includes restrictive trader licensing, widespread quantitative controls, systematic foreign exchange allocation under the Foreign Exchange Demand and Supply Plan, intervention in export-import settlements, required advance deposits (which have been as high as 200% of import value), and capricious customs practices. An important example is that prospective importers must realize minimum export earnings before becoming eligible to import; these obligations began at $10,000 in 1962 and have increased over time to $1 million in 1982.

Pack and Westphal conclude that "through import restrictions, selectively promoted infant industries were often initially granted whatever levels of effective protection were required to secure an adequate market for their output as well as a satisfactory rate of return on investment. Initial rates of effective protection were frequently in excess of 100 percent." The country also utilizes an informal system of indicative planning-type protectionist measures. In South Korea, tariffs are primarily collected on final goods and intermediate inputs for domestic sales rather than exports. As Robert Wade notes, tariff rates appear much higher when they are averaged over non-export-related imports only. Finally, Peter Petri presents data that leads him to conclude that Korea has "an unusually protection-prone export bundle."

Thus in the Korean case, import controls may be called a "handmaiden" of successful industrial export promotion. In the first instance, many export industries begin as infant industries requiring protection. Pack and Westphal stress that as a result of the export promotion reforms of the early 1960s, "imports destined (either directly or indirectly as inputs) for the domestic market remained subject to tariffs and quantitative controls."

However, the system of controls on these imports was rationalized and thereby converted from a mechanism of socially unproductive rent seeking into an instrument of industrial promotion." Second, as Luedde-Neurath notes, the developing industrial sector functions as a whole and benefits from externalities and linkages between firms, making a market failure case for general protection. Finally, Amsden has pointed out that in South Korea cross-subsidization across divisions within firms as a company enters new export markets, such as shipbuilding, is intentionally facilitated by government. Diversified companies understand that they are expected to use the monopoly rents that they earn from these various import barriers as working capital for expansion into new sectors. The state also offers supplemental support for entering new markets as needed.

As Pack and Westphal summarize the evidence, "something approximating neutrality" applies to "established industries... But there has been substantial industry bias in favor of the promoted infant industries."

Given the central role of technological progress in this type of development strategy, it may be asked what role multinational corporations played in transferring technology. There is a large literature exploring the pros and cons of multinational firm presence for development and analysis of policies intended to maximize these benefits and minimize these costs.

A major World Bank study by Larry Westphal, Yung W. Rhee, and Gary Pursell has concluded that "Korea's export industrialization has overwhelmingly and in fundamental respects been directed and controlled by nationals... technology has been acquired from abroad largely through means other than direct foreign investment." The role of multinational corporations in the economy has been much smaller than in most other middle-income countries.

Unquestionably, in the late 1980s and early 1990s, South Korea substantially liberalized. The lesson question is whether they would have done as well had they liberalized sooner. This is a question that can never be answered with certainty. Some economists have argued that South Korea would have industrialized even faster if it had maintained a free trade policy from the beginning. In any case, active industrial policy continues to this day, emphasizing Korean entry into the most leading-edge, high-technology fields.

Recently, South Korea's Ministry of Trade and Industry targeted new materials, computer-controlled machine tools, bioengineering, microelectronics, fine chemistry, optics, and aircraft as fields in which it predicted that the country could catch up with the

U.S. and Japan economically and technologically. Government is involved with the whole process. As South Korea becomes a candidate for developed country status, targeted industrial policies oriented toward technology enhancement are continuing to play a central role. Samsung has already become one of the largest world players in semiconductors.

What stands out in the case of industrial policy in South Korea is the selective involvement of government in projects in which technological progress (product, process, or organizational) has been a central concern. This policy theme may be traced from early attempts at achieving technology transfer in relatively basic industries to the current efforts of South Korea to develop original innovative capacity in high technology sectors.

Of course, it is impossible to prove that Korea's industrial policies were responsible for its success. It cannot be ruled out that Korea might have done even better without these policies. Moreover, one can argue as have Joseph Stern and his collaborators that the central role of the state was necessary in industrial policy in large part because of the way that government set up the rules of the economic game, including the allocation of credit. This itself ensured that major initiatives like the chemical and heavy industry drive were impossible without government direction. Because South Korea often looked to the example of Japan in setting industrial policy, one can argue that the country followed a "patterns of development" analysis rather than a classic industrial policy. These views certainly have some merit.

But the central interpretation that seems most favored by the evidence is that the South Korean industrial policy mix has served to overcome market failures involved in the process of technological progress. That such market failures are endemic to original technological progress is a well-known proposition of economics. But there may have been a massive underestimation of the importance and extent of such market failures in the *transfer* of product, process, and organizational innovations to developing countries.

Obviously, because these policies have been used successfully in South Korea does not automatically negate the arguments that such policies may in general be subject to the corruptions of rent-seeking activities. Understanding how South Korea was successful in this regard while so many others failed will likely be a major focus of development studies in coming years.

As a preliminary conclusion, the case of South Korea suggests that it is a combination of industrial policies addressed to specific market failures, and consistent with underlying market forces (as well as the local political economy) that promotes industrial development. Without proper attention to incentives (for both market and rent-seeking activities), these same industrial policies can prove counterproductive. Countries that cannot find the political will to use protection as a highly selective and strictly temporary instrument of industrial policy in cases where large, identified market failures can be shown to exist are probably better off abandoning this instrument altogether; the case of Bolivia is probably a good example of this.

In the 1990s, Korea's now democratic government is making a series of adjustments designed to make its market economy function in a more mature way. In the past, the government encouraged giant conglomerates, or *Chaebol,* to expand and enter new markets as a way of achieving economies of scale and scope, to facilitate exporting, and to facilitate its control over the economy by keeping the number of companies it had to stay in close contact with small.

Now that the Korean economy is established, the Chaebol are seen as liabilities to further growth. They are also seen as political liabilities, or as companies that unfairly received government advantages in the past from which other companies did not benefit. Antitrust regulations are now being enacted and enforced; this will probably make the Korean economy much more competitive in the future. As the Korean economy approaches maturity, government's role in the productive sector continues to recede.

But the lesson for developing countries that would like to emulate South Korea's success is that until the world technology frontier is approached, government does have an important role, even in the productive sector, until domestically-based private industry can establish itself.

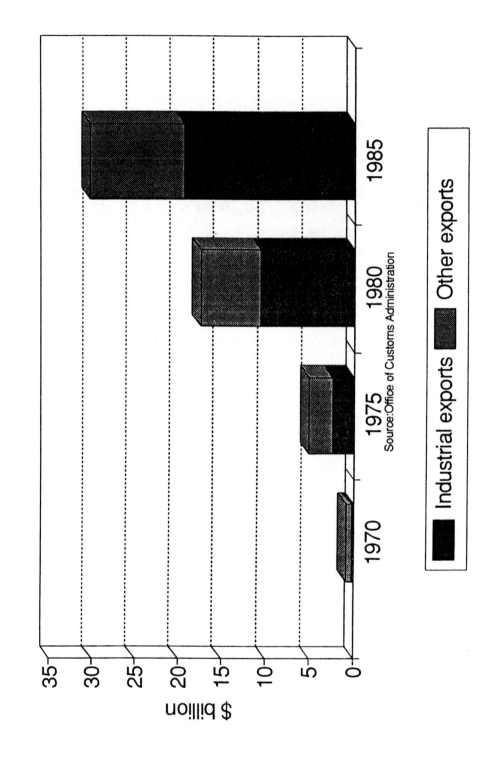

KOREA
Exports 1970-85

$ billion

35 30 25 20 15 10 5 0

1970   1975   1980   1985

Source:Office of Customs Administration

Industrial exports   Other exports

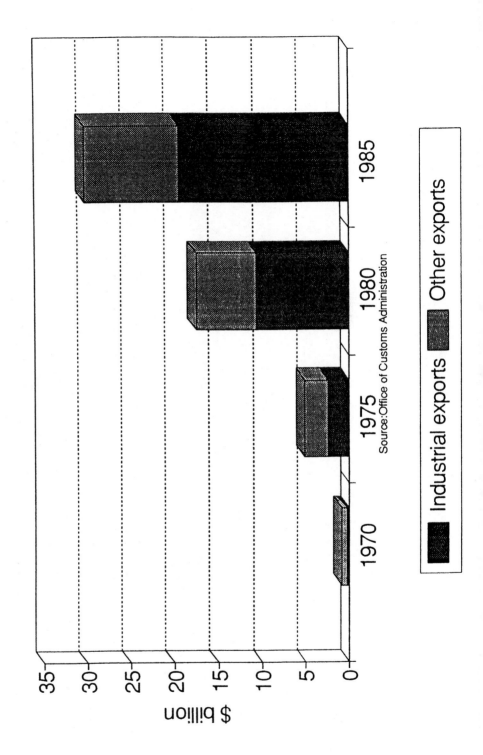

KOREA
Exports 1970-85

Source:Office of Customs Administration

■ Industrial exports   □ Other exports

165

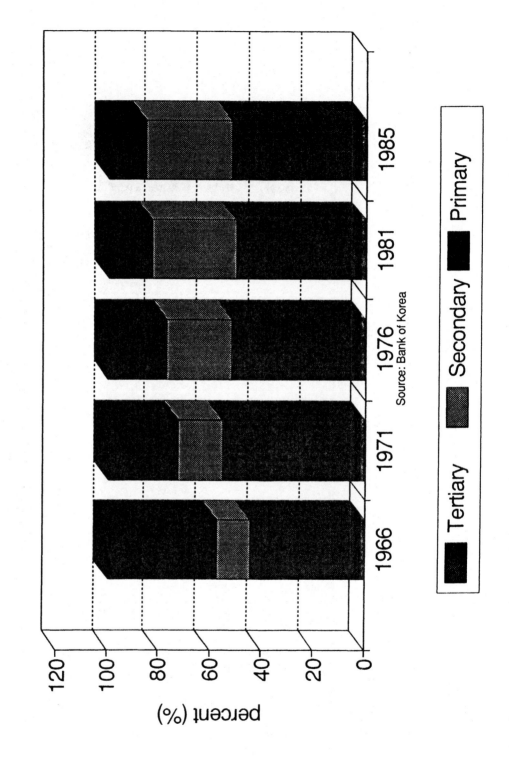

KOREA
Sectors' share of GNP

Source: Bank of Korea

Tertiary   Secondary   Primary

percent (%)

KOREA

Motor Vehicle Production

Source: Korea Auto. Indus. Coop. Assoc.

No. of vehicles produced (Thousands)

1970 1975 1978 1980 1981 1982 1983 1984 1985

0 50 100 150 200 250 300 350 400

167

Sources

Amsden, Alice. *Asia's Next Giant: South Korea and Late Industrialization.* Oxford: Oxford University Press, 1989.

Balassa, Bela. "The Lessons of East Asian Development: An Overview." *Economic Development and Cultural Change 36,* Supplement S273–290, 1988.

Chenery, Hollis, Sherwin Robinson, and Moses Syrquin. *Industrialization and Growth: A Comparative Study.* New York: Oxford, 1986.

Dahlman, Carl J., Bruce Ross-Larson, and Larry E. Westphal. "Managing Technical Development: Lessons from the Newly Industrializing Countries." *World Development 15* (1987): 759–75.

Financial Times, May 28, 1993, and other issues.

Frank, Charles R. *Foreign Trade Regimes and Economic Development: South Korea.* New York: Columbia (for NBER), 1975.

Heo, Yoon, Fred Joutz, and Stephen C. Smith. "Do Manufactures Export Subsidies Work? A Vector Autoregression Analysis of South Korean Performance." *George Washington University Economics Discussion Paper,* 1996.

Keesing, Donald B. "The Four Successful Exceptions. Official Export Promotion and Support for Export Marketing in Korea, Hong Kong, Singapore and Taiwan, China," *United Nations Development Program-World Bank Trade Expansion Program Occasional Paper 2,* 1988.

Luedde-Neurath, Richard. *Import Controls and Export-Oriented Development: A Reassessment of the South Korean Case.* Boulder: Westview, 1986.

Pack, Howard, and Larry Westphal. "Industrial Strategy and Technological Change: Theory versus Reality." *Journal of Development Economics 22* (1986): 87–128.

Petri, Peter. "Korea's Export Niche: Origins and Prospects." *World Development 16* (1988): 47–63.

Porter, Michael. *The Competitive Advantage of Nations.* New York: Free Press, 1990.

Rhee, Yung Whee, Bruce Ross-Larson, and Gary Pursell. *Korea's Competitive Edge: Managing the Entry into World Markets.* Baltimore: Johns Hopkins (for the World Bank), 1984.

Smith, Stephen C. *Industrial Policy in Developing Countries: Reconsidering the Real Sources of Export Led Growth.* Washington, DC: Economic Policy Institute, 1991.

Stern, Joseph, Ji-hong Kim, Dwight Perkins, and Jung-ho Yoo. *Industrialization and the State: The Korean Heavy and Chemical Industry Drive.* Cambridge, MA: Harvard University Press, 1995.

Wade, Robert. "The Role of Government in Overcoming Market Failure: Taiwan, Republic of Korea and Japan." In Helen Hughes, ed., *Achieving Industrialization in East Asia.* New York: Cambridge University Press, 1988.

Westphal, Larry E., Yung W. Rhee, and Gary Pursell. "Korean Industrial Competence: Where it Came From." *World Bank Staff Working Paper No. 469,* 1981.

Westphal, Larry E., Yung W. Rhee, Linsu Kim, and Alice Amsden. "Exports of Capital Goods and Related Services from the Republic of Korea," *World Bank Staff Working Paper 629,* 1984.

White, Gordon, ed. *Developmental States in East Asia.* New York: St. Martins, 1988.

World Bank. *The East Asian Miracle: Economic Growth and Public Policy.* New York: Oxford, 1993.

World Bank. *Korea: Managing the Industrial Transition,* in 2 volumes, Washington, DC: World Ban, 1987.

19. Mexico: A Pioneer in Successful Debt Reduction

In August 1982, Mexico triggered the Third World debt crisis when it announced that it could not pay its debt service, and would begin a moratorium of at least three months on debt payments to private creditors. Creditor banks, led by Citibank, formed an advisory committee. Mexico sought and received emergency assistance from the IMF and U.S. financial institutions. In September, Mexico nationalized its banks and introduced rigorous exchange controls.

In late September 1982, the annual World Bank-IMF meetings took place in Toronto in what is frequently described as an atmosphere of panic. The greatest fear was that the stability of the international banking system was in peril if significant defaults on loans threatened the major banks. The crisis swept through Latin America, Africa and other developing countries such as the Philippines and Yugoslavia. A plan was devised that saved the banking system, but led to what is often called the lost decade of development in Latin America and Africa.

Mexico was not only the first country to enter a debt crisis but a pacesetter in finding resolutions to it. The chart at the end of this case study compares some key external debt ratios for Mexico in 1980, just before the onset of the debt crisis, with those prevailing in 1991, when the debt crisis is widely thought to have gone into remission.

This case study will examine the strategy it followed. It is largely based on the excellent book on the subject by Sudarshan Gooptu. The debt crisis has now been declared over by many observers, and the pioneering role played by Mexico has been an important part of recovery. But it may be premature to declare the crisis over and Mexico's case suggests how the seeds of new crisis could have been sown anew.

The genesis of the debt crisis is well known. The oil shock of 1973 led to world recession. Developing countries such as Mexico found their export markets smaller while facing a larger oil bill. The price elasticity of oil in the short run is very small, and it was not easy to reduce the amount of oil imported without major economic dislocations.

For decades, it had been hard for Latin American countries to secure bank loans from major developed country banks; and before 1973, the external debt of Mexico, like most LDCs, was relatively small, primarily official, and often based on concessional lending. But major OPEC countries received a huge cash windfall from the 1973 oil price rise, and to sterilize this foreign exchange, they deposited much of the funds in

170

major American banks. These banks had to lend the money to earn interest, out of which to pay interest to the OPEC depositors. Mexico and other Latin American countries had a ready demand for these loanable funds. Commercial banks, recycling petrodollars, began issuing general-purpose loans to LDCs to provide balance of payments support and expansion of export sectors. From 1970 to 1992, Third World external debt grew from $68 billion to over $2000 billion.

Mexico did not discover its substantial new oil reserves until later in the 1970s. Following Citibank Chairman John Reed's dictum that "sovereign countries do not default," large banks lent to this region with abandon, often overlooking normal criteria of country lending risk. The value of loans outstanding increased by ten times in less than a decade.

Fate was sealed in the resulting crisis when Mexico and other borrowing countries failed to increase domestic investments apace with borrowing to levels capable of producing adequate levels of viable exports. Investment as a share of GDP hardly increased at all in this period of massive borrowing. This meant that Mexico and other borrower countries did not have the added capacity to produce the exports that could have generated foreign exchange to repay the debt without necessitating a fall in living standards.

Problems in Mexico were aggravated by very large fiscal deficits and inflation. After Mexico discovered additional large oil reserves and began producing oil in larger amounts in 1977, the country was merely tempted to borrow more money with oil as an implicit collateral. But this money, too, was not wisely invested, and the oil industry was operated with considerable inefficiency. Exchange rate appreciation hurt other exports (an example of "Dutch disease," in which exports of a commodity raise exchange rates and crowd out manufacturing and agricultural exports), and non-oil industries were neglected.

If the first oil shock triggered international lending through the combination of loan demand and recycling petrodollars that expanded the supply of loanable funds, the second oil shock in 1979 triggered a reversal of this process, as interest rates rose, stagnation reduced the demand for LDC exports, and already high debt levels made further borrowing to accommodate high oil prices all the more difficult. When real interest rates rose dramatically after 1979, Mexico's debt burden became untenable. In early 1982, Mexico's financial position began to deteriorate rapidly. The country needed to borrow some $20 billion that year to finance its existing loans and meet its expected deficit. As the year progressed, bank loans were harder to arrange and required a substantially higher interest rate. Inflation rose and a series of devaluations began. When the crisis finally broke in August it should not have come as a surprise.

For Mexico, the early years of the crisis were harsh. An economic adjustment program under the auspices of the IMF was initiated to restore economic order. Typical elements of IMF stabilization packages included liberalization of foreign exchange and import controls, devaluation, interest rate rises, deficit reduction, wage restrictions, decreased price controls, and a general opening up of the economy. It was widely argued in Mexico that this would lead to adjustment without growth, with negative development consequences. Indeed, this "austerity" program was much resented by Mexican leaders, but they saw no alternative.

This "IMF period" of the debt crisis had as its explicit objective the stability of the world financial system, and this meant ensuring the stability of the major money center banks. Mexicans and the Mexican economy were clearly suffering. Real income fell dramatically from 1982 to 1985. The IMF was asked to provide funds under less stringent conditions. Their standard public relations reply was, "We are the fire department. You call us when your house is on fire. We are not the carpenter. You don't complain when we put an axe to your door or cause water damage with our hoses." But by 1985 it had become clear that while the fire was being contained, it was not going out. There had been some achievements. In particular, the public sector deficit fell from about 17% to 8% as a share of GDP. But there had been a dramatic fall in the level of GDP, and a rise in poverty and inequality.

By 1985, the position of the banks was stabilizing. They were substantially reducing their exposure in Third World debt in relation to their paid-up capital. The immediate crisis subsided somewhat in 1984 when a "multi-year rescheduling agreement" with foreign banks stretched out repayment terms for Mexico's debt. But growth showed no sign of resuming in Mexico or elsewhere among the heavily indebted countries. No new capital flows were forthcoming to heavily indebted countries, and it became clear that a new approach would be needed.

In 1985 the American Secretary of State James Baker introduced a new initiative that became known as the Baker Plan. The idea was to get growth to resume in debtor countries, so they could "grow their way out of debt." Debt forgiveness was still a taboo subject. But new funds would be lent to indebted countries that would let growth resume, drawing on private banks, the World Bank, the IMF, and other sources. In return, Mexico and other indebted countries would introduce market reforms that were expected to facilitate the use of new funds in a more efficient and growth-enhancing manner.

Mexico became one of the first countries to participate in the Baker Plan. Mexico agreed to a major debt restructuring and domestic economy reform program in June 1986. Commercial banks agreed to over $7 billion in loans and a new rescheduling agreement covering some $54 billion of outstanding debt. In return, the World Bank offered a loan of one-half billion dollars. This represented the entry of the World Bank into structural adjustment loans (SALs) as part of the Baker Plan. Previously, such general loans were seen as the exclusive province of the IMF, with the World Bank specializing in project lending.

The IMF also committed new funds. At this time, Mexico was being severely hurt by the big drop in the price of oil of the mid-1980s. The IMF agreed to a "special stand-by" agreement, in which it would make some $600 million credit available to Mexico in the eventuality that the price of oil fell below $9 a barrel. The IMF also offered substantial new credit, to be matched by new credits from commercial banks. Mexico did introduce far-reaching market-oriented reforms in this period. The most important reason why this approach did not work in the end is that commercial banks proved unwilling to "do their part" in net new lending. These banks committed only a fraction of the loans anticipated in the Baker Plan. The banks' main concern at this time was still to reduce their exposure to developing country debt, and certainly not to increase it.

Mexico had been one of the countries at the forefront of a major trend of the 1970s, limiting the allowed role of foreign multinational firms to participating only in approved minority joint ventures in most sectors. One effect of the debt crisis was that these restrictions were largely lifted. Full subsidiaries were allowed. The level of direct foreign investment (DFI) increased steadily.

In the mid-1980s Mexico became one of the pioneers of debt-for-equity swaps as an instrument of debt reduction. In these swaps, restrictions on DFI are lifted when foreign investors pay for the asset by presenting Mexican debt paper. These are acquired, usually at a substantial discount, from banks that wish to reduce their Third World debt exposure. The secondary market for Latin American debt has an average discount of perhaps 50% of face value (sometimes with far steeper discounts). The investor presents the loan to the central bank, which in turn issues local currency (pesos in the case of Mexico) that can be used only to purchase a local firm's assets. Sometimes the firm may be a state owned enterprise, so the transaction facilitates privatization. But debt equity swaps carry the inherent risk of generating inflationary pressures, because they usually involve swaps of public debt for private assets. Because the central bank issues currency for the investor to buy a local asset, this represents a direct addition to high-powered money.

Mexico suspended debt-equity swaps in November, 1987, officially because of their inflationary effects. A part of the real reason may have been political pressures to limit the share of foreign ownership and control in the economy, though swaps of private debt for private equity continued to be permitted. In any case, concerns about large-scale foreign ownership would represent another limitation on the ability to use debt-equity swaps as a major element of a debt reduction program.

In 1988, as the debt-equity swap strategy lost momentum, Mexico pioneered a new approach to debt reduction. Mexico would exchange some of its outstanding debt, perceived as high-risk, for new debt called "Aztec Bonds," that would be backed by U.S. Treasury bonds bought by Mexico and held in Washington as collateral. An auction would be held, in which banks would bid on how much discount on the face amount of their existing loans they would accept in exchange for the new, more secure bonds. In March 1988, some $2.5 billion of bonds were exchanged for $3.6 billion in bank debt, an average discount of about 33%. A total of some $6.7 billion was offered by banks, but Mexico rejected some of these bids as offering too small a discount. If the results were disappointing in their magnitude, they represented an important innovation, later built on in the Brady Plan.

Eventually it became clear to all parties that substantial Mexican growth could not resume until its large debt burden was substantially reduced, not just rescheduled. With the major U.S. money center banks out of immediate danger after several years of reducing developing world exposure, notably their large additions to loan loss reserves in summer 1987, debt reduction could be considered without risk of financial panic. A debt reduction plan was floated by U.S. Treasury Secretary Nicholas Brady in March 1989. Although the plan was market based, it had an important public role designed to help overcome free rider problems. Each lender would like other lenders to reduce the amount of debt owed to them, because this would increase the probability that their own debt would be repaid. But unilateral reduction of debt by any one bank only benefits other banks holding debt. Thus, some coordinating role, generally of government, must be played to overcome this basic market failure.

Mexico was the first country to negotiate debt reduction under the new "Brady Plan." Banks were given three options: (1) to exchange loans for floating rate bonds with collateral at a 35% discount, (2) to exchange loans for bonds with the same par value but receiving a lower, fixed interest rate, or (3) to lend new money to finance Mexican interest payments, keeping nominal value of the debt they were owed intact. In 1990, 49% of the banks exchanged some $22 billion in debt for lower-interest, fixed-rate bonds, and 41% exchanged $20 billion in debt for the discounted floating-rate bonds. This constituted Mexico's creditor banks' "revealed preferences" from among the options.

Provided that Mexico continues to successfully service this debt, the bonds on deposit in Washington as collateral will earn interest that Mexico will receive, which can eventually be used for debt reduction or investment. These exchanges saved Mexico payments of about $1.3 billion per year. From the banks' point of view, the trade-off involved giving up higher yielding but higher risk debt for lower yielding but lower risk debt. Following Mexico's example, other countries reduced their required payments under the Brady Plan, and the debt crisis went into remission.

In the early 1990s, successful debt reduction, combined with market reforms and the investor enthusiasm over the prospects of the North American Free Trade Agreement (NAFTA), returned net positive capital flows to Mexico. Capital inflows soared in Mexico in the early 1990s. This enabled Mexico to return to current account deficits. Inflows of capital to Mexico amounted to almost 8.5% of GDP in 1992. Current account deficits were over 6% in 1992 and close to 8% in 1993. Mexico's trade deficit in 1992 was some $19 billion. Its net investment inflows were some $23 billion.

But this capital inflow success raised the question of whether it could be sowing the seeds of renewed crisis. In the late 1980s and early 1990s, exports did not grow nearly as fast as imports. Prescient observers concluded that Mexico's exchange rate was too high. They argued that despite the commitment of the Mexican government to a stable currency, the ensuing deficits could not be maintained indefinitely. While growth can be restarted with the stimulus of these large capital inflows, over the longer term it cannot be sustained by them.

Certainly, there were some important differences from the 1970s. Because much of the inflow was in the form of equity rather than debt, not requiring interest and principal payments on a fixed schedule, a repayments crisis was less plausible. At the same time, foreign private investment tends to be extremely volatile, especially foreign stock market investments. Investments can pour out of a country as rapidly as they pour in, as Chile discovered in its financial crash of the early 1980s.

In any case, as before, there is a risk that living standards will be lower in the future if the inflows are not invested in ways that will promote higher exports. Published statistics did show that investment as a share of GDP was rising in Mexico in the early 1990s. Unfortunately, the way Mexican statistics are assembled makes it impossible to judge whether funds were going to the right investments. Some of what is being invested may not pay off in greater capacity for producing exportables. For example, some of the new investment was going into commercial and residential real estate.

In sum, if the debt crisis is defined as a threat to the large commercial banks, it is largely over. If it is defined as a threat to development prospects, for many developing countries, even for Mexico, it is not over. The fact that Mexico is borrowing in dollars to finance road construction—tolls would be paid in pesos—is a symbol of a potential new phase of the debt crisis in the future.

In late 1994 and early 1995, some of the critics' worst predictions seemed to come true, as government attempted to carry out a small, orderly devaluation of the peso. But the market saw this step as too little too late, and concluded that the action was likely merely a prelude to much larger devaluations in the near future. Speculators, acting on these expectations, forced the hand of the government, which let the peso float until it had lost over half its value. This debacle precipitated a crash of the Mexican stock market. In the ensuing recession, imports dropped dramatically. Mexican companies, receiving far more pesos for a dollar's worth of exports than before the crisis, greatly increased their exports. The adjustment was a classic case of markets overwhelming the ability of a government to maintain faulty policies.

By mid-1996 it looked as though the worst of the crisis had passed. Yet the experience of 1994-1995 showed that the danger of international debt crises will be on the international agenda for many years to come. Indeed, Russia and other transition economies not affected by the debt crisis of the 1980s have already faced debt crises of their own in the 1990s.

One of the important lessons of Mexico's experience is that to treat a genuine debt crisis as a liquidity problem only delays finding a solution. Moreover, it is clear that some public role will be needed to overcome lenders' free rider problems. In the future, it will be important to try to ensure that borrowing is matched by productive investments, though this will be very difficult in practice.

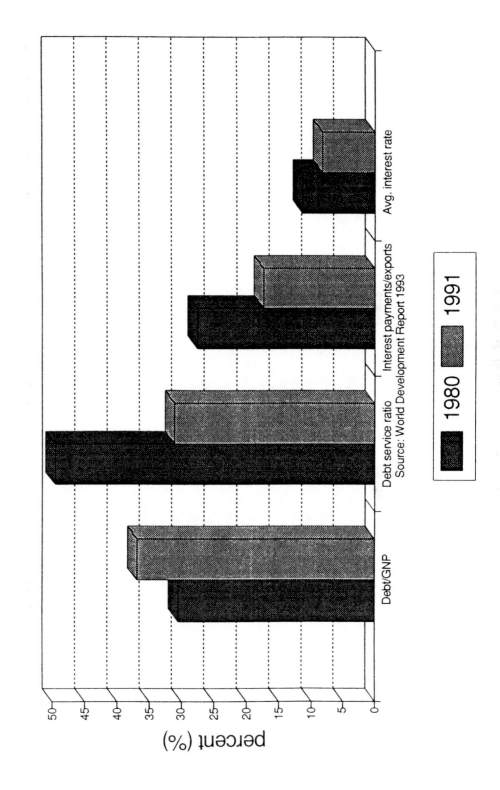

MEXICO:
External debt ratios 1980 and 1991

Source: World Development Report 1993

1980 1991

percent (%)

Debt/GNP   Debt service ratio   Interest payments/exports   Avg. interest rate

Sources

Business Week, "The Mexican Worker," April 19, 1993.

Erzan, Refik. "Free Trade Agreements with the United States: What's in it for Latin America?" *World Bank Policy Research Working Paper 827,* 1992.

Financial Times, various issues, including July 30, 1992; Feb. 12 and March 29, 1993.

Gooptu, Sudarshan. *Debt Reduction and Development: The Case of Mexico.* Westport, CT: Praeger, 1993.

Hufbauer, Gary, and Jeffery Schott. *NAFTA: An Assessment.* Washington, DC: Institute for International Economics, 1993.

Pastor, Robert F., and Jorje G. Castenada. *Limits to Friendship: The United States and Mexico.* New York: Vintage, 1988.

Prestowitz, Clyde, et al. *The New North American Order: A Win-Win Strategy for US–Mexico Trade.* Economic Strategy Institute, 1991.

20. Restrictive Policy toward Multinationals: Argentina and Korea

One of the most enduringly controversial issues in economic development is the role played by multinational corporations (MNCs). This case study will examine the major issues behind this controversy. It will then examine the broad features of the MNC policies of two middle income developing countries, Argentina and Korea, that have historically sought to restrict MNCs, though in different ways, and consider recent changes in those policies.

The Multinational Corporation and Development Policy

By definition MNCs manage production units in more than one country, including joint ventures (JVs) and management contracts, as well as wholly owned subsidiaries. This definition deliberately excludes licensing, conventional exporting, and other international business activities that do not involve direct managerial control by the parent company. The parent has a home-base country—for the purposes of this case study, a developed economy such as the U.S. or Japan—from which it operates subsidiary operations abroad—in this discussion, in a developing country.

MNCs undertake "Direct Foreign Investment" (DFI), to be contrasted with international portfolio investment, in which foreign investors generally keep at "arms-length" of local management decisions. In the conventional theory of DFI, MNCs exist because they hold monopolistic advantages in the presence of transaction costs of sufficient magnitude to offset inherent informational and other disadvantages of operating outside a firm's national home base. These disadvantages include barriers of language, culture (including business culture), knowledge of reliable local suppliers, contacts, and special government assistance programs available only to local firms. If the transaction costs of operating licensing agreements were sufficiently small, it would be more profitable to avoid the many costs of directly doing business in a foreign country; instead, the parent company would collect a fee from a local company for allowing it to use the rights to the patent, production process, trademark, or other assets providing the MNC its monopolistic advantages. Note that MNCs may produce either for the domestic market or for export; which of these orientations of MNCs predominates in a given country will depend in part on the policy incentives MNCs face.

In theory, MNCs offer many important benefits for economic development. Some of the argued advantages of a significant presence of MNCs include their role in filling three "development gaps": they can increase the available foreign exchange through initial investments and exports, increase the total level of investment, and increase government revenues through the taxes they pay. In addition, MNCs are argued to facilitate transfer of technology and management skills; provide modern sector employment; and help "realize" a country's comparative advantage by supplying complementary inputs, market access, and management skill. Further, by increasing competition, MNCs can spur the economy to providing more and better quality goods.

On the other hand, MNCs have been accused of bringing about several major disadvantages for development. A major criticism is the "decapitalization" argument, that in the long run MNCs drain a developing country of capital, claiming that MNCs raise a high percentage of capital locally, and eventually repatriate their profits to their home country. Note that when MNCs raise capital locally, they may crowd out local firms that are unable to turn to international sources to finance their operations. It has been argued that most of the benefits of MNCs' activities go to foreign nationals, or at best to a few locals with close ties to the MNC. Further, when MNCs set up operations to "produce under tariff barriers," they typically restrict the ability of their subsidiaries to export, so that they do not disrupt the global marketing plan. But this also means that the LDC will not gain foreign exchange through exports. MNCs can also sometimes avoid paying taxes through creative transfer pricing. Under some circumstances, the MNC may overcharge its subsidiary for inputs, or underpay the subsidiary for its output, thus understating the subsidiary's taxable profit. This is most problematic when the inputs and outputs in question are not widely traded on international markets, so the appropriate prices may not be obvious to tax authorities. In sum, MNCs may fail to contribute to filling any of the three gaps.

MNCs are also accused of using an excessively capital intensive technique that together with crowding out of local investment could lead to a possible employment decline. MNCs are also said to disrupt domestic stabilization and other economic policy. For example, when the authorities tighten credit policy, MNCs may simply turn to their international sources of capital, while local firms cannot compete. Taking a broad view, Michael Porter effectively argues that a substantial domestically owned sector is a prerequisite for development.

Which of these factors predominates at a given time and point in the development process; and for a given country, industry, indeed a given project, is an empirical question. Benefits and costs of measures to restrict or encourage MNCs generally evolve in a way that may differ by sector as a country passes through stages of development. Many of the argued costs of DFI, such as their higher use of imported intermediate inputs, decline over time, as the MNC learns which low-cost local suppliers have reliable quality and delivery times. Thus, benefits of DFI may be realized only with a lag.

In general, the debate on merits and demerits of foreign investment in economic development provides few explicit recommendations for an optimal level of DFI. However, if there are benefits as well as costs, it may not be optimal to have either a fully open door policy to MNCs, or a highly restrictive stance. The costs and benefits of any one direct foreign investment proposal will have to be considered for approval on the basis of its individual merits.

In his landmark study of competitive advantage, Michael Porter stressed that:

"foreign multinationals should be only <u>one component</u> (original emphasis) of a developing nation's economic strategy, and an evolving component. At some stage in the development process, the focus should shift to indigenous companies... Government should encourage the formation and upgrading of indigenous companies in related and supporting industries to those in which multinationals operate, not solely with an eye toward import substitution but ultimately as international competitors. This will not take place, however, without the parallel development of human resource skills, a scientific base, and infrastructure in those fields to support higher-order competitive advantages... Multinationals should also be cultivated whose rationale for locating in a nation goes beyond basic factor considerations... The ideal is to make the nation almost a 'home base.'"

Moreover, Porter argues that governments and firms must work toward developing independent national brand names rather than working as an "original equipment manufacturer."

While the focus of this case study will be on economic policy toward MNCs, it is important to recognize that this policy is not initiated for economic reasons alone. Public attitudes toward MNCs, often negative and xenophobic in even the most developed countries, can be very hostile in LDCs. Politicians often use MNCs as a convenient scapegoat. So, while under some circumstances an overreliance on MNCs does present certain real costs to an economy, these are sometimes exaggerated or distorted in the political process.

This case study will consider policies toward MNCs from the viewpoint of two countries, South Korea and Argentina. The former country has at least until very recently had a relatively restrictive attitude to MNCs, though admitting MNC involvement in cases in which officials are convinced of their importance to the economy. Until recently, Argentina has encouraged MNCs to operate locally in a number of sectors within its generally failed policy of import substitution. In response to the failures of the import substitution period, the economy has substantially liberalized, but without the policies that would probably help the country get as many benefits and incur as few as possible of the costs of MNCs involvement. We examine each country in turn. (For an additional comparison between these countries, see Comparative Case Study 1, in Michael Todaro, *Economic Development,* 6th Ed., 1996.)

South Korea

Korea has pursued a policy that has both restricted imports and provided strong incentives for exports (see Case Study 18). MNCs have been restricted from producing for local consumers, but have encountered fewer restrictions producing within Korea for the export market.

The role of multinationals in the Korean economy has been much smaller than most other middle-income countries. A World Bank study by Larry Westphal, Yung W. Rhee and Gary Pursell concluded that "Korea's export industrialization has overwhelmingly and in fundamental respects been directed and controlled by nationals... technology has been acquired from abroad largely through means other than direct foreign investment."

As Michael Porter concluded in his examination of the Korean experience, "government has played a heavy role thus far, directing scarce capital, limiting foreign investment, assisting in foreign technology licensing and protecting the home market. Like Singapore, Korea has invested aggressively to upgrade human resources and infrastructure. Unlike Singapore, Korean development is based heavily on Korean companies though multinationals have some role. To a much greater extent than Singapore, Korean firms and the Korean government have also begun investing in research."

South Korea clearly illustrates the evolution of costs and benefits of policies toward MNCs as a country passes through stages of its development. For decades Korea had one of the most restrictive policies toward MNCs in Asia, a policy that has been closely related to its strongly protectionist stance. In the mid-1990s Korea undertook significant measures to liberalize rules of foreign investment. As the Korean economic miracle continued, economic and diplomatic costs of continuing to restrict multinationals increased while the benefits of doing so declined.

Investment in infrastructure is a good example. When a developing country is constructing basic infrastructure, foreign participation is often unnecessary. Government construction contracts are often a way of getting local companies started. So long as technology and financing requirements are not burdensome for the country, the infant industry protection argument may come into play. But when modern economic growth is well underway, the country's infrastructure needs change. Capital requirements become larger, quality matters more, and technology transfer may be more difficult, especially in communications and other higher-tech fields of infrastructure.

In the case of Korea, a substantial construction industry did emerge during a period of high protection. But with rapid development straining the infrastructure of the economy, $100 billion in construction projects were planned for the second half of the 1990s. Even combined, the public and private sectors in Korea would be hard pressed to raise this amount of capital. This has been one of the driving factors behind the opening of the formerly closed construction market.

Quality is also an important factor in Korea. Many industries have received substantial protection since the Korean War. Industries producing exportable goods, responding to strong government incentives to export, have greatly increased their quality along with their productivity in their quest to be competitive in international markets. Some Korean construction companies have been active abroad. But the quality of domestic construction, at least, has been placed very much in doubt by a deadly series of recent construction disasters, such as the collapses of a Seoul department store and the Songsu Bridge. Engineering studies are now often conducted by foreign firms. Even so, MNCs are continuing to be closely regulated. Many government contracts are being targeted to MNCs with local partners, where the agreements specifically call for substantial technology transfers to the local partner during the project; and the government is actively encouraging local firms to establish technology transfer linkages.

Domestic politics are another important factor. The democratically elected government is embarked on a policy of *segyehwa*, or globalization, that has meant substantially less restrictive trade and investment policies than in the past. The purpose of this policy is, in part, to introduce more competition within the domestic economy. The structure of the economy has been seen as benefitting major corporations rather than Korean consumers. In Korea, four large conglomerates, or *chaebol*, dominate industry: Hyundae, Daewoo, Samsung, and Goldstar. The top four have represented almost one-third of total Korean exports in recent years, and have enormous market power in the domestic economy. The chaebol system was devised by the government to facilitate its industrial and export policies, but now is seen by many Koreans as having outlived its usefulness.

Considerations of diplomacy and international affairs introduced further complications. Earlier in its development, Korea enjoyed many special benefits as a country at the front line of the containment of Communism at the height of the Cold War. In large part, this geopolitical position led the U.S. in particular to overlook many of Korea's protectionist policies, as well as restrictiveness toward MNCs, in a manner analogous to U.S. policy toward Japan and Taiwan. The small size of the Korean economy at that time made it easier for U.S. policy to give Korea special treatment. But as the Cold War drew to a close, the Korean presence in the world economy had become far more significant, and the U.S. was attempting to respond to its chronic trade deficit problems, U.S. policy took a dimmer view of the way Korean policies negatively affected American commercial interests.

Moreover, as Korea sought to join the OECD, it found that it had to harmonize its foreign investment rules with the much more open standards of other members. In 1995, the OECD stated that Korea's general prohibition of majority foreign ownership of firms was a major obstacle to the approval of Korea's application for membership in the organization.

As a result of these forces, Korea has been partially deregulating foreign investment rules. Foreign firms may establish new affiliates as either joint ventures or wholly owned affiliates under rules that have been relaxed over time. From 1997, Korea will now permit friendly takeovers of Korean firms by foreign investors, although hostile takeovers will continue to be banned. In addition, the ban on foreign investment in defense, nuclear power, and communications industries will stay in force. Strict rules on foreign stock holdings of listed companies are also being relaxed to some extent. In sum, only after the country began to approach developed economy status were restrictions on MNCs significantly relaxed.

Argentina

While South Korea has pursued an export promotion strategy for over three decades, until the last few years Argentina's trade strategy has been squarely in the import substitution camp. As part of this strategy, although MNCs have faced some restrictions, they have found it easier in practice to produce for Argentina's domestic market than Korea's. In fact, MNCs have had strong incentives to "produce under tariff barriers" in Argentina; the same forces, overvalued exchange rates, and other high costs of exporting, have provided MNCs almost no incentive to export products they produce in the country.

An economy's outlook on currency, debt servicing, and savings has considerable influence over an MNCs decision to invest in the economy. It is easy for a country to tarnish its macroeconomic reputation, but difficult to rebuild it. Argentina has been undergoing significant market-oriented reforms in recent years. The government has been opening the economy through deregulation, freer trade, privatization, and tax reform. However, it is still unclear whether these reforms have been properly implemented.

The macroeconomic environment for direct foreign investment is very important. Investors perceive the danger of devaluation to be the biggest deterrence to investing in Argentina. A secondary fear is that the country won't be able to service its debt; Argentina had been one of the countries most at risk during the debt crisis of the 1980s, and it still has a very large international debt despite restructuring. The savings rate, down from about 23% in 1980 to around 18% in the mid-1990s, is inadequate to support the investment needs of the economy.

To alleviate concerns over devaluation, Argentina has formally pegged its local currency to the U.S. dollar at a one-to-one ratio, referred to as "convertability." Every peso is fully backed by reserves of U.S. dollars and other assets. This new system has already survived three external shocks, most notably the Mexican peso crisis of late 1994. The new rules have taken much control of the money supply out of the hands of the government, which can no longer effectively print money to finance its expenditures. The government is further restricted because it can no longer extend credit to the private sector. On the other hand, the central bank can't inject liquidity into suffering banks without reserves to back it up. The new system has stopped both currency speculation and inflation. As long as this strategy remains credible, panic selling of the local currency should not set in. But Argentina was facing a still modest but widening trade deficit through 1995. The high exchange rate led to no increases in the level of exports even while imports quadrupled from 1990 through 1993. If these trends continue, the incentive for devaluation will grow, and markets will come to doubt whether the pegged currency policy is sustainable. These doubts may eventually cause the system to unravel.

Another deterrent to potential investors is the prospect of limited and sluggish growth in the domestic market. The rate of unemployment is high and rising. As policy attention is shifted to export promotion, incentives to produce for the domestic market have decreased, while it is still not clear that Argentina is a good choice of an economy from which to export to the world market.

However, MNCs have increased interest in Argentina due to the market access potential of the MERCOSUR common market, uniting Argentina with Brazil, Uruguay, and Paraguay. Specifically, MNCs in the food and energy sectors have maintained their interest despite the recent recession there. Like other southern cone countries, Argentina has made a great effort to improve its infrastructure after a decade of neglect during the debt crisis. Because infrastructure and private investment are generally complements, these efforts have also been a draw for MNC investment.

As they have throughout Latin America, net capital inflows to Argentina increased dramatically in the 1990s. The source of funds is no longer predominantly commercial banks lending to the government and state owned enterprises (SOEs) as in the 1970s, but increasingly is based on DFI. Principal foreign investors are the U.S., Spain, Italy, U.K., Germany, France, and Brazil. The stock of U.S. DFI at the end of 1993 was about $4.4 billion, a share of 30%, up almost $2 billion from 1990. Much of this share was in the energy sector and banking. U.S. firms are also planning to make substantial investments in coming years. Auto firms plan to invest nearly $5 billion in the 1995-2000 period. For example, GM is building a second vehicle assembly plant in Santa Fe province, at a cost of about $300 million. Du Pont is planning a $40 million investment in machinery at its Argentine plants.

In the early 1990s, Argentina attracted attention from investors through the sale of SOEs. The privatization program was one of the largest in the world. Partly as a result, the position of Argentina's four largest industrial groups (Perez Companac, Commercial del Planta, Organizacion Techint, and Astra) has been significantly strengthened. They may now play a larger role in Argentina's domestic economy than the four *chaebol* currently play in South Korea.

The largest financial transaction in Latin American history was Argentina's recent sale of YPF, the state-owned oil company. In this case, the restrictive policy toward MNCs was quite explicit. The government sought both to maximize the number of shares remaining in Argentine hands, and to prevent a major foreign oil company from dominating the company. It is worth noting that this policy extended to local oil firms—government also did not want the company dominated by an Argentine corporate group. In the end, YPF acquired a very diversified ownership, with some 65 to 70% of shares in Argentine hands, and a diverse body of international investors. Once it was privatized, YPF could no longer play the role of artificially generating employment, and the workforce fell from more than 52,000 to just 5,750.

Although the wish to encourage widespread ownership is commendable, the YPF sell-off raises a classic dilemma. The more diffuse the ownership of a company, the lower the incentive for any one small shareholder to monitor the efficiency of the company and the degree to which it follows arms-length policy in dealing with customers and suppliers. In fact, the more diffuse is company ownership, the smaller the stake actually needed for a single interest to maintain effective control of a company. This is one reason why MNCs in Latin America and elsewhere were often able to maintain control of joint ventures in the 1970s, when laws restricted their ownership to 49% or less.

Many U.S. multinationals won bids for privatized firms, especially in electricity, transport, and the oil and gas sector. For example, Enron Corp. of Houston is a major shareholder in the recently privatized gas transmission company. Enron has a role in directing the company's operations and has supplied its chief executive. Nabisco bought one of Argentina's largest food groups for $250 million. However, Italian and Spanish companies have won controlling interests in important sectors, such as the two phone companies and several natural gas companies. Some MNCs have become involved in unforeseen ways in sectors such as real estate. But large-scale, national-level privatizations have now been largely exhausted as a major source of national income and foreign investment—most big SOEs have been sold off.

Efficiency may improve significantly after privatization. In two out of four industries studied, the McKinsey consulting group found that productivity had significantly increased in firms in Argentina that had been privatized with foreign participation. The study found that privatization with DFI had benefitted the telecommunications and steel industries.

Argentina still maintains complex regulations in many areas that cause difficulty for potential investors. Officials are trying to make improvements in such areas, and are regarded as having made significant progress in the area of trade regulation. New legislation in this area gives foreign firms essentially the same treatment as national companies, except for minor payments restrictions. Transportation costs have also dropped through the deregulation of freight and harbor operations. Argentina has also taken steps to prevent pirating by enforcing patent law in order to induce pharmaceutical MNCs to invest. In sum, Argentina has liberalized DFI rules at the beginning of a hoped-for drive to economic maturity, rather than near the end of such a phase as in South Korea.

Conclusion

Both Argentina and South Korea have employed restrictive policies toward multinationals over the past several decades. Both have relaxed these policies in the 1990s. But on closer examination, significant differences emerge between the strategies of these countries in both earlier and later years. South Korea appears to have had a more balanced, intelligible policy throughout. While now much more open to MNCs, South Korea is using complementary policies to help ensure that it will get the maximum benefits from their presence, especially in the field of technology transfer. Argentina, on the other hand, appears to have moved from a policy of trying to encourage MNCs to produce locally within a generally failed policy of import substitution, to a general policy of openness to MNCs and trade, without policies to ensure that the benefits largely remain within the country. The country has also now liberalized DFI rules at an earlier stage of technology acquisition than South Korea.

In sum, economic policies either encourage or discourage MNCs. Some policies are consciously intended to either restrict or encourage MNC activity, in favored sectors or across the board. Other policies, such as those that might affect macroeconomic stability, have the perhaps unintended effect of influencing MNC investment decisions. Thus, economic policy will affect MNCs whether intended or not, so a country's perspective on the appropriate role or scope of MNCs in its economy should be considered explicitly in the formulation of policy. Policymakers must consider the role they expect MNCs to play in economic development, such as to facilitate technology transfer, then devise policies to encourage them to play this role—seeking to maximize the benefits and minimize the costs.

Sources

Bornschier, V. "Multinational Corporations and Economic Growth." *Journal of Development Economics 7,* no. 2 (June 1980): 191–210.

Caves, Richard E. *Multinational Enterprise and Economic Analysis.* New York: Cambridge University Press, 1982.

Financial Times, various issues.

Haddad, M., and A. Harrison. "Are there Positive Spillovers from Direct Foreign Investment," *Journal of Development Economics 42* (1993): 51–74.

Jenkins, Rhys. "Comparing Foreign Subsidiaries and Local Firms in LDCs: Theoretical Issues and Empirical Evidence." *Journal of Development Studies 26* (1990): 205–228.

Levy, Brian. "The Determinants of Manufacturing Ownership in Less Developed Countries." *Journal of Development Economics 28* (1988): 159–174.

Porter, Michael. *The Competitive Advantage of Nations.* New York: Free Press, 1990.

Smith, Stephen C. "Multinational Corporations and the Third World: Bargaining Power and Development." *Towson Journal of International Affairs,* fall 1984.

Svejnar, Jan, and Stephen C. Smith. "The Economics of Joint Ventures in Less Developed Countries." *The Quarterly Journal of Economics 98* (1984): 149–168.

Todaro, Michael P., *Economic Development,* 6th ed., Reading, MA: Addison-Wesley, 1997.

U.S. Department of Commerce, various documents and Internet materials.

Wall Street Journal, various issues.

Washington Post, various issues.

Westphal, Larry E., Yung W. Rhee, and Gary Pursell. "Korean Industrial Competence: Where it Came From," *World Bank Staff Working Paper No. 469,* 1981.

21. Marketization and Privatization in Chile

The government role in the Chilean economy and society was once one of the most pervasive in Latin America. Beginning with the 1973 military coup, Chile began the longest-running marketization and privatization program in the developing world. Although this program continues, since the 1990 election of President Patricio Aylwin, the government in Chile has moved to chart a middle course, acknowledging an important role for the state in development, but usually outside of productive enterprises. Throughout this history, Chile has moved in fits and starts that epitomize the problems of finding the right balance between market and public regulation. In principle, privatization can offer numerous benefits to an economy, such as greater efficiency and incentives for innovation, and as a means to jump-start stock markets. The role of privatized firms in Chile's emerging stock market is summarized by a chart at the end of this case study. To date, Chile has had more success with privatization than any other developing country.

In the 19th century, state-owned enterprises (SOEs) played an important role in Chile's early development, in sectors such as the post and telegraph, railroads and ports, and financial services. Like many Latin American economies, SOEs were greatly expanded in number and scope beginning in the late 1930s. Obstacles to international trade and finance brought on by World War II, and to some degree earlier by the Great Depression and its trading blocs, were the proximate motivations. CORFO, a public investment bank and holding company, financed SOE start-ups in oil refining, steel, sugar beet and other sectors. Later, it acquired private firms, usually after they defaulted on CORFO-provided credit.

In 1970, Salvadore Allende, an avowed Marxist, was elected president. While he strongly supported political democracy, he was committed to turning Chile into a fully socialist economy. His most controversial action was the nationalization of copper mining activities, by far the country's most important export industry, and which was largely controlled by foreign interests. Allende took other actions that angered traditional elites, such as carrying out rapid, extensive land reform.

Chile had a history of democratic government and a military with a strong commitment to constitutional rule. But with the support of the country's elite, as well as President Nixon in the U.S., the military joined in with the Latin American trend toward military dictatorship of that period and overthrew Allende in 1973, killing him and thousands of supporters.

After the 1973 coup, the Chilean government headed by Augusto Pinochet sought successfully to reverse all of the changes of the Allende era. Deregulation, trade liberalization, and privatization were the three main components of that reversal. Every market was largely freed from government control with the exception of the labor market, as Alejandro Foxley noted.

Over an 18-year period some 550 firms employing 5 percent of the country's workforce were privatized. Market forces were brought to bear on areas of the economy unknown in other parts of the developing world, including private social security for all but the poorest citizens. Mandatory individual retirement accounts, replacing the former social security system, set the stage for increased savings and an expanded range of financial instruments.

Chile, even under Pinochet, was never really purely laissez-faire. Some hidden subsidies and inducements remained, including a massive government rescue of the financial sector, amounting to 4.6% of GDP from 1982 to 1986. Many banks that had been privatized in the preceding years had to be renationalized in the 1982 financial crash. In privatization itself, subsidies were offered to the private sector through the sale of assets at little more than half their real asset values. The nearly 50 remaining SOEs in Chile still accounted for almost 15% of the country's GDP by 1994, a share that is likely to fall primarily as a result of the growth of the private sector. These SOEs are predominantly found in electric power and the important mining sectors.

Fishing companies were privatized in the 1970s, but an extensive government role remained, including export market development, technical assistance, and ecosystem regulation. Agriculture is the sector in which the lion's share of new nontraditional exports have been realized, especially in fruits, and in the 1990s in wine. There, government has played an active role in targeting potential export sectors, providing infrastructure, developing markets, supporting research, and providing extension services to help realize higher productivity. Today, Chile's exports represent 35% of GNP, and are more diversified than ever before in its history. Chile runs a trade surplus with Japan, its largest trading partner.

Chile's export promotion activities have represented a modest but successful sector policy, and has played an important part in the favorable growth performance of the late 1980s. But it remains unclear if policies for exports of fruit and other specialty farm and forest products centering around larger farms (latifundia and agribusiness) provide a sufficient development strategy in the longer term. Within agriculture, most farms are very small, and most of these seem to have benefitted little from government campaigns to produce nontraditional exports. It is encouraging, though, that in the sugar beet sector, agribusinesses have found it is in their interest to provide small farmers a secure market, a source of credit, and technical assistance.

Chile's new democratic government is continuing a broad commitment to market-oriented reforms but is also responding to the apparent need to expand the supporting government role. Thus, while privatization has an important role to play in most developing countries, it must be understood in context, and does not succeed by simply banishing government from the economic scene.

Privatization in Chile proceeded over several overlapping stages. In 1974 and 1975, 360 firms that had been nationalized in the early 1970s were returned to their previous owners; most of the rest of these were reprivatized by 1978. This was far easier to accomplish than the privatizations of long-term SOEs carried out by Chile in subsequent years. Of the 110 enterprises divested from 1975 to 1983, a large share were SOEs formed in the Allende regime of the early 1970s. Many others were existing private companies in which that government had bought a percentage of the outstanding shares.

From 1978 to 1981, privatization of social services commenced; government officially continued to provide social services only for the poorest citizens, and focused on subsidizing demand rather than supply. By 1981, public enterprises represented 24% of GDP, down from 39% in 1973.

Chile experienced rapid growth in the 1976 to 1981 period following three years of severe recession. But this expansion had the earmarks of a speculative bubble, including wild stock speculation. Financial market deregulation took place too quickly and went too far. After the bubble burst in 1982, stocks crashed (falling 36% in 1982 and an additional 33% in 1983), there was a huge wave of bankruptcies, including a fifth of all manufacturing companies employing over 50 workers; output fell dramatically and unemployment reached 24%. The onset of the debt crisis was a contributing factor. Many of the companies privatized in the 1970s were purchased with a high ratio of debt-to-equity financing. These companies often failed in the recession period, forcing renationalizations in many cases.

From 1983 to 1986, many enterprises "rescued" (nationalized) by Pinochet in the 1982-83 financial crash were reprivatized. Eight of the 15 largest corporations in Chile were privatized in the 1980s. After the Chilean government assumed a large part of the foreign debt in 1983, debt-equity swaps came to play a major role in privatization. Here, considerable use was made of special competitive restrictions and joint venture arrangements, reducing fears of exploitation at the hands of multinational corporations with greater financial sophistication and high bargaining power. From 1986 to 1990, and continuing to the present though at a slower pace, at least 27 large industrial enterprises that had been in state hands for a longer time were privatized.

The renewed growth of the late 1980s and early 1990s had a qualitatively different character, owing to more judicious regulation of the financial system and macroeconomic management. From 1990 to 1995, Chile's gross domestic product rose an average of 7.4% annually. GDP grew 8.5% in 1995 and was projected to grow at around 6.6% in 1996, with the leading sectors being investment and exports.

At the same time, inflation has fallen to about 12%. World Bank data show that annual inflation was about 20% for the 1980-1990 period, and about 130% from 1965 to 1980. Chile's inflation rate was projected to be just 7% in 1996, an impressive achievement in the face of continued rapid growth. One difference between Chile's recent high growth and previous booms is that growth is investment-led rather than consumption-led.

Increasingly, U.S. corporations are producing in Chile not only for the domestic market but for export. Foreign investment continues to flow into Chile in the 1990s, having reached some $1.38 billion by the end of 1992. There is some concern that the rapid inflow will drive up the value of the peso and make exports less competitive, as happened in the late 1970s.

But Chile has experienced an apparently permanent drop in the share of manufacturing in GDP, especially in sectors not intensive in their use of local natural resources. This makes its experience to date different from the long-run top performing countries such as Korea and Taiwan, and may pose a challenge if opportunities for productivity gains are concentrated in manufacturing sectors. On the other hand, in Chile, manufacturing companies were often import substitution industries that were, to say the least, not growing up very fast.

Privatization from the mid-1980s onward was achieved through public auction, negotiation, sales to pension funds, and through "popular capitalism" (to small investors) and "labor capitalism" (to employees). Sales of the latter two types represented about 20% of privatization. Finally, even SOEs not slated for privatization were subject to major internal reorganization with the result that efficiency and profitability increased. A World Bank study suggests that efficiency gains have been made, most dramatically the increased sales after the privatization of Chile Telecom. Of course, these actions were taken in the context of an expanding economy. In addition, the World Bank concluded that the largest part of the gains were realized from expanded freedom to hire and fire workers.

"Popular capitalism" was intended to spread ownership among many small individual investors, in part to increase popularity and acceptance of privatization. To become eligible for generous discounts, participants had to be taxpayers with no back taxes owed. Two major banks, Banco de Chile and Banco de Santiago, were privatized under this plan.

Under labor capitalism, workers could acquire a percentage of shares in their own companies, up to the value of 50% of a worker's pension fund that could be received in advance for this purpose. Retirement funds could be used as collateral for below-market government loans to buy additional shares. At retirement, workers could elect to trade these shares back for the value of their pension fund, so this provided the workers with an essentially riskless investment. About 21,000 workers, 35% of those eligible, took part; other shares were purchased by groups of workers organized as investment societies.

Between 1985 and 1990, 15 SOEs were sold using some employee ownership, including three that became 100% employee-owned. Another three became 44, 33, and 31% employee owned, and the remaining nine had an average of about 12% employee ownership. These privatizations have been remarkably successful. Not only have productivity and share values risen substantially, but employment has risen. Employees seem to be working more conscientiously (e.g., taking better care of company equipment) and, in some cases, firms are allowing workers to use greater judgment on the job.

To date, the conventional wisdom that employee ownership may decrease attractiveness has not been borne out. An example is the National Sugar Industry in Chile, privatized in 1986, in which workers hold a total of 45% of the shares. Despite this, several foreign investors purchased good-sized minority shares, and it is a highly regarded investment. Many U.S.-owned firms are familiar with Employee Stock Ownership Plans and similar programs in the U.S. or other countries, and may have introduced ESOPs themselves or seen firms with which they are familiar do so, precisely to improve labor relations and efficiency. Employee stock purchases represent a positive market signal to other potential investors from a group possessing unique insider information. Employee ownership in privatization may also help countries reduce the drastic increases in inequality that often accompany liberalization.

Inequality has increased in Chile. In 20 years of almost constant "structural adjustment" in Chile, the top 10% has gained but the bottom 90% remains worse off. Absolute poverty has also increased: The Inter-American Development Bank reports that the share of families in the Greater Santiago area living in poverty has grown from about one-third to about one-half from the late 1960s to the late 1980s. The sharpest jump occurred in the 1969 to 1976 period, when the percentage of the poor increased from 28.5 to 57%, a historic high. Poor is defined here as having an income less than twice the cost of the "minimum food basket." When we consider only those whose income is even less than the cost of this basket, poverty grew even more dramatically, from 8.4% in 1969 to 22.6% in 1987 (the last year available), after reaching a high of 24.7% in 1986. The poverty rate was also found to be related to the growth rate of the economy, with a two-year lag. A modest increase in resources targeted to the poorest of the poor has also played a role in mitigating absolute poverty.

In the late 1980s, high growth rates at last were reached—followed by a short slowdown at the start of the 1990s as the economy had become overheated. Poverty and inequality are major concerns of the new democratic government. The Finance Minister, Alejandro Foxley, was one of the most able critics of the excesses of the ultraorthodox economic policies under Pinochet.

Privatization in Chile has been facilitated by the country's liberal trade and investment rules, and by growing confidence in its macroeconomic stability. Dominique Hachette and Rolf Luders present some empirical evidence that Chilean markets were functioning well enough to provide fair sale prices and to induce efficient operation of privatized enterprises.

The two largest remaining SOEs are the national copper company, CODELCO, nationalized in 1971, and the National Oil Refinery, ENAP. These are considered very unlikely candidates for future privatization. A 1981 constitutional court ruling prohibited active copper mines from being nationalized. However, the new government has authorized CODELCO to initiate joint ventures with private companies for projects not currently active or unlikely to proceed without cofinancing. But certain hydroelectric projects are considered possible candidates for privatization in the near future.

Despite the limitations on devising an optimal plan for privatization and market development, privatization is best not implemented as an isolated part of a development strategy, but as part of a general program for market development. The benefits of privatization will not occur automatically. The role of the state in the economy becomes significantly modified, but is certainly not eliminated.

The supporting institutions of the market will have to grow and develop. Privatization is easier when SOEs began as the result of nationalizations, especially recent ones, rather than as government start-ups. Good examples of this are provided by Chile's reprivatizations of the 1970s. Privatization is also easier when markets are already well-developed, when there is strong political will for privatization, and when ordinary employees and citizens perceive themselves to have a positive stake in privatization. The proper balance will vary from country to country and may not be easy to find. Any one country may have to go through years of experimentation before finding the right balance, suited for its own conditions, as the case of Chile reveals.

Indicators are at times conflicting, and Chile's wild swings of expansion and contraction makes an accurate assessment of long-term trends difficult. But it would appear that Chile today is in an excellent position to move toward a "drive to maturity," in Walt Rostow's phrase. The country began a strong emphasis on education and human development in the 1920s; superior conditions of basic education and health survived the dictatorship period, and Chile enjoys the fruits of this long-term program today.

Despite some errors of excess, for which a price was paid in the form of the financial crash, the modern market institutions that are the foundation of a developed economy were successfully created under the Pinochet regime. One repeated criticism was the "lack of transparency in divestitures," as Dominique Hachette and Rolf Luders put it. As a result, rightly or wrongly, many Chileans came to feel that the process of privatization, particularly in its first phase, was financially benefitting favored circles and discriminating against ordinary Chileans. This was partly rectified with the "popular capitalism" and "labor capitalism" programs of the late 1980s.

But while undertaken undemocratically and against the will of the majority, and in a political context of often brutal repression, polls suggest that the core of these market reforms is now accepted by the majority in Chile, and likely will not be reversed under democratic rule. At the same time, the new democratic government is wisely giving greater attention to concerns for equity, reversing the cutbacks in social spending of the Pinochet regime by expanding programs in education, basic health care, nutrition, housing, water, and sewerage. Tax reform passed in the first year of President Aylwin's government raised $1 billion for social projects and better pay for schoolteachers.

The government is also expanding public investment in other vital infrastructure, such as roads, ports, and irrigation systems. It is also beginning to diversify the scope of its moderate industrial and export policies to assist development of manufacturing sectors. A first in Latin America, Chile seems to have permanently tamed inflation. By the mid-1990s, Chile appeared well-positioned economically and socially for successful long-term growth. It has a strongly market-based economy, in which government competently plays an active but targeted role in the areas in which it is most needed.

The country has traveled a rocky road to get there, but today the outlook is very hopeful for Chile's extensively privatized economy, supported where needed by a constructive government role. And, while there may be some doubts about the applicability of the experience of Chile to other countries—for example, it is a modest size country, with a population of only about 13 million—it is an economy that bears watching closely in the coming years.

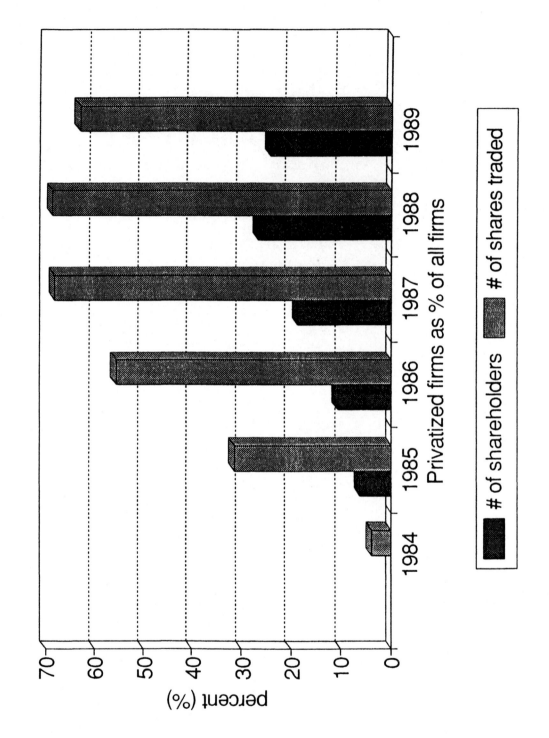

Chile Privatization Shares/Shareholders
Source: CORFO & Stock exchange

Sources

Business America. *Chile: A Status Report on Privatization.* May 18, 1992.

The Economist, June 13, 1992.

Financial Times, Nov. 10, 1992.

Foxley, Alejandro. *Latin American Experiments in Neoconservative Economics.* Berkeley: University of California Press, 1984

Galal, Ahmad et al. *Welfare Consequences of Selling Public Enterprises.* World Bank, 1992.

Hachette, Dominique, and Rolf Luders. *Privatization in Chile: An Economic Appraisal.* San Francisco: ICS, 1993.

Inter-American Development Bank. *Chile: Socioeconomic Report.* Aug. 1991.

Santamaria, Marco. "Privatizing Social Security: The Chilean Case." *Columbia Journal of World Business,* spring (1992): 38–51.

Smith, Stephen C. "Comparative Case Study on Chile and Poland." In Michael Todaro, *Economic Development,* 6th Ed, Reading, MA: Addison-Wesley, 1997.

Smith, Stephen C. "On the Law and Economics of Employee Ownership in Privatization in Developing and Transition Economies." *Annals of Public and Cooperative Economics 65,* no. 3 (1994): 437–468.

Vickers, John, and George Yarrow. "Economic Perspectives on Privatization." *Journal of Economic Perspectives 5,* spring (1991): 111–32.

Wall Street Journal, Jan. 22 and Jan. 25, 1993.

World Bank. "Techniques of Privatization of State-Owned Enterprises." *World Bank Technical Paper 90,* in 3 volumes, 1988.

World Bank. *World Development Report,* 1992.

22. Development on a Large Scale: Sri Lanka's Mahaveli River Project

Julie Brinker contributed to this case study

The Mahaveli Development Project provides an excellent case study of what the state can do to foster large-scale economic development, and also of the importance both of utilizing market forces and popular participation in decision-making to bring such development projects to fruition.

For many years, Sri Lanka has had a reputation as one of the most forward-looking of the poorer developing countries. The island nation was widely known and respected internationally for implementing progressive systems of health care and education. Despite modest achievements in economic growth—GNP per capita is still just $540—Sri Lanka has made remarkable progress in eradicating absolute poverty. Its literacy rate is almost 90%, some 93% of the population has access to health services, and life expectancy is 72 years.

For the last several years, however, Sri Lanka has found itself in the news most often for the sometimes violent conflict between the predominantly Buddhist majority Sinhalese and the predominantly Hindu Tamil minority, who settled on the island over the last several hundred years from the nearby Indian state of Tamil Nadu. Tamil separatists, sometimes holding some legitimate grievances, have been active since 1983, drawing scarce government funds into the defense budget and scaring off foreign investors. The country's development efforts have been sorely tried as a result. The achievements of one major such effort is all the more impressive as a result.

The Mahaveli Development Project is an ambitious attempt to manage Sri Lanka's largest river, the Mahaveli, while providing for an extensive system of irrigation and hydroelectric power. (A common alternative spelling is Mahaweli; the phonetic variant is adopted here.) The project was begun in 1967 after the completion of a major UN study of the utilization of national water resources that had been requested by Sri Lanka. The United Nations Development Program (UNDP) had surveyed an area spanning 39% of Sri Lanka's total land area (6.32 million acres), including 55% of its dry zone. The study proposed that the waters of the Mahaveli River be diverted into this dry zone; Sri Lanka decided to implement the project over a three phase, 30-year period. At the end of this period, the irrigated portion of the island was to be increased by 70%, bringing the total irrigated area from .94 million acres to 1.59 million acres. Another quarter million acres would benefit from improved irrigation.

Interestingly, in implementing the project, engineers laying out channels for the irrigation system found the archeological remains of ancient irrigation systems. So development planners past and present have adopted similar strategies and even went about implementing them in similar ways.

Implementation of the Mahaveli Development Project raises many of the most important issues in economic development. The project was intended to address agricultural development, education, infrastructure, unemployment, and international trade problems. It is administered by two agencies, the Mahaveli Engineering and Construction Agency, and the Mahaveli Economic Agency (MEA), responsible for resettlement and economic development in the zone, including research, agricultural extension, and marketing. The total cost of the project is expected to be approximately $3 billion, supported in large part by some 15 bilateral and multilateral development agencies. The plan includes 15 dams, of which eight would have power stations; a ninth power station would be located on a transbasin canal. By 1995, the system already produced over 40% of the island's hydroelectric power, while hydro power is the source of most of the country's electricity production.

Sri Lanka's hydro power has been widely touted as an sensible alternative to costly dependence on foreign oil. In fact, dependence on hydro power has come with its own problems. In 1996, a severe drought led to drastic declines in hydro power output, with costs felt by industry as well as consumers. In the future, Sri Lanka plans to turn to a more even balance between hydro and thermal and perhaps solar sources of power, at least to provide the economy with backup power in the event of another drought.

In addition, the ecological impact of the hydro projects were never given proper consideration in decision making, and indeed has never been fully calculated; environment was not a major concern in the design and implementation of the Mahaveli system. New projects of this kind in Sri Lanka or virtually anywhere else in the developing world would undoubtedly be subject to far greater local and international environmental review than those begun a generation ago.

One purpose of the project was to assist Sri Lanka in its drive to diversify its economy through an increase in the manufacturing sector. Another goal was "food self-sufficiency." In the early 1960s, Sri Lanka imported about 30% of its rice supplies, the chief staple food of the country. More than half of the labor force worked in the agricultural sector, and the ratio of farmers to farmland area was high and labor productivity low; thus the project was seen as an important opportunity to boost rice production, productivity, incomes, and employment (or to reduce underemployment). This case study will focus on the impact of the project on small-scale development, particularly on settlers in drylands newly opened up by Mahaveli irrigation.

The project study found that 1.5 million acres were suitable for irrigation, of which about 1.2 million acres were underdeveloped forest or dry lands owned by the State and the remaining 300,000 acres were already under some cultivation. Water resources were calculated to be sufficient for about 900,000 acres on a year-round basis. Areas already under cultivation were to have first priority. Irrigation would require 14 irrigation systems under the plan; eight would be located in the Mahaveli and Maduru basins to irrigate 470,000 acres, and the remaining six would be in the north central part of the program area.

In the newly cultivated lands, each settler receives an approximately two-and-a-half acre irrigable plot of farmland, and a half-acre homestead on higher ground. The plot size is designed to support a family with 6.5 persons on average. In addition to the small farms, some more mechanized medium-size farms of about 15 acres, and larger-size farms of 200 to 5000 acres, were designed to demonstrate advanced farming methods and promote greater production. Both residential and hired labor would be used. The plan was to encourage double and, in some cases, triple cropping and improved agricultural practices in both new and existing irrigable areas. Combining new acreage with an increase in the number of crops harvested each year from one to two or three, total crop acreage was projected to increase from 340,000 to about 1,800,000—a more than five-fold increase in all.

The planned settlements designed each village as a composite of 400 to 500 households dispersed into four or five satellite units. The centrally located village would be the site of the supporting services for its surrounding area. The entire scheme had a fractal-like structure in which sub-settlements would be located within larger settlements.

The first project of the master plan, the Polgolla Division, was initiated in 1970. With its completion along with the Bowatenna complex in 1976, 128,000 acres of existing rice paddy areas in the Anurdhapura, Polonnaura, and Tricomalee districts benefitted. An additional 71,000 acres of new land was irrigated in the Kandalama and Kalawewa areas. By 1988, nearly 56,000 families had moved in and settled in new areas throughout the project area.

A major decision to accelerate the Mahaveli plan was reached in 1977, in part due to the impact of the energy crisis on the Sri Lankan economy. The Mahaveli project was a way of both cutting down on the demand for oil, providing for more import substitution, and increasing exports. A separate Ministry of Mahaveli development was put in place at this time. Over 60% of project costs were met with foreign aid contributions, mostly in the form of outright grants.

To date, over 50,000 farm families have already been resettled in former dryland areas now irrigated with water from the river. This entailed a massive infrastructure project of its own, as towns, roads and agricultural storage and distribution systems had to be constructed from scratch. By 1994, the zone provided about 25% of Sri Lanka's rice crop, its share having risen steadily since 1978. The zone also produces more than half the dried chilies and about 20% of other crops. Moreover, the yield per acre in the Mahaveli region is now higher than the national average.

The average family income is estimated to be two-and-a-half times what it was before the project, on average. A study of the left bank of the pioneering settlement System H found that inequality had decreased significantly while more than 60% of the settlers were earning incomes that were greater than 98% of the rural population. This does indicate a significant success. Of course, this may also suggest that development benefits have been overly concentrated on the minority of families fortunate enough to become part of the project.

The Mahaveli Development Project was a pioneer in settler participation in decision making, which was portrayed in a widely praised Nova public television program in the late 1980s. The irrigation system was suffering badly from lack of public participation. Such matters as the timing and amounts of water discharges through the canals and crop selection were decided by Mahaveli officials with virtually no input from the affected farmers. The results included theft of water by those near the main canals (headenders) and great scarcity of water for those unfortunate enough to have a farm located near the end of a canal branch (tailenders). Moreover, government proved unable to ensure timely delivery of needed inputs such as fertilizers, seeds, and chemicals.

Eventually, in part at the advice of some of the donor agencies, the MEA turned to farmer participation plans. Responsibility has been shifted to farmers, with the official goal of substantial participation—albeit short of real self-management—in such matters as local water management, crop selection, and marketing. Much remains to be done in this area. The government still maintains many smaller, downstream ditches, and local peasants might do a better job of local maintenance. A fee structure for the use of water might begin to replace the extensive management oversight costs.

Planning now starts at the basic level of the Unit Block; results are combined with input from each unit and are finally aggregated to the MEA's Master Plan. Among the major goals for future development are greater agricultural diversification, including fisheries, poultry, and milk production activities. The Draft Animal and Dairy Development Program has been working to upgrade practices of keeping farm animals as well as to expand the market for dairy products.

One major reason for the promotion of agricultural diversification is the growing scarcity of water. Rice paddy is a very water-intensive crop. As more and more irrigated areas are opened up by the Mahaveli Project, this leaves fewer potential gallons of water per farm. In addition, crop rotation is beneficial to protect the soil quality and prevent paddy areas from becoming a source of disease and pests. Among the new crops that have been promoted among the farmers are black and green grams, chilies, corn, cowpea, gingelly, peanuts, and yams. Fresh fruits and vegetables are now understood to offer greater potential profitability and are being actively promoted. In addition to education and training, the MEA also provides production inputs and help with storage and marketing of alternative crops.

The MEA has declared its intention to provide credit, sometimes using guarantees through the Peoples' Bank, Bank of Ceylon, and the Hatton National Bank. However, only a small fraction of settlers have used these facilities, and the MEA is uncertain as to the reasons. However, little use seems to have been made of peer-based credit union lending on the Grameen Bank model (see Case 5); instead, frustrating attempts to use major commercial banks with special facilities have continued. As many governments around the world have done, eventually Sri Lanka may realize that the Grameen model may point in the direction of a strategy for credit development that would be consistent with the move to decentralize decisions and encourage settler participation in all aspects of the program that directly affect them.

An innovative dimension of the program is the creation of Export Promotion Villages (EPVs). For example, the Kalawewa Mahaveli EPV produces green chilies for export to the Middle East, and won a presidential award for excellence in export promotion in 1987.

Agencies such as USAID have been focusing on encouraging greater entrepreneurship of Mahaveli settlers, including business training, provision of credit, and office support services. The initial focus has been commercial agriculture, but an expansion into service and craft sectors is foreseen. Most employment expansion had been expected and targeted for larger agribusiness, though services were to be made available to all settlers. A study commissioned by USAID found that a relatively low level of services was really being directed to the poorer microentrepreneurs. Yet in a result that neither donor agencies nor the Sri Lankan government apparently expected, despite comparable experience around the world, most employment has been created in small firms; only some 15% of jobs were created in medium and large firms, well below targets.

One area for small entrepreneurs is in all manner of services to support the farming sector, the maintenance and improvement of equipment, in some cases even small scale manufacturing. Over 500 new self-employment projects have begun along side numerous new enterprise developments. Training programs for such ventures outside of agriculture have also been developed. As of 1993, the training facilities cover staff, settler, and second-generation training, with a total participation by 1993 of 131,945. For example, there are programs for women settler farmers, youth skill development programs, and middle-management training for staff. Not surprisingly, studies have found that assistance works best when it is based on actual client demands, not formulated by distant policymakers.

The government reports that by 1993, in part as a result of the acceleration program, 120,067 families had been settled in the Mahaveli areas, including 31,934 non-farm families. A total of 112,328 hectares, or 277,450 acres, have been developed under irrigated agriculture. A 1995 study found that a total of 56 Sri Lankan rupees had been spent on the project up to mid-1993, of which Rs. 30 billion were in the form of foreign aid. The recovered costs in agriculture and power generation have reached Rs. 57, without even considering important social benefits, such as a higher standard of living for participating families.

Paddy remains the major crop in both seasons and all systems except system H, where the emphasis during the Yala season is now on cultivation of other crops, mainly chilies. But heavy export taxes and perhaps other factors have led to stagnation in tea, rubber, and coconut plantation crops. This is a serious problem, because other countries such as Thailand appear to have the international comparative advantage in rice, and further moves to diversification would benefit the economy. Thus, while some useful steps toward export promotion have been taken by the Mahaveli project, a serious look needs to be taken at the incentives of the economy as a whole. Continued protection of rice may send the wrong signals to farmers. Moreover, the limited size of the domestic market and inadequate technologies have offset some productivity and quality gains in rice paddy.

The Mahaveli project has been generally successful, but new issues are always coming to the fore. A new and growing dilemma is how to employ the second and third generations of these farming families, because the allotted plots cannot be viably divided into smaller plots. Inheritance laws actually state that the holding cannot be fragmented, leaving only a single child as legal inheritor. According to USAID, some of these disinherited children and their families have slipped into poverty. One solution is to increase the level of training for these young people. But employment has not been sufficient even for trained workers.

Lack of a clear property rights structure may pose difficult problems. Private ownership is very rare in many parts of the country. The government owns large tracts of land on which squatters are permitted to farm. Government often legitimizes these squatters by giving them some form of legal claim on lands they have worked for some time. This has obvious advantages in addressing absolute poverty, but also discourages agribusiness ventures on public land, something the government has said it wishes to encourage. Some trade-offs will have to be made here, for example, in the use of other antipoverty programs—a case where the government cannot have it both ways. Unclear property rights also creates problems for small and large farmers alike in securing credit, and provides disincentives to make investments in improving the land.

It is also worth noting that it is now clear that costs of maintaining the system were greatly underestimated. Needed repairs and maintenance are sometimes going unheeded. Still, the economy has benefitted from this massive project. Further progress will require well-prepared liberalization and further emphasis on market incentives and diversification of production and exports.

The ethnic conflict between Tamils and Sinhalese continues, and does have some unfortunate spillover to the Mahaveli system. Due to the conflict, the northern portion of the project area, designated for Tamil settlement, has not been pursued. But the Tamils see this as yet another case of discrimination, in which income becomes more concentrated among the Sinhalese.

Another area that needs closer attention is environmental impact. Part of this concern is at the national level, involving the Mahaveli Engineering and Construction Agency, so it is outside the focus of this case study. But it is worth noting that much damming has occurred, and significant amounts of water have already been diverted from the island's major river. A significant amount of soil salinization has occurred and has caused a decrease in usable land in system H. Poor land use management there has caused soil erosion. Uncontrolled expansion of squatter-cultivators is jeopardizing watershed management by cutting down the vegetative cover in critical areas and eroding the soil. Poor management practices on tea plantations are contributors as well. Encroachment on elephant territory has occurred, and significant deforestation of ecologically critical areas has proceeded apace. Recent studies have shown that the irrigated areas are using about twice as much water as originally projected.

Beyond the adverse impact of the hydro projects, environmental issues are also of concern at the grassroots level, in the daily lives of those who have moved to the newly-irrigated areas. Poor farming practices may cause soil nutrients to be lost, for example. Today, a reforestation program has been implemented, and plans are underway for the installation of 35 kilometers of electric fencing by the Wild Elephant Hazard Program. It remains to be seen how effective these measures will prove in practice.

Sources

Alexis, L. "Sri Lank's Mahaweli Scheme: The Damnation of Paradise." *The Ecologist,* Sept./Oct. 1984: 206–215.

Attanayake, Abhaya. *Mahaweli Saga: Challenge and Response.* Colombo, Sri Lanka: State Printing Corp., 1985.

Ekayanake, S. A. B. "Location Specificity, Settler Type and Productive Efficiency: A Study of the Mahaweli Project in Sri Lanka." *Journal of Development Studies* July 1987: 509–521.

Embassy of Sri Lanka. *Mahaweli Programme,* 1993; various interviews.

Fields, Gary. *Poverty Inequality and Development.* New York: Cambridge University Press, 1980.

Jawardena, Jayantha, ed. *Impacts and New Directions in Agriculture: The Mahaveli Experience.* Mahaveli Economic Agency, 1993.

Karunatillake, Dingi. *A Study of Socio-Economic Conditions and Investment Potentialities of the Settlers of the Mahaweli Development Project.* Colombo: Sri Lanka: Peoples' Bank, 1977.

Mendis, M. W. J. G. *The Planning Implications of the Mahaweli Development Project in Sri Lanka.* Colombo, Sri Lanka: Lake House Investment Ltd., 1973.

Ministry of Mahaweli Development. *Mahaweli Projects and Programme.* Colombo, Sri Lanka: State Printing Corp., 1988.

Ministry of Mahaweli Development. *Mahaweli Projects and Programme.* Colombo, Sri Lanka: State Printing Corp., 1985.

Ministry of Mahaweli Development. *Mahaweli Projects and Programme.* Colombo, Sri Lanka: State Printing Corp., 1982.

Raby, Namika. *Professional Management in Irrigation Systems: A Case Study of Performance Control in Mahaweli System H.* Colombo, Sri Lanka: Aitken Spence Printing, 1989.

Richards, Peter, and Wilber Gooneratne. *Basic Needs, Poverty and Government Policies in Sri Lanka.* Geneva, Switzerland: ILO, 1980.

Siriwardhana, S. S. A. L. *Emerging Income Inequalities and Forms of Hidden Tenancy in the Mahaweli H Area.* Colombo, Sri Lanka: Peoples' Bank, 1981.

U.S. AID. *Development in Sri Lanka: A Review,* 1991.

U.S. AID, various project assistance documents.

World Bank. *World Development Report,* various years.

World Bank. Interviews with South Asian Dept. staff.

23. Tax Reform in Bolivia

Developing countries almost always face a difficult task in raising tax revenues. Accounting is often rudimentary or nonexistent, and tax evasion is common. As a result, governments have resorted to the use of highly distortionary methods of raising revenues, such as taxes on exports, which can in effect be counted on the dock, and inflation taxes, enforced through financial repression (see Michael Todaro, chapter 17).

In recent years, many developing countries have undertaken tax reform. From experiences before and after tax reforms, development economists have learned some important things.

First, it does not work to impose tax policy strictly on the basis of Ramsey rules and other staples of conventional optimal taxation theory. (The Ramsey rule is to equalize the "deadweight loss" per unit of tax revenue, to minimize the efficiency cost of taxation.) In developing countries particularly, feasibility and costs of collection of each type of tax proposed must play an important role in the choice of tax instruments. In other words, as Joel Slemrod has put it, we must consider "optimal tax systems" rather than "optimal taxes" in the abstract. Thus the "technology of tax collection" must be considered, which includes the cost of tax administration and enforcement of compliance.

One finding is that "fiscal carrots" seem to work better than "fiscal sticks." Another is that the value added tax, or VAT, may not be the best tax in theory, but it is usually the best tax in LDC practice. It costs less to administer, results in better compliance at least at modest tax rates, is at least not strongly regressive in that large consumers pay proportionately more, and provides an incentive for saving. More broadly, tax reform is best introduced in conjunction with other trade, macroeconomic, and monetary reforms, which should be developed pragmatically and flexibly. Spending reform must proceed in tandem with tax reform. But too extreme an adherence to purely orthodox or to the various "heterodox" alternatives is fraught with danger.

Serious tax reform is exceedingly difficult to implement. It becomes politically feasible only in the most dire economic circumstances. When such windows of opportunity open, they must be used quickly, before they shut. Finally, tax reform is never really complete. Whatever is achieved must be guarded vigilantly. Unfortunately, all tax systems lead to perverse incentives and have other serious drawbacks. All tax systems are compromises across objectives of simplicity, compliance, fairness and, of course, producing adequate government revenue.

One of the most dramatic overhauls of a developing country tax system took place in Bolivia. The Bolivian experience illustrates these tax reform principles and pitfalls.

In the early- to mid-1980s, Bolivia was widely perceived as one of the world's basket-case economies. The world recession and the effects of the debt crisis hit Bolivia hard. Official unemployment was over 17%. The government printed money in lieu of collecting taxes and inflation reached a peak annual rate of 24,000% during 1985. Inflation had been 4,000% for just the first seven months of that year. The import of Bolivian currency, which was printed abroad, became a significant part of the import bill. Debt servicing consumed a growing portion of export revenues. There was a complete lack of faith in the Bolivian peso, and the U.S. dollar had effectively replaced it as a store of value and unit of account—what is called "currency substitution." Many factors led to this result. The debt crisis was a proximate cause, which resulted from the unchecked borrowing of foreign money by a military dictatorship in the 1970s.

The elected government that followed in the early 1980s was mandated to reduce Bolivia's startling inequality, but was unable to achieve this, and social strife proliferated. Manuel Pastor has argued that the government simply had few degrees of freedom given inflexibility on debt repayment in this period.

The political economy of civil strife led to a total loss of fiscal discipline. In the mid-1980s, the government collected a mere 1% of GNP in taxes, a fiscal policy of "all spending and no taxes." The large budget deficits that followed were the proximate cause of the hyperinflation and subsequent economic collapse.

In 1986, the newly elected government of President Victor Paz Estenssoro was able to pass a complete overhaul of the tax system, as well as a wide range of other market liberalization measures. Together these reforms were known as the New Economic Policy. A dramatic tax reform was approved in mid-1986, to become operational one year later. Paz coupled this reform with the toughest balanced budget fiscal policy on record: each day, government would authorize payments of only as much as it was collecting in taxes. The policy was presided over by the tough planning minister, Gonzalo Sanchez de Lozada, one of Bolivia's richest citizens. Bolivia became one of the vanguards of the 1980s marketization movement.

Thanks in large part to tax reform, Bolivia's government budget deficit has been brought under control, and the hyperinflation that derived from it eliminated. Eventually, growth was restored—but at a big upfront cost of income declines, and a seemingly permanent legacy of widened inequality.

One goal of the Bolivian "tax revolution," as it is called, is to use some parts of the tax system to gain information that may be useful in enforcing other parts of the system. This is a potentially important aspect of designing an optimal "tax system" as a whole.

Most developing countries have a hard time collecting sales taxes. Individuals and storekeepers often collude in tax evasion, splitting the savings from not paying sales taxes. Taxes are hard to enforce if records of sales are not kept.

Under the Bolivian tax reform, there is a 10% withholding tax on income from all sources—but this tax can be offset to the extent that individuals furnish proof of having paid VAT taxes in that amount. This proof is normally in the form of a sales receipt. These receipts can then be used by the new Ministerio de Recaudaciones (Ministry of Tax Collections) to do spot checks on the honesty of retail stores. This is an excellent example of a "fiscal carrot," or positive incentive to play by the tax rules, as distinct from the "fiscal stick" of legal sanctions. Another is the elimination of direct contact between low-level tax officials, who were notoriously easy to bribe in Bolivia under the old system, and taxpayers.

Commercial banks have been enlisted to collect taxes. They get to see the tax returns of their customers, and as an incentive receive 0.8% of taxes they collect. The creation of a new ministry to enforce tax laws acted as a signal to Bolivians that tax avoidance would no longer be taken lightly. Harsh penalties have been introduced for fraud. Most impressively, a tax registration campaign more than doubled the number of officially enrolled business taxpayers (though there is no rigorous evidence that this new registrant information has itself been effectively used to increase compliance).

Tax simplification was an important part of the reforms. Most importantly, individual and corporate income taxes were abolished and replaced with a VAT; companies were to pay a flat 2% tax on net worth (this was later increased to 2.5%). The old system was simply too complex for Bolivia to administer. The income withholding and rebate is used only to ensure compliance with VAT rules. Further, small taxes whose collection costs were high and were easily flouted were eliminated.

Tariff collection is not an efficient source of government revenue, as it can be highly distortionary. Countries that cannot find the political will to use tariff protection as a highly selective and strictly temporary instrument of industrial policy in cases where large, identified market failures can be shown to exist, are probably better off abandoning this instrument altogether. A uniform tariff of 20% was adopted, later reduced to just

10%. The government of Bolivia has become much less dependent on tariffs as a source of revenue. Thus, the incentive for protected firms to produce for the home market rather than for export has been reduced.

Another new measure is a 1% transactions tax. One goal is to collect information that could be useful in other aspects of tax enforcement. This is simple to administer, but causes high rates of tax on sectors that have a very low degree of vertical integration. By the same token, it also creates incentives for an inefficiently large level of vertical integration mergers, both to avoid the tax and to avoid providing the government with information.

Equity concerns are always an issue in designing a tax system. Equity and efficiency do not always represent trade-offs in development, as the earlier case study of girls' education demonstrates. Unfortunately, the tax system is one place where we are often presented with a harsh tradeoff. Progressive taxation is fair, and provides taxation with wide political legitimacy. But steeply progressive taxation leads to rampant tax evasion (legal and illegal) by high-income taxpayers, and distorts economic decisions such as where and how much to invest. Complex tax codes encourage tax avoidance and corruption. Lower and flatter marginal tax rates are easier to administer and enforce.

On the other hand, very low marginal tax rates for the very rich are politically unsustainable in virtually all countries, as the recent experience in the United States demonstrates. Tax codes biased in favor of the rich may contribute to inequality, and inequality may lead to lower growth. Once issues like tax rates are reopened, so too are the doors for new tax breaks and loopholes for well-connected interest groups; and efficiency gains may prove fleeting.

There is no science of tax rate progressivity. A progressive structure must be chosen that is perceived as fair but is not so steep that it produces large distortions in economic behavior. A tax code must be written that is simple but recognizes that some activities, such as equipment investment, should be treated differently from other activities such as company perks.

But the case of Bolivia is dramatic. By abolishing the income tax altogether, and replacing it with a VAT, Bolivia is open to the charge of abandoning progressivity altogether (and perhaps creating regressivity). A progressive tax on real estate and vehicles does partially compensate, however. Moreover, Bolivia's previous tax system, while nominally progressive, was flagrantly violated by the rich, and the code may have well been significantly regressive in practice.

Another question is whether nonprogressivity on the revenue (tax) side can be balanced by progressivity on the expenditure side, that is, whether the government spends more money proportionately on important services for the poor, such as agricultural extension, basic education, prenatal and infant nutrition, and so on. Even so, it remains to be seen if the lack of an income tax for the very rich is politically sustainable in Bolivia. Widespread complaints, which are essentially arguments that the tax system is not progressive enough, can be heard voiced throughout the country.

Major efforts have been made to reduce corruption by reportedly more honest parts of the bureaucracy, such as the Comptroller-General's office, which is armed with tough new auditing powers. But forces of corruption, including resurgent power of drug traffickers, are proving tenacious in Bolivia as in much of Latin America.

Certainly Bolivia's tax and broader market reforms have achieved some important successes. Inflation was only 9% in 1992, lowest in Latin America in that year. In 1993, Sanchez de Lozada was elected president in a free election, which shows that making politically daring decisions like implementing tax increases and cutting wasteful government spending does not have to mean political suicide. If reform ultimately brings an overall improvement for most voters, they will forgive their loss of specific benefits—at least if politicians are also astute at making grand political gestures, such as naming a native Bolivian as his vice-presidential running mate, as Sanchez de Lozada did in Victor Hugo Cardenas. Sanchez de Lozada has ambitious growth targets and a "popular capitalism" privatization plan that would distribute substantial proceeds to the Bolivian people.

By 1990, the government was collecting 14% of GNP in taxes, up from 1% five years earlier. GDP growth has been positive but modest: 2.2% in 1987, 2.8% in 1988, and 2.5% in 1989. But with population growth close to 3%, real GNP per capita was still declining several years into the program. In the 1990s, Bolivia continues to struggle economically, though the bleak period of the 1980s has clearly been left behind. By 1996, Bolivia had logged a decade of steady growth, with inflation under control and the currency stable, despite banking-sector problems. The consumer inflation rate for Bolivia in 1994 was just 8.5%. But despite the tax reform, fiscal balance is under continued threat, and the government stays afloat partly thanks to the considerable multilateral development assistance it receives.

The World Bank has described Bolivian poverty as at "sub-Saharan levels." The main exports are still tin, natural gas, and, despite efforts to eradicate it, cocaine. Balance of payments problems have not been successfully resolved.

The promise of restored growth of the Bolivian "tax revolution" and related market reforms has yet to be fully realized. After a decade, the jury is still out on Bolivian tax reform and the wider political and economic transformation of which it is a part.

Sources

Abente, Diego. "The Political Economy of Tax Reform in Venezuela." *Comparative Politics* (Jan. 1990): 199–216.

Bird, Richard M. "Tax Reform in Latin America: A Review of Some Recent Experiences." *Latin American Research Review 27,* no. 1, 1992: 7–36.

Cabezas, Ramiro. "Bolivia's Tax Reform of 1986." *Tax Notes International 2* (1990): 529–39.

The Economist, various issues.

Financial Times, various issues.

Gillis, Malcolm, et al., eds. *Tax Reform in Developing Countries.* Durham, NC: Duke University Press, 1989.

Khalilzadeh, Javid, and Anwar Shah, eds. "A Symposium on Tax Policy in Developing Countries." *World Bank Economic Review 5,* no. 3 (1991): 459–573.

Mann, Arthur P. "Bolivia: Tax Reform 1986-89." *Bulletin for International Fiscal Documentation 44* (1990): 32–35.

Musgrave, Richard. "Fiscal Reform in Bolivia." processed, Harvard Law School, 1981.

Newbery, David, and Nicholas H. Stern, eds. *The Theory of Taxation for Developing Countries,* New York: Oxford, 1987.

Pastor, Manuel. *Inflation, Stabilization and Debt: Macroeconomic Experients in Peru and Bolivia.* Boulder, CO: Westview, 1992.

Slemrod, Joel. "Optimal Taxation and Optimal Tax Systems." Journal of Economic Perspectives 4 (winter 1990): 157–78.

Michael Todaro, *Economic Development,* 6th Ed., Reading, MA: Addison-Wesley, 1997.

24. Property Rights Reform: China's Township and Village Enterprises

In many LDCs, the dominant system of manufacturing has been large public or quasi-public enterprises operated either directly by government ministries or by independent management. These firms are know as state-owned enterprises (SOEs). The dominance of SOEs in manufacturing has been particularly prevalent in China until the current market reforms. The world's largest developing country has been governed by the Chinese Communist Party since 1949.

There are several crucial roles for government in developing countries, including health, environment, education, and infrastructure, but there is an emerging consensus that governments should generally avoid direct involvement in the production process. In agreement with this broad consensus, many developing countries have been selling off their SOEs to private investors. (For a discussion of issues concerning privatization, see the Comparative Case Study on in Chile and Poland in Michael Todaro, *Economic Development,* 6th Ed., 1996, pgs. 669–675.)

However, China has avoided privatization, despite the large subsidies its SOEs consume. As Wing Thye Woo and his colleagues conclude, recent experience strongly implies that the traditional Chinese state-owned firm is not the optimal form for achieving modernization and development. Gary Jefferson, Thomas Rawski, and Yuxin Zheng showed that when financial rewards and decision-making initiative are decentralized to plant managers, performance of Chinese firms has improved but serious incentive problems remain.

In addition to private enterprise, the Township and Village Enterprises (TVEs) represent a quasi-public alternative enterprise form in China. These are firms regulated at the local township or village level, rather than by the central or provincial government. The phenomenal growth of TVEs in China, with an average annual growth rate of output of over 30% in the 1981–94 period, has begun to draw much international attention. These firms employed about 25 million workers when China's market-oriented reforms began in 1978. By 1990, TVEs employed over 90 million workers, about 17 percent of China's total labor force. This figure rose to some 112 million workers by 1993, and the best current estimate is a total employment of some 125 million, far outnumbering those employed by the SOEs.

Some 60% of TVE employees are estimated to work in industry. Of these industrial employees, approximately 60%—about 32 million—work in "collective" industrial enterprises closely affiliated with township and village government. In 1990, these firms represented about 80% of the gross value of output of TVEs. They have no designated owners, though they are implicitly owned by the people in its local community. Before reforms, managers can in many cases be appointed by the village chief, and may be subject to the chief's intervention in management decisions. The TVE's capital cannot be transferred or sold. Profits are not disbursed, except as wages, retained earnings, and local government taxation income.

Property rights refers to the legal right to decide on the use of assets, to benefit from the income that derives from them, and to dispose of the asset. This sometimes but not always is determined by who owns the shares in a company. Such rights are sometimes held by different individuals or legal entities. In some countries and for some purposes, these rights are explicitly defined by law and regulation; in other cases they may rest on implicit understandings.

A key feature of China's market reforms is to make vaguely defined property rights more clear and explicit. There are three important actors involved in TVEs: workers, managers, and local government officials. One of the most striking features of these TVEs is their hybrid institutional form. While in effect municipally owned, they also share features with both conventional private firms and employee-owned industrial cooperatives. Effective pay appears to be linked to firm performance, and both managers and regular employees appear to have considerable say in enterprise decisions. In practice, TVE employees have ownership rights to a share of the profits and ultimate disposal of assets, but these are not explicit (in other words, they have de facto but not necessarily de jure property rights). Despite management and employee control over short-run decisions, local authorities appear to closely guide, or at least have veto power over, many strategic decisions.

A major accepted model for property rights reform is the so-called cooperative shareholding system, in which some shares may remain collectively held by all implicit owners, some may be explicitly held by employees and management, and some may be held by outside investors. Some special forms require that all owners play a part in the production process. Tian estimated that by 1994, about 10% of collective TVEs had adopted this reform to some extent.

The unusual institutional features of TVEs might be little more than a curiosity if not for the dramatic, unplanned growth and current prevalence of TVEs in the Chinese economy. This record of success raises some basic questions. Would conventional ideas about property rights have predicted this development? What role do independent management and municipal authorities play in the management of these systems? Is this form of enterprise merely a temporary phase in the transition between plan and market in China? Or do TVEs have some features of long-term benefit to the Chinese economy?

It is not hard to make a case that the TVEs' system of de facto property rights (or property rights in practice) are closer to those of Western corporations than are traditional Chinese SOEs. In particular, the public officials ultimately responsible are "closer to the ground," and so can better monitor TVE performance. And those local officials charged with monitoring firms are more likely to reap a larger share of the rewards from their monitoring efforts. When central controls began to be loosened from 1978 onward, these local firms, which had long experience trying to secure inputs and markets without assistance from the planning authorities, were more agile than the long dependent SOEs. No doubt these differences represent some of the explanation for the superior productivity and financial performance of TVEs over SOEs. Studies differ on whether there has been substantial total factor productivity growth progress among SOEs in recent years (Compare Svejnar, in Byrd and Lin (1990), with Woo et al. (1994)), but the superior performance of TVEs over SOEs has not been put in doubt by any study to date.

It is much less clear whether TVEs' property rights advantages over SOEs can serve to explain TVEs' superior absolute performance when measured against comparatively unfettered private enterprise in other developing economies. Some observers have found TVE growth to be too sustained and consistent to be explained by a once-for-all shift resulting from market liberalization: these dynamic efficiencies are apparently greater than seen in any type of firm in East Asia. In other words, the TVE enterprise form might have advantages beyond the simple observation that they look more like free enterprise than do SOEs. And cultural explanations, such as the traditionally cooperative nature of economic life in Chinese villages, may offer insights but do not seem sufficient to explain TVEs' outstanding record.

One alternative explanation would be that TVEs directly or indirectly reward the efforts of those who work in them, in a manner similar to employee-owned firms in Western economies. Such employee-owned firms, while still comparatively rare, enjoy an impressive record of efficient performance and rapid growth. It might improve the efficiency of Chinese TVEs to make these *de facto* property rights explicit—and stable over time—through partial employee ownership.

To put the matter somewhat differently, the advantages of markets over central planning are quite obvious. But does it follow that the traditional, purely wage-paying corporation is thus the best alternative model for firm reorganization in a country such as China? Most Western economies are moving toward much more "participatory" forms of enterprise.

In the past decade there has been an enormous expansion in the number and variety of employee stock ownership plans, profit and gain sharing, and decision-making participation arrangements throughout the OECD economies.

There is some evidence that the growth rate of employment in TVEs has slowed in recent years while output growth has remained high (see Ody, 1992). These changes reflect rapid total factor productivity growth and increased capital-labor ratios and at least in part reflect improvements in TVEs' efficiency. But they may also reflect a reluctance of employed "insiders" to share economic rents with unemployed "outsiders," one of the major hazards to be watched for under effective majority employee control of firms.

On the other hand, the earlier extraordinary growth of employment in TVEs—and their continued rapid growth by world standards—may indicate that employment is an objective of TVEs or their township and village governors. This employment objective does not seem to extend beyond the local township or village, however. Where TVEs are at their most developed, closer to the coast, unemployment of local citizens is a much smaller problem than what is found further west.

These questions were recently explored through eight case studies of TVEs in Zhejiang Province on central coastal China. Experiences of employee participation in equity ownership, profit and gain sharing, and decision-making participation in Township and Village Enterprises (TVEs) in China during the current property rights reform efforts were examined, along with management and municipal attitudes to property rights reform. While the evolving property rights reform in TVEs, including the employee role, differs from region to region, the issues faced in Zhejiang are similar to those faced elsewhere in China. Moreover, as Zhejiang Province tends to be more advanced in its reforms than elsewhere in rural China, some general perspective is gained from an in-depth look at the evolution of TVE organization in that region. Little is known in the west about TVEs, especially on crucial reform matters as examined here, and thus the role of this information is very important; this case study will refer to specific firms visited for this reason.

The TVE site visits and interviews were conducted in August 1994. In most cases the chief executive officer was interviewed, along with a number of other senior man-

220

agers in most cases. Although it was not possible to arrange formal interviews of ordinary production workers, in each case one or more plant site was toured, conditions of work could be closely examined, and short, informal exchanges with ordinary production workers did take place in most factories.

All firms interviewed operated in the manufacturing sector, with products ranging from major capital goods to light consumer nondurables. Products of two of these firms were highly diversified. Because the methods by which the firms were selected locally was not fully clear, the firms should not be considered a strictly random sample. Although the direction of any bias is not self-evident, the firms are probably more privately owned and managed in practice than most Chinese TVEs.

Firms ranged widely in size from 90 to 4,100 employees, one of the largest TVEs in China. Some TVEs not visited have just a handful of employees. None of the firms visited were established before 1967.

TVEs come in many different forms. Some look like conventional firms, others like pure cooperatives, and still others like municipally owned companies. Most embody some features of each. Among the case study TVEs, five were shareholding cooperatives, although two of these were for practical purposes conventional private firms, and one other firm called itself a private company. The remaining two were more traditional township and village enterprises, respectively, although each had some formal employee ownership and one of these had outside shareholders.

Levels of formalized ownership for ordinary employees showed an enormous variability from 0 to 35%. In the six firms for which information is available, five have a piece rate or bonus system related to enterprise results, and the remaining firm offers an effective 50% employee share purchase discount. All firms for which information is available offered a significant pension scheme through either public channels, a private program, or both.

Most firms have a consultative "workers' council" in accordance with standard Chinese practice. The role of these workers' councils is modest compared with, say, workplace councils in Germany. But the level of involvement in "workers' councils" in many TVEs is often quite high compared with the rest of the developing world. Other participation channels include annual employee meetings, shareholders meetings, and managers' "open door policies." In Europe, such mechanisms are widely appreciated and supported by management; it may take some time before China's emerging entrepreneurs develop the same appreciation. For example, one of those interviewed said, "I do not like to have my employees participate as owners or in decisions because they are poor men and they think like poor men."

While retained earnings appeared to be unusually important, other financial sources proved to be extremely diverse. Each firm was asked how its investment decision was made and, specifically, whether a payback period criterion was used, and if so how long. This is important among other reasons because there may be concern that employee-owners will have a shorter time horizon than conventional owners, with resulting depressing effect on investment levels, although empirical research shows little difference between payback periods between firms with no and full employee ownership. Each of the four TVEs for which information could be obtained reported a short payback period (time before income from an investment fully pays for the initial financial layout), ranging from three months to five years. Certainly these periods are well within the working lifetime horizon of the typical manager and employee, suggesting that the retirement horizon was not providing a binding constraint on investment choice. Moreover, this short payback period reflects the short life of most of the capital goods under consideration; interviews suggested that managers believed there was no real flexibility in the type of capital goods they could utilize in their industry (there was no way to verify whether this was true).

It is common to find provisions for bonding of workers, that is, inducing them to stay working at the TVE as long as the company wants to retain them. One manager said of his firm that, "If a worker leaves before his contract expires, he must pay for his training fees and forfeit a 200 Yuan escrow." Another firm uses employee share ownership as a means of generating a bond that relies on carrot rather than stick. As he put it, "We created our stock system to bond skilled labor to the firm. But we keep a limit on how much can be held by individuals so that the whole village can get rich together."

The eight TVEs visited use a wide variety of strategies for innovation. While three firms cited ordinary employees as an important source of innovation, other cited sources included trained engineers, national agencies, ideas from customers, joint ventures with multinational firms, and other foreign buyers. This eclectic pattern may reflect differences in company history, organization, ownership, incentive plans, and capitalization. Most likely, the innovation strategies of these firms are not in any equilibrium, and may be refined at a later point.

TVEs have a close connection to the local economy. Most employees live in the township or village in which they work, and most capital is raised from local sources such as savings, retained earnings, and employee investments. These are conditions in which industrial districts operating in similar industries, though with higher technology, flourish in Europe, such as the Italian apparel districts. But the case studies provided little evidence that TVEs tend to be geographically clustered by product. Recent research suggests that industrial districts may be important to the economic development of developing countries. Encouraging such clustering by product might be a way to further enhance TVE efficiency.

What explains the success of those TVEs that have not reformed their property rights? The existence of a "cooperative culture" may be part of the explanation for the success of TVEs to date, despite their unconventional property rights. As soon as property rights become well-defined, all parties can see who has received the most shares. This source of potential conflict would spoil an atmosphere of "mutual sacrifice for the betterment of the firm." The manager of a large, well-known and highly diversified TVE said, "We prefer to keep property rights somewhat vague. Clarifying them would cause more conflict than it would resolve."

But many TVEs have been motivated to assume a more formal, Western-style system of property rights as a result of many current or anticipated forces. As one manager said, "Our property rights reform results from the pressures we expect from four sources: (1) reformed SOEs, (2) private firms, (3) joint ventures, and (4) GATT. We want to bind workers to the financial well-being of the firm."

In some cases, a reformed system of property rights may generate somewhat greater efficiency, but the costs of transition may outweigh the benefits. Certainly if the cooperative culture is lost, costs can be high, and may outweigh other benefits. But as one manager put it, "Property rights transition costs have been very high. But second- and third-level managers had become disillusioned as they saw colleagues making more money in outside enterprises. We had to reform property rights to retain key employees."

Perhaps the safest strategy for TVEs would be to adopt property rights reforms that fit with the culture but also guard against possible future incentive problems. No matter how strong the cooperative culture, incentive issues must be taken seriously, even if their effects have not been observed in practice. At least as a long-run proposition, culture does often change with economic development. Full privatization of TVEs is not on the political agenda in China as of this writing. If any future privatization allots shares to those who have made investments in the firm, managers and employees as well as the local town or village will likely become part owners.

To survive changes in the prevailing political winds, many TVEs seem to alter official definitions of their property rights without actually making any real underlying changes. Two examples will illustrate. Some TVEs were started with private funds, and little or no outside investment was contributed. These firms may be expected to have little or at least much less difficulty converting to conventional, fully private ownership, as long as general political conditions permit. One manager of a TVE in Wenzhou, a city long known for its Hong-Kong-style freewheeling market, said, "When we started we called ourselves a collective for political reasons. In 1988 we 'took off the red hat' and declared ourselves what we really are, a private firm." TVEs that are essentially conventional firms but designate themselves as collective TVEs to receive benefits such as local loans are known in China as "red-hatted enterprises"; they are relatively small in number. On the other hand, some firms had a major municipal and employee role from the beginning. As a manager in a different town said, "We started as a collective township enterprise, but since most of our customers were SOEs, we began calling ourselves an SOE. Then we reverted to a collective and now are a partial shareholding cooperative."

For most TVEs, carefully designed, partial township, employee, and management ownership rights, along with conventional private ownership to encourage riskier but potentially high-return investment, may be the best compromise. Such diversified ownership and control would provide checks and balances on unwarranted and short-sighted confiscatory taxation and other interventions by municipal authorities, which are sometimes corrupt. At the same time, this reform would increase incentives for employees to work hard, develop skills, and innovate. Both rights and limitations of employee decision-making participation would be spelled out formally and enforceably.

Moreover, profit sharing and other incentive plans provide motivation along with lower base wages; they do not have to involve share ownership to work. However, the formula for such schemes work best when made clear and explicit; reforms along these lines are underway in parts of Zhejiang province.

A reasonable level of job security, contract enforceability, and internal cooperation in the firm are natural complements. Employees would then experience profit sharing as an effort, skill development, and innovation incentive for the long term. Employees could better monitor whether they are receiving a contractual reward, which is good both for simple incentives and for employee morale. And an explicit profit sharing contract can help monitoring authorities, such as local government, to determine whether employee compensation is excessive. If sufficient variability exists in the structure of TVEs, it could be tested before instituting legal changes.

To improve efficiency, TVEs might want to form leagues across regions that would pool risks and make capital available where its return is highest. They might also want to form consortia, to facilitate exporting, research, and development; or for other purposes, such as joint bidding on large contracts. All of these activities are found among leagues of successful Italian industrial coops, which have been compared to collective TVEs. In Italy, government has also provided export and "industrial extension" services, with which there may be an analogy with the services of the analogous Spark Program in China. Evidence is that TVEs have started in low-tech operations but have upgraded rapidly in quality, a trend that corresponds to European experience.

In sum, the TVE sector has grown dramatically in China but has begun to come up against some limits. Its collective ownership form may no longer function well in the rapidly changing Chinese economy, yet it is still unknown what forms of property rights will ultimately take its place. The transition will be full of difficulties and uncertainties. Regardless of the outcome, the process of TVE reform deserves close attention because of its effects on the well-being of the Chinese population. Over 125 million employees now work in these firms, a number exceeding the workforces of almost all other countries. Moreover, most of the issues facing TVEs are found in less dramatic form in many other LDCs. Paternalistic employment systems, only partially clarified property rights, government meddling in management, and other problems are issues that must be addressed in many LDCs. Brought into high relief by the Chinese TVE reform experience, lessons learned from this transition will bear important lessons for the reform process throughout the developing world.

Sources

Bartlett, Will, et al. "Labor-Managed Cooperatives and Private Firms in North-Central Italy: An Empirical Comparison." *Industrial and Labor Relations Review 46* (1992) 103–118.

Becattini, G., F. Pyke, and W. Sengenberger, eds. *Industrial Districts and Inter-Firm Cooperation in Italy.* Geneva, Switzerland: ILO, 1990.

Blinder, Alan S., ed. *Paying for Productivity: A Look at the Evidence.* Washington, DC: Brookings, 1990.

Byrd, William, and Alan Gelb. "Township, Village and Private Industry in China's Economic Reform." *PRE Working Paper WPS 406.* World Bank, 1990.

Byrd, William, and Qingsong Lin, ed. *China's Rural Industry: Structure, Development and Reform.* New York: Oxford, 1990.

Fan, Gang, and Wing Thye Woo. "Decentralized Socialism and Macroeconomic Stability: Lessons From China." *Economics Working Paper 411,* University of California, Davis, 1992.

Jefferson, Gary, Thomas Rawski, and Yuxin Zheng. "Growth, Efficiency and Convergence in China's State and Collective Industry." *Economic Development and Cultural Change 40* (1992): 239–266.

Jefferson, Gary, and Wenyi Xu. "The Impact of Reform on Socialist Enterprise in Transition: Structure Conduct and Performance in Chinese Industry." *Journal of Comparative Economics 15* (1991): 45–64.

Jefferson, Gary, and Thomas Rawski. "Enterprise Reform in Chinese Industry." *Journal of Economic Perspectives 8* (1994): 47–70.

Nadvi, Khalid, and Hubert Schmitz. "Industrial Clusters in LDCs: Review of Experiences and Research Agenda." *Discussion Paper 339.* Sussex, England: Institute of Development Studies, 1994.

Ody, Anthony J. "Rural Enterprise Development in China, 1986–90," *World Bank Discussion Paper 162,* 1992.

Smith, Stephen C. "Employee Participation in China's Township and Village Enterprises." *China Economic Review 6,* no. 1, (1995): 157–167.

Smith, Stephen C. "Property Rights Reform in China's Township and Village Enterprises: Implications from the Economic Theory and International Experience of Employee Ownership." Paper presented at the International Symposium on Property Rights of TVEs, Hangzhou, China, August 6–8, 1994.

Tian, Guoquiang. "The Property Rights Structure of Chinese Township-Village Enterprises and its Reform." Working paper, Texas A&M University, 1994.

Weitzman, Martin and Chenggang Xu. "Chinese Township-Village Enterprises as Vaguely Defined Cooperatives. *Journal of Comparative Economics 18,* (1994): 121–145.

Woo, Wing Thye, Wen Hai, Yibiao Jin, and Gang Fan. "How Successful Has Chinese Enterprise Reform Been? Pitfalls in Opposite Biases and Focus." *Journal of Comparative Economics 18* (1994): 410–437.

25. Governance and Civil Service Reform: Mali

Diana Evans, Angela Reading, and Rachel Rigoli contributed to this case study

Good governance is one of the fundamental prerequisites of successful economic development. Government has an important role to play in health, education, infrastructure, capital market regulation, macroeconomic stability, safety net provision, the legal system, creation of a good business environment, and environmental protection, all of which are both preconditions and basic features of the developed economy. If government does these things well, the economy is likely to prosper. If the government does them poorly—or makes matters worse through inefficiency and corruption—development is much more difficult to achieve and sustain.

When discussing governance, most people think of preeminent politicians or other leading figures in authority. Certainly, the quality of political leadership does make a difference in setting appropriate goals and a establishing a moral tone of leadership. But the quality of a country's civil service, which carries out the daily tasks of governance that affect most peoples' lives directly, and can be done in a manner that is more or less efficient, honest, and perceptive of local needs, is in the aggregate far more important for the achievement of economic development than the actions of a few visible leaders.

Good governance has been a particular problem in Africa. The lack of good governance there has been a major cause of the decline of the sub-Saharan Africa (SSA) region (see Case 26). Thus, reform of governance in general and the civil service in particular will be a major prerequisite for pulling SSA out of its decline and onto the path of sustainable development. This case study will examine the problems of civil service reform in Mali, a low-income SSA developing country.

In many SSA countries, current civil service problems can largely be traced to the end of the colonial period. Part of the problem was the negative legacy of colonialism, and part was the unrealistic expectations of the population about what government could and should do for the economy once independence was achieved.

At the time of independence, it was widely believed in SSA that the central government was responsible for ensuring the public welfare. This included providing jobs when needed to raise living standards. In practice this has meant creating and expanding the practice of hiring "ghost workers" who receive government paychecks but actually do little or no work for the public sector. Usually, this is simple political patronage, or to put it bluntly, a theft of public resources.

At the same time, traditional local ties remained strong among civil servants and many officials nominally working for the central government had their first loyalty to their family, village, and ethnic group. As a result, the civil service became plagued by clientelism. Objective criteria of efficiency were rarely the standards for government decisions, and even justice was often a less important standard than loyalty. While some ethnic groups gained from this system, others were excluded from a share of power and government largesse. Alienated groups often sought to replace unresponsive officials with their own representatives by legal or illegal means.

As an expert on African institutional reform, Mamadou Dia explains: "Aware of the insecurity of their hold on power (lack of traditional legitimacy), most African regimes became persuaded of the need to assure ascendancy of the state over civil society to strengthen their power and chances of survival. Without countervailing legislative, judicial and other checks and balances, and transparency, this stranglehold on the economy was ultimately misused to build ethnic bases and clientelism as substitutes for moral and political legitimacy."

From the African experience, Dia has defined a "patrimonial state" as generally including a one-party monopoly with discretionary power using clientelism instead of legally defined political processes; a lack of accountability, including the absence of government oversight and weak interest groups; and a lack of transparency, including government control over the media.

Patrimonialism is still strong and the misuse of government control over the economy is rampant in countries where one ethnic group dominates others or where two or more groups compete. Many African leaders lack either the aspiration or the ability (or both) to implement fundamental civil service reforms.

Even where government leaders are well intentioned, the civil service suffers from low wages and wage compression, keeping the pay of highly trained and dedicated civil servants not far above those performing unskilled work or working inefficiently. Obviously, this creates poor incentives for qualified personnel to join or remain with the civil service, or to excel at their jobs. In contrast, successful developing countries such as South Korea have generally paid their civil services above norm salaries for their per capital income levels. Other important factors for successful reform are to separate political party machinery from the civil service, development of legal and regulatory frameworks, and creation of formal institutions and informal channels to facilitate communications between the public and private sectors.

The Case of Mali

In the case of Mali, serious attempts at reform have revealed the extent and intractability of the civil service problems faced in many developing countries. Established in 1960 after independence from France, Mali has experienced an unstable political environment in which several different factions of the government have struggled for power and several coups have occurred. The political instability of the country has led to the government spending well beyond its means to try to appease citizens, even at the expense of more important spending priorities.

Mali is a large country with about 9 million citizens, located in the Sahel region below the southern boundary of the Sahara desert. With a per capita income of about $280 and a life expectancy of just 48 years, Mali ranks as the 16th poorest country in the world among those with a population over one million. Even so, these statistics rank the country among the middle of the group of poor SSA nations.

A USAID study noted that after independence, Mali had "a small, French-dominated export sector, virtually no modern industrial sector, a limited private sector, a highly regulated and centralized economy and administration, a very small number of university-educated Malians who quickly became civil servants at high levels, and a strong bias toward viewing positively the role of public sector employment." Even after independence the French continued to control the private sector. The primary source of employment for Malians was the public sector.

With the introduction of socialist ideology under the rule of Modibo Keita, the civil service quickly expanded. The practice of guaranteeing employment in the civil service for all graduates of secondary schools and universities, coupled with an enormous expansion of higher education, contributed significantly to this expansion. Under Moussa Traore's military rule from 1969 to 1978, reforms were introduced to decrease the size of the civil service. But in practice, the number of employees actually increased in the central government, rising from 16,340 in 1969 to 19,329 in 1974. The expansion of rural development agencies put about 20,000 additional individuals on government payrolls. Finally, the expansion of state-owned enterprises (SOEs) further increased these numbers, which reached over 45,000 by 1980.

In the early 1980s, concern over the uncontrolled expansion of the civil service was met with policies to control their number and quality. By 1983, the number was decreased to 32,000 as a result of massive layoffs, the introduction of competitive exams for entry level positions, and a hiring ceiling on new recruits. At this time, over 20% of the total labor force was comprised of civil servants, while the total public sector accounted for 62.6% of the labor force. Recognizing that this share was too high, the government resolved again to reduce these numbers. This recognition coincided with a gathering economic crisis in which real per capita income dropped substantially.

In 1985, the U.S. announced that Mali was selected to become one of four African beneficiaries of a special assistance program. Mali's three-year Economic Policy Reform Program (EPRP) received $18 million of funding by USAID. Its objectives included fiscal reform, better equipment, and improved service, but reduction of civil service size was the top priority. This was accomplished through a voluntary early departure program (VED) and a hiring ceiling program.

The VED program included severance pay at approximately five times annual base pay, pension guarantees for those with 15 or more years of service, a credit loan guarantee program for those who wished to start private businesses, and a fund for the financing of their business feasibility studies. In the first phase of the program, there were 40,000 government employees, of whom 352 applied and 212 were selected. An estimated 400 employees were selected for the second phase. This number is obviously very small compared to the number of civil servants and the great expense involved; even the benefit-cost study undertaken by USAID showed a ratio of 1.085, so that the benefits outweighed the costs by less than 9%. Moreover, this type of program has some perverse effects. The most able civil servants, those capable of thriving in the private sector, are the most likely to take advantage of this windfall. Those least able to do well outside their government sinecures are the most likely to remain in government.

In contrast, the hiring ceiling program was more effective, and is estimated to have decreased the recruitment budget from one billion CFA francs in 1985 to half that amount by 1987. Unfortunately, the program was met with great hostility on the part of the general public, because it was seen as a threat to economic opportunity and a source of growing unemployment.

The government failed to adequately explain the goals and methods of the programs, which contributed significantly to the public's rejection of them. Another problem was lack of data. An adequate "census" of actual and ghost civil servants and other public employees such as soldiers was never completed. The program was also too limited in scope. It considered reduction of the number of public employees, but not accountability, efficiency, and wage erosion and compression. Finally, the government itself perceived the program as largely dictated by foreign donors. Mali had little input into the design of the programs and, as a result, did not push hard enough to ensure their success, especially in the face of growing public opposition. In the end, the economic limitations of the VED program and the political opposition to the hiring ceiling meant the programs had little net effect on the civil service in Mali.

By 1987, the economic reform package in Mali had come to an almost complete halt and the government ceased to comply with IMF-World Bank structural adjustment requirements. Fear of unemployment made it almost impossible to continue civil service reforms.

The case of Mali demonstrates how difficult it can be to implement constructive changes in the civil service even for a government that has signed an international agreement and receives substantial foreign assistance to carry it out. This shows that reform will be all the more difficult for countries reluctant to carry out needed reforms and not under the pressure of an economic crisis to do so.

A new Malian civil service reform program was being considered in the mid-1990s. To make it a success, more attention will have to be paid to full Malian role in design and implementation, proper data collection and analysis, public relations efforts, simultaneous efforts to increase accountability and efficiency, and other reforms, to make the market more efficient.

Sources

Dia, Mamadou. *A Governance Approach to Civil Service Reform in Sub Saharan Africa.* Washington, DC: World Bank, 1993.

Dia, Mamadou. International Development Studies lecture, George Washington University, Oct. 20, 1994.

Financial Times, various issues.

Moore, Richard. *Report on Civil Service Reform Efforts with Particular Reference to Sub Saharan Africa.* Washington, DC: U.S. AID, 1990.

26. Africa Falls Behind: Debate over the Causes

The poor performance of sub-Saharan Africa (SSA) compared with other developing regions over the last two decades has been of deep and growing concern in the development community. Extremely rapid population growth, environmental degradation, and steady increases in the number of absolutely poor people have been widely noted aspects of the SSA crisis. Absolute poverty refers to an income level so low that those with this standard of living may be said to be in absolute human misery. Often calculated at a dollar per person per day, the income is set so that those falling below this level have their basic health in jeopardy. (For details, see Michael Todaro, *Economic Development,* Sixth Edition, chapter 5.)

Life expectancy at birth in the region is only 53 years. Infant mortality is still over 100 deaths per thousand live births. The population growth rate is over 3% per year. The World Bank has noted that in at least 16 African countries a child is more likely to die before the age of five than attend secondary school. The adult illiteracy rate is over 50%. Today, some 19 countries in SSA are poorer than they were a generation ago.

Numerous causes of poor SSA performance have been hypothesized—18 are introduced in this case study. These are organized according to factors that could be considered largely exogenous, those reflecting government failure, and those representing mixed exogenous and policy failures. The major categories are first outlined to provide an overview of the topics of this chapter.

Exogenous factors

1. Legacy of the colonial period
2. War
3. Commodity price declines

Government failure factors

4. Poor governance/corruption
5. Low investment in human capital (education and skills)
6. Poor macroeconomic policies
7. Excessive state ownership in industry
8. Poor business climate; harassment of entrepreneurs
9. Neglect of agriculture

10. Disincentives for exports
11. Low incentives for foreign investment

Mixed exogenous and policy failures

12. Debt crisis
13. Low savings and investment in nonhuman capital
14. High population growth
15. Environmental degradation and climate change
16. Poor advice and harsh conditionality from international agencies
17. Inequality
18. Underdeveloped institutions

It seems clear that only some of these are primary root causes, and others are symptoms or secondary, proximate causes. But which ones? In this case study, we will look at the arguments on each of these factors. As we will see, many of these explanations are closely interrelated. The debate is still very active, and it will require many more years of experience before the relative merits and demerits of these arguments will become more fully clarified.

An examination of possible factors in the poor performance of sub-Saharan Africa

Exogenous Factors.

1. *Legacy of Colonial Period*

Much of Africa was colonized by European powers, beginning in the 19th century and extending to the 1960s. There is no doubt that Africa was particularly victimized by colonialization. Unlike other colonized regions, such as the Americas and South Asia, little attempt was made to educate and train local residents, bring them into the local colonial administration, or even help them to get involved with local commerce. Colonial borders were defined with an eye to divide and rule. Residents were divided without regard to language, religion, ethnicity, or any of the other factors that help make a cohesive nation state in Europe and elsewhere. This type of diversity may have benefits for a nation's progress, but this requires an overriding identification with the nation, something that was not present in Africa at the time of decolonization. It was not uncommon for countries in Africa to become independent with just a handful of university graduates among its citizens. The slave trade that preceded colonialization for centuries probably did much to set the stage for the later problems of the region.

Thus the legacy of the colonial period should not be dismissed as an important explanation of Africa's current problems. At the same time, it should be noted that Africa's performance in the 15 years immediately following decolonialization was substantially better than that seen in the two decades following. Some very poor choices, apparently made in the early years of independence, continue to have important consequences today. The better, early performance may have been due to unsustainable practices. Colonial powers cannot be entirely to blame for this, though they may have given bad advice and incentives to follow poor policies. Moreover, 35 years after many countries have become independent, it is no longer very helpful to focus exclusive attention on a cause for problems for which policy can today do little to redress. Thus it is very important to examine other possible causes, on which today's governments may make a positive (as well as negative) difference.

2. War

Partly as a legacy of colonialism, Africa has had more than its share of regional wars, and especially civil wars, over the past two decades. These wars have debilitated some of Africa's most promising economies, such as Angola. In the last 30 years, war has led to the direct or indirect deaths of about 7 million Africans, and caused enormous destruction to SSA economies. Most famines in Africa have been caused or at least greatly aggravated by civil wars. With the end of the Cold War in 1989, the external support for many of the protagonists in these wars has slowed to a trickle or dried up entirely. With African countries taking the lead, international efforts should focus on resolution of remaining conflicts, and do a much better job of monitoring emerging conflicts and seeking to broker peaceful agreements. Wars can also have persistent negative effects on economic growth. And, of course, war is not always imposed on governments—it can be the result of poor economic policies as well as bellicose international diplomacy. But we will need to look elsewhere for the key sources of better or poorer performance after wars are concluded.

3. Commodity Price Declines

Prices of commodity exports declined significantly in the 1980s, and evidence shows that there is a downward drift in the long-term trend of these prices. (See Michael

Todaro, *Economic Development,* Sixth Edition, chapters 12–13; and Reinhart and Wickham, 1994). Certainly Africa was negatively affected by the commodity price declines of the 1980s. This has been a major factor in SSA's severe debt crisis, and has worsened the poverty of farmers; as we will see, this in turn has helped spur high population growth and environmental degradation.

Commodity export expansion has often resulted from development advice to follow traditional comparative advantage. Major aid agencies such as the World Bank have promoted commodity exports from developing countries. Aid agencies and even their departments have worked in relative isolation to promote exports from specific countries or regions. Because most of these countries are small in the context of the world economy, prices are taken as given in much economic analysis. Yet a World Bank study found that the expanded sugar export projects in which the bank participated in the 1974-1985 period would account for about 20% of world sugar exports. The focus of aid agencies is now on structural adjustment, and aid agency policies may play a small part of the overall explanation, but better coordination of aid policies may be called for.

In any case, commodity price declines is not a sufficient condition for the scope and magnitude of Africa's economic problems, and it does not offer an explanation for the failure of these economies to diversify into other products.

Government Failure Factors.

External factors are a significant part of the explanation and cannot be dismissed. Yet they are not the whole story, and poor policy responses to existing problems have worsened more than improved them. Attributing responsibility entirely to external forces also tends to turn perceived dependency into a reality, or into more of a reality. A significant part of the problem can be traced to failures of the governments themselves.

4. Poor Governance, Autocracy, and Corruption

Sadly, many of the most corrupt governments in the developing world are to be found in SSA. Corruption is found throughout the developing world, and in developed countries such as Italy; the problems with corruption in Africa can be seen as more of degree than of kind. Corruption and autocracy need not go hand in hand, and democratic countries may have corrupt governments. But certainly in the 1990s democratization has not been an obstacle to needed liberalization, or to good policy choice in general, in economies as disparate as Taiwan, the Czech Republic, and Argentina. The 1991 World

Bank *World Development Report* summarized evidence that fast-growing East Asian economies have been exceptions in their high-growth/authoritarian government combinations. Moreover, while it is widely argued on political economy grounds that democracies tend to overspend, the empirical evidence shows that democracy is no worse for fiscal balance than its alternatives. (Some contrary evidence has been published, but it relied on low apparent deficits of Communist countries in the 1970s, which had central planning to collect revenue and whose data is unreliable.) An open question is whether aid should be conditional on democratic governance. But certainly it does little good to provide aid if most of it will be diverted from the intended recipients. For details on perhaps the worst such case, and the international response, see Case 2 on Zaire.

5. *Low Investment in Human Capital (Education and Skills)*

The contrast in investment in education in SSA and East Asia could not be more dramatic. In the early 1960s, when the income levels of these regions were not far apart, East Asian countries invested considerable resources in primary education, and continued a substantial commitment in this field. They did so at income levels comparable to those of SSA today, which shows that Africa's educational failures are not due simply to the lack of resources, but of political will. Indeed, though aid is generally thought to have become more difficult to obtain, there is more foreign aid available for education now than in the early 1960s. Instead, for many countries—and there are exceptions, such as Botswana—other priorities have simply been considered more pressing. SSA countries spend about the same budgets on the military as they do on education. By contrast, in East Asian countries, often thought of as located in a militarily tense area, spending on education far exceeds defense outlays. These ratios are even more lopsided regarding another important dimension of human capital, investments in health. The evidence is overwhelming that investment in girls' education is particularly beneficial in reducing fertility, raising productivity and improving the well-being of children; yet the enrollment gender gap is especially high in many SSA countries. It should also be noted that the AIDS epidemic in SSA has particularly affected more educated, urban workers. If the epidemic is not contained, it will place further constraints on growth. (See Case 8).

6. *Poor Macroeconomic Policies*

The large, money-financed budget deficits in the SSA region lead to high inflation, which in turn shifts investment to unproductive commodity hoarding. The region is badly in need of thoroughgoing tax reform, yet only a few countries, such as Ghana, have begun serious efforts in this direction. Exchange rates have been chronically overvalued.

Abrupt changes of course in macro policy are sometimes followed by equally abrupt reversals. Savings is low and the financial system is very underdeveloped. Again, the contrast with East Asia could hardly be more dramatic. The World Bank's East Asian Miracle report found that macro stability was a clear source of the East Asian region's success. As a precondition for much else in economic development, improved African macro policy must be a priority.

7. *Excessive State Ownership in Industry*

Privatization has been coming much later to Africa than to Latin America, Asia, and the transition countries. Economists almost universally believe that governments are least efficient—and least needed—in the directly productive sector. Resources and attention are thereby diverted from the sectors, such as health care, education, and environment, where governments can make a large, positive difference.

8. *Poor Business Climate and Harassment of Entrepreneurs*

Business is often unpopular with the citizenry in SSA, and officials find that it can be politically popular to harass successful entrepreneurs. But the effect of this harassment on development is very costly. In most SSA countries, rewards have not been linked to economic performance. There is little doubt that these poor incentives play a part in explaining the problems of the region.

9. *Neglect of Agriculture*

Although the share of national income accounted for by agriculture tends to decline as an economy develops, it certainly does not follow that policy can neglect agriculture and concentrate on industry and services. In fact, an increase in agricultural productivity has been the hallmark of early stages of economic development since the dawn of the modern era. The SSA region has had extremely poor extension and research services, poor transportation and storage infrastructure, and discriminatory pricing policies. These policies have discouraged farmers from raising productivity and shifting from subsistence, slash-and-burn agriculture to cash crops and practices that could raise productivity and incomes. Moreover, women are now responsible for over 70% of all agricultural work in SSA. Yet extension, credit, and other agricultural services that do exist are typically oriented toward male farmers, despite some changes (see Case 6). Finally, wages are artificially high in urban areas, encouraging the best educated and most ambitious rural residents to migrate.

10. Disincentives for Exports

Expansion of exports represents an important element in development strategy. Overvalued exchange rates, high export costs, bureaucratic red tape, and corruption have all served to discourage firms from trying to increase their exports. This is almost certainly an important factor in the relatively poor performance of the region, closely connected to the poor governance explanation.

11. Low Incentives for Foreign Investment

An economy would be hard-pressed to develop successfully without a strong base of domestic firms, but direct foreign investment (DFI) does have a significant role to play in economic development (see Case 20). Governments in the region have discouraged foreign firms from investing by creating a poor general business climate, allowing corruption to continue unchecked, carrying out poor macro policies, and putting ill-considered barriers to investment in place.

Mixed Exogenous and Policy Failures

12. Debt Crisis

Over the last 15 years, most popular discussions of the debt crisis has centered on the Latin American region. This is due in part to the much larger sums of money owed by this region and the dangers the crisis there posed to U.S. banks. But in terms of impact on people, the debt crisis in SSA has been much more substantial. The debt of the SSA region is actually much larger in comparison to their much smaller economies, and the absolute poverty of many citizens in the region has made the debt a much greater burden to bear. The debt crisis has been caused partly by exogenous forces such as the decline in commodity prices, but also by very poor policies, including wasteful use of government directed investment funds, inefficient management and outright theft of assets, as well as an incentive system tilted toward encouraging imports and discouraging exports. Note that the increased capital flows to LDCs prominently advertised for Latin America and elsewhere have yet to benefit the SSA region, so this important avenue for debt crisis resolution has been unavailable. Policy reform may well be a precondition for any significant increase in these flows to SSA. But a World Bank study concluded that a major lesson of the debt crisis is that the private sector cannot be counted on to finance investment in the poorest countries, and official development assistance will continue to be needed; indeed, this conclusion suggests that aid should be strongly focused on the SSA region.

13. *Low Savings and Investment in (Nonhuman) Capital*

The government has only a limited ability to affect individuals' willingness to save, and it is not surprising that in economies with very low incomes we observe low saving rates and a large part of the population living below the absolute poverty line. But a climate of high inflation, insecure investment, capricious taxation, and harassment of successful business people has certainly contributed to low savings. Certainly the now fast-developing East Asian economies managed a much higher savings rate at a time when their incomes per capita were comparable to much of SSA today. Better incentives for domestic savings will have to be put in place.

14. *High Population Growth*

Population growth rates in Africa have been the highest of any region in recorded history, and all observers agree that this has been a factor in holding down per capita income. As is well known, the poor have high fertility in part because children soon contribute to family income, and later to their parents' support in their old age. Population issues cannot be separated from the status of women, who may be particularly dependent on children for economic support in old age. Women often are barred from owning property or benefitting from other legal protections. World Bank studies have confirmed that gender inequalities have played a major role in population growth. Increasing employment and income earning opportunities for women should be a top policy priority. (More on population in the next section.)

15. *Environmental Degradation and Climate Change*

The SSA region faces a wide range of environmental problems, including deforestation and degradation of farmland, with damage to wetlands and grasslands, the loss of biodiversity and hunting, increased air and water pollution, poor waste disposal, drought, floods, and insect outbreaks. Certainly some of the severe environmental problems that SSA has faced in recent years, such as spreading desertification, are to some degree the result of factors outside of human influence. However, much of the environmental threat in SSA can be clearly linked to human activity.

Much of this environmentally damaging activity results from high poverty. Conditions of absolute poverty induce the poor to become agents as well as victims of environmental degradation. The absolutely poor have an incentive for high fertility to increase the number of potential income earners in the family and provide for old age income. The poor have every incentive to run down the fertility of their soil if they know they—and their children—may not survive to benefit from conservation. Indeed, the poorest are known to eat their next year's seed corn to avoid starvation this year, and this serves as a telling metaphor for the general time horizon problem. Even if survival is not at stake, when farmers have insecure land tenure rights as the poor often do, there is an incentive to treat land as a short-term resource. Lack of access to credit can have the same effect. Poverty is closely linked to the low status of women, who often have roles as guardians of natural resources, are responsible for (especially marginal) agriculture, and have an ultimate responsibility for fertility. All these factors are very active in SSA today. Environmental degradation is a major source of economic stagnation and decline; it is worsened by poverty and other social problems, for which government policy can promote improvements.

16. *Poor Advice and Harsh Conditionality from International Agencies*

Some critics have argued that the problems of the SSA region are largely caused by following the irrelevant and possibly damaging advice of the World Bank and other aid agencies, and the ill effects of IMF or World Bank conditions on their structural adjustment lending. Aid agency advice to specialize in commodity exports is one possible source of problems (see point 3). Of course, a country generally only seeks IMF loans if its macroeconomic condition has deteriorated enough to need them, which is generally in part the result of past poor policy choices; so, to some extent, this factor too has some endogenous elements. But certainly adjustment programs have had very harsh effects on the poor in SSA, as they have had in other regions. Development agencies could have done much more to alleviate the desperate plight of the absolutely poor in the SSA region. More must now be done to create basic social safety nets to shield the poor from the harshest effects. At the same time, the evidence is that most governments in the SSA region follow World Bank advice less than those in other regions, such as South America. And, as we have seen, the conditions of absolute poverty that are so prevalent in the region lead to many of SSA's other severe problems, such as environmental degradation and rapid population growth. A renewed emphasis by the development agencies on programs to assist the absolutely poor might do as much as any other strategy to reverse the region's decline.

17. *Inequality*

There is evidence that high inequality is inimical to growth, especially in the post-1980 period. In Africa, inequality started at a low level—because very low incomes were widespread—but, has increased significantly. Where income growth has taken place, much of it has accrued to relatively well-off families. Once again, programs directed at alleviating absolute poverty might have a positive effect on growth as well as social welfare.

18. *Underdeveloped Institutions*

Many institutions playing a role in the regulation of the economic and political spheres, especially at the local level, such as business and citizens' associations that are taken for granted in developed and even middle income countries, are absent or seriously underdeveloped in the SSA region. Many non-governmental organizations are now active in this sphere, but improvements cannot be expected quickly, especially without changes in governance.

The absence of democracy is a related possible factor in explaining poor policy, as we have seen. Certainly many of the authoritarian governments of the region have operated virtually without regard to the popular interest. It should be noted that several East Asian economies, such as South Korea and Taiwan, have been very successful economically despite having authoritarian governments until quite recent democratization. However, some political scientists argue that these East Asian governments were never as dictatorial as many SSA countries are today.

In sum, SSA stagnation has several important root and proximate causes. Some of these factors are out of the control of local governments, but despite some of the adverse conditions Africa continues to face, there are clearly many policy steps that can be taken to improve on the current situation. In general, it is hard to put reliable quantitative values on the relative importance of any one factor in the economic development problems of SSA. To some extent, the sheer number of negative factors and their interactions go a long way to explain the severity of problems in SSA.

In coming years, it will bear watching closely whether the SSA region begins to exhibit some of the policy initiatives and economic changes that characterized the beginning of East Asia's economic rise a generation ago (see Case 3 on economic development in Taiwan). But those concerned with economic development must view the deteriorated economies in SSA with alarm, and treat the predicament of the region as an urgent call to action.

Sources

Brown, James G. "The International Sugar Industry: Developments and Prospects." *Commodities Working Paper No. 18.* Washington, DC: World Bank, 1987.

Cheru, Fantu. "Structural Adjustment, Primary Resource Trade and Sustainable Development in Sub-Saharan Africa." *World Development 20,* no. 4 (1992): 497–512.

Cleaver, Kevin, and Gotz Schreiber. "Population, Agriculture and the Environment in Africa." *Finance and Development,* June 1992.

Cornwell, Richard. "War and the Decline of Africa." *Africa Insight 21,* no. 2 (1991): 74–77.

Logan, Ikubolajeh Bernard, and Kidane Mengisteab. "IMF-World Bank Adjustment and Structural Transformation in Sub-Saharan Africa." *Economic Geography 69,* no. 7 (1993): 1–21.

Persson, Torsten, and Guido Tabellini. "Is Inequality Harmful for Growth?" *American Economic Review 84,* (1994): 600–621.

Reinhart, Carmen M., and Peter Wickham. "Commodity Prices: Cyclical Weakness or Secular Decline?" *International Monetary Fund Staff Papers 41* (June 1994): 175–213.

Summers, Larry. "The Challenges of Development: Some Lessons of History for Sub Saharan Africa." *Finance and Development,* March 1992.

Turner, Conley. "African Development," processed, World Bank, 1996.

Van de Walle, Nicolas. "Political Liberation and Economic Policy Reform in Africa." *World Development 22,* no. 4 (1994): 483–500.

Wall Street Journal, various issues.

Washington Post, various issues.

World Bank. *The East Asian Miracle: Economic Growth and Public Policy.* New York: Oxford, 1993.

World Bank. *Report on SSA and Structural Adjustment Results,* February 1994.